Integration Matters

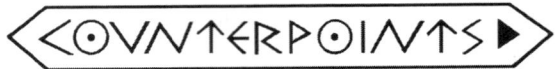

Studies in the
Postmodern Theory of Education

Joe L. Kincheloe and Shirley R. Steinberg
General Editors

Vol. 337

PETER LANG
New York • Washington, D.C./Baltimore • Bern
Frankfurt am Main • Berlin • Brussels • Vienna • Oxford

C. P. Gause

Integration Matters

Navigating Identity, Culture, and Resistance

PETER LANG
New York • Washington, D.C./Baltimore • Bern
Frankfurt am Main • Berlin • Brussels • Vienna • Oxford

Library of Congress Cataloging-in-Publication Data
Gause, C. P.
Integration matters: navigating identity, culture, and resistance / C. P. Gause.
p. cm. — (Counterpoints: studies in the postmodern theory of education; vol. 337)
Includes bibliographical references and index.
1. African American men—Education. 2. African American young men—Education.
3. African Americans—Race identity. 4. Educational change—United States. I. Title.
LC2731.G38   371.829'96073—dc22   2008006182
ISBN 978-1-4331-0202-8
ISSN 1058-1634

Bibliographic information published by **Die Deutsche Bibliothek**.
Die Deutsche Bibliothek lists this publication in the "Deutsche
Nationalbibliografie"; detailed bibliographic data is available
on the Internet at http://dnb.ddb.de/.

Cover design by Joni Holst

The paper in this book meets the guidelines for permanence and durability
of the Committee on Production Guidelines for Book Longevity
of the Council of Library Resources.

© 2008 Peter Lang Publishing, Inc., New York
29 Broadway, 18th floor, New York, NY 10006
www.peterlang.com

All rights reserved.
Reprint or reproduction, even partially, in all forms such as microfilm,
xerography, microfiche, microcard, and offset strictly prohibited.

Printed in the United States of America

I dedicate this book to the memory of my mother, the late Ernestine Laverne Lewis-Gause, who inspired me in life and in her death to remain true to my calling and purpose in life and to my spiritual brother and friend Willie Moye who provided so much support and wisdom during the time of this writing; may their spirits continue to whisper love and joy in our lives and hearts.

TABLE OF CONTENTS

Foreword		ix
Preface		xiii
Acknowledgments		xvii
Introduction	American Democracy: *E Pluribus Unum*—Lost in Translation	1
Chapter 1	Integration Matters	15
Chapter 2	Black Masculinity	37
Chapter 3	From Preachers, Pushers, and Pimps to Hoochies, Heifers, and W(Ho)res: Leaders of the New School	61
Chapter 4	Rap, Race, and Resistance	87
Chapter 5	Still Shouting, but Not with My Voice	107
Chapter 6	Law and Order: Policing the Village	123

Chapter 7	Collaborative Activism: Keys to Transforming Learning Communities	137
Chapter 8	The Courage to Lead: Navigating Identity	157
	Afterword	177
	References	181
	Index	195

FOREWORD

Integration Matters: Navigating Identity, Culture and Resistance carefully articulates the burdens carried when we care about the quality of work we enact against institutional racism and inequity. Black males in our society, as Gause poignantly discusses, wear this burden, more heavily, and given the cloak of political correctness or assumed reparations in a post–civil rights era, most continue to ignore or overlook the deeply embedded insidiousness in our culture that allows such wrongs. The book is one of its kind in the way it carefully unfolds the many layers of educational leadership, identity politics, and praxis. Will educational leaders head the wisdom and information presented here? Will it serve as a catalyst for new possibilities? This book leaves the reader no other conscionable choice.

Why does integration matter? Because despite alleged progress, as the book title implies, U.S. culture still resists integration and diverse identities while succumbing to stereotypes and misinformation. Gause shares a classroom experience where students felt entitled to defy his pedagogical authority, translate passion/commitment/urgency into anger, and isolate race as their impediment (not that articulating their thoughts led to awareness of how they implicated themselves in racism, on the contrary). Nonetheless this is but one incident common in today's college classrooms and all to often similar misreads in academic unit meetings. Bottom line is we have not come as far as we should in the ways we understand race, gender, class, sexual orientation, language, culture, religion, ability, or any other identity factor as these impact educational contexts, work environments, and knowledge production. Despite the wealth of interdisciplinary literature on these issues, mainstream educational leadership has a propensity to favor managerial paradigms that devalue critical perspectives on access, equity, and power.

Integration Matters: Navigating Identity, Culture and Resistance situates cultural expectations in a post-civil rights era. The reader discovers there is no guarantee of progressiveness as they delve into the introductory chapters which map the contributing factors of history, popular culture, capitalism and corporate expansion to conspire against the changes necessary in society. Most importantly this book pinpoints the injustices and inhumanity in our schools, the complacency to maintain the status quo and the lack of courage to make a difference. Gause chronicles lived and constructed black male identity through popular culture, law and order, and schools. Black masculinity, as stated earlier, is carefully analyzed and presented as an important/ terribly complex entity in our social and educational culture. Gause highlights educational leaders in various "schooling" contexts including making parallels between key figures of the Hip Hop generation who consider themselves leaders of the "new school." Readers are engaged by various case studies of African American educators documenting their struggles to educate students in a system working against them.

The chapter on collaborative activism is a call for readers to not only engage these discussions, but also become intricately involved. The point here is that our educational system is in desperate need of repair, assistance, and vision. By contextualizing schooling within a world context Gause allows his readers to get a better appreciation of what is at stake, what students should learn to assess and critically analyze, and what educational leaders should see as imperatives in their leadership. He contends, "Our freedom depends upon the development of enticing and exciting democratic learning communities where the pursuit of knowledge is the primary objective and students are given the tools to critically examine the world they inhabit." As an undoubted bonus the chapter provides keys for collaborative activism tailor suited to administrators, teachers, parents, and students.

The last chapter, "Courage to Lead and Navigate Identity" focuses on the courage we must develop with increased critical awareness about we are within the context we find ourselves in order to act. The needed risk we must take to go against the grain, to bear the bruising of making a difference, of being unpopular for calling it like it is, and having the imagination to craft a new path. This is not done alone, nor as a rogue agent, but as a student of society, the current educational system, people, patterns, history, theory, and priorities. The priorities cannot be test scores or salaries, but people, in specific children, youth, families, and colleagues. And we cannot forget, ignore, other, or turn a blind eye to race, gender, sexual orientation class, language, religion place, and all other identity factors as these impact the lives of individuals today and their access to the future (it's the haunting promise of proleptic moments).

Integration Matters: Navigating Identity, Culture and Resistance connects cultural, historical, political, and educational dots in undeniable ways. Gause documents what he's witnessed in his career and lived experiences situating these as pedagogical springboards and curricular imperatives for civic involvement. This is a deeply personal and public analysis intended to educate, move, and trouble. Let it move you, your students, and community.

Leila E. Villaverde
University of North Carolina at Greensboro

PREFACE

We need mass-based political movements calling citizens of this nation to uphold democracy and the rights of everyone to be educated, and to work on behalf of the ending domination in all its forms—to work for justice, changing our educational system so that schooling is not the site where students are indoctrinated to support imperialist white-supremacist capitalist patriarchy or any ideology, but rather where they learn to open their minds, to engage in rigorous study and to think critically.
—*bell hooks, 2004, Teaching Community*

Schooling is a process intended to perpetuate and maintain the society's existing power relations and the institutional structures that support those arrangements. Education, in contrast to schooling, is the process of transmitting from one generation to the next knowledge of the values, aesthetics, spiritual beliefs, and all things that give a particular cultural orientation its uniqueness.
—*Mwalimu Shujaa, Education and Schooling*

The stigmatization of African American males has been embraced not only by European Americans, but by African Americans as well. The dominant culture continues to perpetuate negative imagery of African American males through media, film, and music. National networks telecasting African American males being apprehended by law enforcement locally and regionally is a daily ritual. This imagery further perpetuates the demise of the African American male.

Over the past forty years of my life I have witnessed the rise and fall of the black male in America. I use black and African American interchangeably in this work because identity is fluid and multiple. Identity construction is forged within historical, political, racial and sociocultural contexts in the United States. Conversations around identity, particularly black identity must be positioned in terms of the legacy of slavery and the history of civil rights in this country.

From the onset of our arrival as slaves in this new world to the current digital representations of our commodified bodies as athletes, thugs, entertainers, and nihilistic showmen, I have watched, waited, and witnessed: I watched at times with disbelief how we treat our family, loved ones and ourselves. I have waited for the promise of redemption by self-appointed and self-proclaimed leaders and I have witnessed the destruction and venom we as black men unleash upon our communities and one another. Turn to any local, national and/or cable news network and you see the black male imprisoned by his words, actions, and deeds.

The personalities spread across every profession and class structure. From politician to preacher, entertainment to professional sports, I and my brothers, we are being called into question. The names of the accused, alleged, and convicted are presented in twenty-second sound bites across the digital airwaves in fifteen-minute cycles. From Michael Vick, the disgraced Atlanta Falcon, to the newly appointed governor of New York, David Patterson; from the rapper Young Jeezy to Detroit's mayor Kwame Kilpatrick, black males and their place in American society is contested, critiqued and challenged. This type of reporting at times seems conspiratorial in nature. All black men are not involved in sex scandals, raping college coeds and murdering innocent bystanders. Many of us are raising families, gainfully employed in professional careers, and striving to make a difference in our lives and the life of others. Yes, there are some who are engaged in the underground economy, who have not completed high school and/or college and who choose a life of criminality; however, those individuals represent a small percentage of the black male population in America.

Integration Matters: Navigating Identity, Culture and Resistance offers the reader insight into issues on identity politics, education, and popular culture. I specifically speak of issues raised by educators and myself, on black masculinity, democratic education, and leadership in the African American community. This text is a set of critical explorations and is not intended to be a linear argument about the socio-cultural dynamics of the African American community. However, it does explore the manifestations of *identity, cultural difference,* and *resistance* in African American culture. The types of difference explored our gender and sexuality, the construction of black masculinity and identity, and the manner in which post–civil rights educators negotiate teaching the hip-hop generation. The object of my critical exploration is to find out how broad American culture conceives the African American community; specifically the black male in "crisis" and how integration contributes to these conceptions. Because of the controversial positions often articulated, pseudonyms have been have been used to protect the anonymity and confidentiality of individuals interviewed. The magnitude of issues on violence within our community continues to increase exponentially even at the time of writing this book. During the time of this writing, eleven black males and four Latinos were murdered in Greensboro, two female college students were murdered, one being the Student Body President of the University of North Carolina-Chapel Hill, a sister institution; and one of the oldest high schools in the city experienced a turf battle on school property of two rival Latin and African American gangs.

In the current socio-cultural and political climate of our society and the ever-growing evolution of negative digitized mediated popular culture, this work is an expression of remaining hopeful in times of despair. I am reminded of a visit to a school in a village north of Lulea, Sweden on my way to the Arctic Circle while attending the Commonwealth Conference of Educational Administration and Management in 2002. The school was a PreK-8th grade school and all the students were Scandinavian. There were no students of color. As I and my colleagues disembarked from our tour bus and made our way into the school, I noticed many students coming to the window and several of them were pointing at me. We were invited to visit their classes and talk with them, which was a great opportunity. While being escorted by the headmaster to an upper school classroom a group of preteen boys ran out of class toward our group and began speaking in Swedish to the headmaster while pointing at me. The headmaster laughed and then asked me in perfect English, *"the children would like to rub your skin; they have never seen a black person in real life, only on television."* I laughed and said, "of course." Entertaining many of their questions, one of the young men asked, *"Why do you shoot people all the time?"* The headmaster rebuked him, apologized and stated, *"I tell them all of the time, American television is filled with violence and you can't believe everything you see."* Another student asked if I knew Michael Jordan or Tiger Woods and I had to regretfully tell him not in person only through the television. During that moment, I became very sad and troubled. Here I am several thousand miles away in a foreign country and meeting a group of native Swedes whose only image of me, a black man is one portrayed by the media. An image of violence is what I represented during that moment, and I wanted to answer his question with his own, why do we shoot people all of the time? Why do we continue to be victims by creating victims? Why do we participate in the assassination of our own identity? How can one of the greatest works of living art by the Divine Creator survive the Middle Passages and die at his own hands? Black masculinity is often regarded as a response to white male racism; but what about the destructive identities we perpetuate, glorify, and perform in response to our own despair?

What has happened to our love for education, truth, and the multiple forms of communities we call family? Where is the love for us and one another? The many opportunities we gained fought, demanded, marched, and died for, we no longer seek in our communities. The critical and radical consciousness we gained and taught our young people has been replaced by fame, fortune, and fear. Our communities suffer with inadequate health care, educational opportunities, and economic independence; but we yet believe "*God will deliver us if we just wait on Him.*" Well, God is tired of us waiting on Him and not doing what we need to do for ourselves and our communities right now! We must use our radical consciousness to transform our community and humanity not for fame and riches but for the continuation of our humanity. We must critically engage who we are and what we believe to move our lineages forward; however, not at the expense of "*othering.*" This is not an easy task.

Working with educators to transform schools has been one of the most challenging career paths that I have journeyed. I have worked in various social service agencies, including those that provide safety, custody and control of child murderers, rapists, and teen drug lords. I have served and cooked fast food at most of the national fast food chains in the United States while living on my own and trying to receive a college education. While searching for my place in this world, I have worked with developmentally disabled youth, crack-addicted mothers and babies, and youth in children's homes and foster care. Working with educators has been the most difficult yet the most rewarding experience. The field of education is one of the most important professions in our society. We take tired, downtrodden and depressed youth who enter the halls of our schools and strive to turn their nights into days, their challenges into victories, and their sorrow into joy. We do this believing students will become loving and caring adult members of our society. Like seedlings they are alive. We must allow them to grow together, for by growing together they will learn to respect one another. Only then will we live in harmony. *Integrations matters*!

C. P. Gause, Ph.D.
March 2008

ACKNOWLEDGMENTS

A project of this nature could not be brought to fruition without the contributions of so many people. I would be remiss if I did not acknowledge and give thanks to those who paved the way, contributed their time, and supported me throughout this process. I dedicate the spirit of this work to my father, Walter T. Gause, Sr. who has been a steady presence in my life; my brother, Walter T. Gause, Jr. who taught me how to fight; my sister, Celeste Ramona Gause who taught me how to be and give my best, and; to my favorite aunt, Isoline Gause who taught me *"without family you're nothing."*

I am deeply grateful to my partner and life-mate T. L. Hargrove who taught me how to love and forgive. We came to know love at a time when no one knew or thought that love could exist. Thank you for the ten years of friendship, challenge, and intrigue.

To my best friends and "keepers of the flame," Willie Moye and Gary Guinyard, we have remained true to our vision of life for more than twenty-five years. Your love, patience, kindness, support, and prayers have sustained this brother! Thank you for being true to your love and black masculinity; it has served as a model for this work.

To my dearest friend and confidant, Calpurnia Able, I am thankful to God for our friendship and "special" relationship. Seeking your wise counsel has provided me with the space to engage in life-changing reflection throughout the years and thank God for "unlimited minutes!"

To my dearest "girlfriends," Tomie Brown and Dara Nix-Stevenson, I am grateful for your love and friendship. Our journey has been filled with wonder and amazement.

To the one who showed me the way TLB2, Tony Lamair Burks II, for all things I am grateful.

To Felicia K. Robinson, I am grateful for your love, wisdom, and marching orders.

To my dear friend and adviser Lillian Hawkins, thank you for your support, love, and friendship. Without you this project would not have come to fruition. I appreciate the opportunity you gave me in January 2001; it changed my life forever.

I am thankful to the following individuals and institutions for their support throughout the years:

Richland School District One, Florence School District One, Williamsburg County School District, North College Hill School District, Trinity University-South Florida Campus, Columbia International University, the University of South Carolina-Columbia, the faculty, staff, and students of the Department of Educational Leadership at Miami University, the faculty, staff, and students of the Department of Educational Leadership and Cultural Foundations at the University of North Carolina-Greensboro. To Peter Lang Publishing and my editors Drs. Shirley Steinberg, Joe Kincheloe, Leila Villaverde, and Roymico Carter, thank you for supporting this project. I give thanks to the Divine Creator without whom none of this would have been possible.

INTRODUCTION

AMERICAN DEMOCRACY: *E PLURIBUS UNUM*— LOST IN TRANSLATION

Mommy Kimberly is calling me black and shiny and she is trying to get Boogie (her dog) to bite me!
—*Celeste Ramona Gause, 1976, Age 7*

People find it very difficult to act on what they know. To act is to be committed, and to be committed is to be in danger.
—*James Baldwin, 1963, The Fire Next Time*

The American democratic experiment is unique in human history not because we are God's chosen people to lead the world, nor because we are always a force for good in the world, but because of our refusal to acknowledge the deeply racist and imperial roots of our democratic project.
—*Cornel West, 2004, Democracy Matters*

I witness the pain of being a black man in America daily. I witness the frustration others have had with black men over my lifetime. I feel the weight of wearing my black skin like a noose around my neck. I did not choose my skin color, it chose me. I am often hated and despised by some, loved and worshipped by others. I am a black man in America just trying to make it like everybody else. C. P. Gause (February 23, 2006)

More diverse now than at any given point of time in her history, the United States continues to marginalize and disenfranchise many of her citizens. Yes, our country is home to multiple beliefs, languages, and ethnicities; however, the affirmation of our plurality is not always evident. For example, who I am and what I represent as a black male are dismissed and overlooked. How? Via popular mediated images and twenty-second sound bites on the daily news; through the legislation and rulings of policymakers, politicians and judges on Capitol Hill, and by producers, directors, and financiers of the entertainment industry. American popular culture that includes motion picture films, television shows, print and television advertisements, and heavily rotated music videos sends out the message that I am worthless and troubled. These powerful images authored and distributed by corporate media giants often appear to be conspiratorial in nature and I often ask myself when I see young brothers participating in the media machinery's assault on our image, is this life emulating art or art emulating life?

The black male identity is relegated to nihilistic behaviors for the purpose of selling products. If you got the *"bling, the booty,* and *bodacious,"* then you eat, drink and drive product "A," "B," and "C." We are represented as bestial, hyperaggressive, and hypersexualized animals who have no regard for our family, community, or nation. We are often judged as anti-intellectuals with the desire to only "shuck and jive," "buck and coon," and/or "dance and laugh," our way through society. I am of no use unless my image can be co-opted, commodified, and repackaged for consumption. Who I really am is not as important as how much I am worth. The contributions my foreparents made in making America a superpower are often forgotten and this further exacerbates the production of negative representations of my identity. I believe it is simple. If you forget my lineage, there is no frame of reference for my identity and if there is no frame of reference for my identity, you will not acknowledge who I am or the culture that I inherit. If you do not recognize the culture, beliefs, values, and ideologies inherent to my lineage, I only exist in ways that are constructed from your own belief systems that are hegemonic in construction. The present belief systems represented in American culture are primarily white, male, middle class, and heterosexual. "Others" are relegated to the margins. As an outlier, one on the margins, your voice is silent and your image is visible to the dominant culture only when it can be used as a tool for production. This is where our current debate on immigration enters to American society. Immigrants are important, particularly in American politics because in many places their votes are needed. The outliers are important because they are now a very important tool of production, as they were when the first slaves arrived in the new world.

Immigration Politics and Economic Expansion

The memories of my ancestor's arrival in Jamestown in 1619 remind me of how people view the lost books of the Holy Bible; everyone knows they exist but refuses to acknowledge or allow them to be canonized. Slavery was a form of forced immigration for economic expansion. As our nation grew and fulfilled its version of manifest destiny, a large workforce was needed. The use of human beings as property and tools, as forms of capitalism, is morally wrong; however, as sad and disparaging as this part of our history is, we have yet to learn the lessons from the past. We are in a new period of economic expansion in the 21st century America. The role of immigrants, as well as the growing impact of globalization on rural farming communities, continues to redefine our country. Old farming communities have been annexed into many cities across the United States. The Southeast has seen significant growth and is creating new urban regional city centers to attract industries to bolster local economies. Cities across the United States are encouraging the revitalization of downtown areas so that citizens can work and live in the same areas. These "green" projects are marketed to consumers as a way to save the environment by cutting back on carbon emissions and greenhouse gases while creating a new sector for the economy, "green jobs."

Furthering our economic expansion has become the priority and many ethnic and linguistic minorities are afforded opportunities to participate in this expansion, except the black male. All across America there is an ever-increasing debate on skilled and unskilled labor. This debate has centered on undocumented workers who enter this country illegally for employment. Many Americans are calling for the closing of U.S. borders to stop the flow of illegal immigrants; however, politicians continue to be pressured by business lobbyists and special interest groups to allow workers to enter the country to do jobs Americans no longer find appealing. I have heard citizens from all walks of life speak of the notion that even black Americans who once monopolized the service sector of our economy no longer want menial jobs. I don't buy the argument; however, I believe many of our people know the story of indentured servitude and slavery all too well and refuse to be used as cheap labor while their white counterparts are given more wages. Historically, African Americans have worked for less wages in menial jobs without job security and benefits. The post–civil rights era brought many educational and career opportunities for black America. Access was granted to jobs other than teaching and the ministry. African Americans were given scholarships to integrate into historically white institutions of higher learning and they found themselves entering corporate America. The great golden period of African American assimilation ended thirty years after it began with the reversal of many landmark court decisions by new ones. Interestingly enough, African Americans were assimilated but not integrated into American culture and society.

Corporations and small businesses in our nation are seeking a cheap labor force to fulfill the demands of the service industry as well as the need for workers in the field of bio- and nanotechnology. I believe members of the African American community desire those jobs and are willing to compete for them, if given the proper resources. Dell Computer, Honda, Jet, Federal Express, and many other companies are relocating their workforce from the western and northeastern part of the United States to the southeastern part to gain access to growing tax breaks, nonunion workers, and the large amount of raw material readily available there. States such as North Carolina, Georgia, and Alabama are competing for these companies because of the loss of manufacturing jobs owing to the North American Free Trade Agreement. These states need to bolster their economies and are granting companies large incentives to bring new industries to the area. The continued expansion in North Carolina has presented problems for our public schools. Educators are trying to find new ways of serving diverse populations in districts with limited resources while keeping up with the ever-increasing student population. This period of adjustment is often filled with constant change; however, one group of individuals who have not maintained pace with this constant change and significant growth is the black male. African American males in America continue to lag behind their counterparts in every measurable educational variable as outlined by the No Child Left Behind legislation.

The American public educational system after undertaking "great" reform efforts continues to not close the academic achievement divide between African American children and children of color on the one hand and their white counterparts on the other. African Americans and Latinos living in urban and rural poverty school districts lag behind their white counterparts in education, health care, and economic conditions. African American households continue to lag behind all other households in access to technology. African American male university enrollment and high school completion continue to decline. In spite of the educational, social, and economic opportunities presented to American society over the past fifty years since the landmark decision in the 1954 *Brown vs. Board of Education* case, black males as a group still struggle. Bill Maxwell, in his article, "On Campus, Grim Statistics for African-American Men" in the *St. Petersburg Times* found that "the obstacles to black males earning college degrees are many, some seemingly intractable. They include inferior public education before college, the absence of black men as role models, low expectations from teachers and other adults, low self-esteem, black men's own low aspirations and their tendency to drop out of high school in disproportionate numbers."

The academic achievement divide has long been a burden of the American public educational system inherited by a "separate, but equal" educational delivery system that began at the inception of modern public education. Title I of the Elementary and Secondary Education Act of 1965, which served as the mandate for Compensatory Education in the United States, was designed to address the issues of urban education and remedy the problems with desegregation; however, more than thirty years later, children of color and children in poverty still receive an education far inferior to that received by their white counterparts. Although gains have been made and many minorities have benefitted from programs and initiatives instituted by local, state, and federal legislation, as the population of the United States increases ethnically and racially, separation by class and race is becoming more evident in our public schools. The result is increasing inequity:

> ... fewer prepared classmates, less-experienced teachers from weaker teacher-training institutions, more-limited curriculum, more remedial and less advanced work in school, weaker reputation, more instability in the school, more kids with health problems, more kids with emotional-abuse problems—all things that relate to poverty. (Orfield, as cited in Jones, 2002, p. 21)

Statistics from the National Assessment of Educational Progress (1996, 1998, and 2000) and school report cards mandated by No Child Left Behind (NCLB) legislation report nearly half of African American students are not performing at grade level and most are nearly four years behind their white counterparts. The black male according to this data continues to fall behind all subgroups reported. The black male is also overly identified for special education programs and suspended from school far more than any other student group according to the same disaggregated data reported under NCLB. The right of African American, Latino, and students in poverty to become educated is one of the greatest social justice issues of the 21st century. Our classrooms, where reading, writing, and arithmetic are being challenged by rap, race, and resistance (Gause, 2001), have erupted with pedagogical conflicts.

Integration Matters: Navigating Identity, Culture and Resistance goes beyond providing educators, parents, and students a critique of present educational experiences for those who are the "other" in America, particularly the black male. By conceptually integrating queer legal theory, the tenets of critical spirituality, and notions of collaborative activism, *Integration Matters* offers a "blueprint" for realizing academic achievement and academic success for all students regardless of condition and/or circumstance. This work integrates the stories, perspectives, and narratives of post–civil rights African American educational leaders juxtaposed with the black male members of the hip-hop generation who consider themselves leaders of the "new school." One group's primary mission is to educate students in public schools to be democratic citizens of our society. The other group's mission is to educate their students on how to survive the *streets*. As I write this text, many may wonder why I am interested in understanding the narratives of black school educators and black male street educators; I believe this strange dichotomy is an integral part in the development of our culture, identities, and how we make sense of what it means to be black in America.

Why Study Postintegration African American Educators?

With such a huge opportunity to document the experiences of African American educators, the amount of research in this area has been surprisingly miniscule. The literature on African American educators is limited to a small number of biographies of famous African American educators who have made significant contributions to the field of education; however, these accounts do not chronicle the experiences of thousands of African American educators who have played an important role in educating children and African American children in particular. With such a significant number of African American women and men serving as educators and teachers, there is a conspicuous absence of their "voice" in the discourse. And because of integration, which afforded African American educators with the opportunity to "teach" students of ethnically diverse backgrounds, the absence of this marginalized group has become more pronounced; in fact their voices have been silenced and silent. Narratives from these individuals speak of providing positive educational experiences to assist young people in developing healthy academic, social, and cultural identities. Their stories and life histories reveal the complexities of their experiences. This text offers critical insights into their beliefs, values, and pedagogy in the areas of teaching and learning. The use of first-person accounts to record and encode the experiences of these black educators serves as a valuable source of information for seeking to understand the black educational community and the black community.

Narratives of African American teachers in multiethnic public junior-senior high schools in America who were dealing with the first wave of students from parents of the hip-hop generation were nonexistent at the time research was conducted to write this text. Given the resegregation of America's schools, I believe the stories of these educators will offer insights into the importance of equality of representation in our society. There were many sites in the United States where an investigation of this nature could have been conducted; however, I chose four African American educators who practiced their craft at Case Junior-Senior High School, an integrated public school located in the midwestern part of the United States. I explore through the voices of these educators the cultural commodification of gendered identities by the "free market" and how this creates spaces of victimization and anti-intellectualism in schools and public life.

The African American educators of Case Junior-Senior High were committed to the liberation of young minds and believed in social justice and equity. I was often reminded by each of them, *"it is our moral duty to transform the lives of these students, most importantly the black students; because of what our forefathers and foremothers endured."* They were beneficiaries of the post–civil rights movement, desegregation, and integration, and they also witnessed the genesis of rap music and hip-hop culture during their lifetime. These educators understood the plight of the black male and were committed to making a difference in their lives by assisting many of their students to navigate the multiple identities they were asked to construct particularly while attending public schools. These educators also understood and interrogated their own positions on the intersections of race, class, and gender. By critically analyzing the stories of African American educators, I suggest ways in which schools and colleges of education can restructure to accommodate the teaching of popular culture. I also suggest ways in which individuals can further use narratives of the "other" to inform their practice.

Why Study African American Males and Black Masculinity?

Black males are the only group in American society stylized, idolized, worshipped, and hated at the same time. Black males are excluded from school in ever-increasing and disproportionate numbers. Researcher and policy analyst, Dr. Shaun Harper speaks of these disparities in *Black Male Students at Public Flagship Universities in the U.S.: Status, Trends and Implications for Policy and Practice*. He notes the following statistics in his executive summary:

- In 2002, black men comprised only 4.3 percent of all students enrolled at institutions of higher education, the same as in 1976.
- Between 1977 and 2003, black male degree attainment increased by an average of 0.2 percentage points. The most significant gains were at the associate's degree level. Only 147 more doctorates were awarded to black men in 2003 than in 1977.
- In 2000, black men represented 7.9 percent of the 18-to 24-year-olds in the U.S. population. Across the 50 flagship universities examined in this report, they comprised 2.8 percent of undergraduate student enrollments in 2004.
- Across all racial/ethnic groups, gender gaps in enrollment are widest among black students, with black women outnumbering their male counterparts by 27.2 percentage points.
- Across all degree levels, white men earned more than ten times the number of degrees awarded to their black male counterparts. (p. vii)

On seeing this data, I decided to review the enrollment data of undergraduates and graduates at the institution in which I teach, the University of North Carolina at Greensboro. I specifically wanted to see the number of African American males and females enrolled. According to 2007 enrollment data, the total undergraduate and graduate student enrollment was 17, 157. African American total enrollment was 3364; total number of females 2621, total number of males 743. By ethnicity and gender to total student population; African American females comprised 15.2 percent of total university enrollment while African American males comprised 4.3 percent of total university enrollment. By gender comparison, the total female university enrollment was 11, 760 and the total male enrollment was 5397; therefore, by gender 22.29 percent of the student population was African American females and 13.77 percent was African American males. This data can be retrieved via the Web at the University of North Carolina at Greensboro's Office of Institutional Research. Given the disparities in educational attainment by African Americans and the historical implication of education within African American communities, what issues regarding race, class, and gender are at work? Even after the many gains brought about through post–civil rights legislation, affirmative action, and access to historically white institutions, why do we continue to lag behind other members of American society in achieving academically? *Integration Matters* makes me ask questions and seek answers to these questions, because, as a black man I know the struggles, sacrifices, pain, and suffering others and I endured to become educated to serve our communities and give back to society, but why as a people and as brothers do we continue to not keep up in this race? Why do we give up and decide that a life of crime, violence, and pain is far better than striving, excelling, and achieving our dreams? Is it how we view and perceive ourselves as men? Maybe it is the way we construct our masculinity?

Masculinities are not expressed in isolation, but are influenced, informed, and shaped by school culture. The continued assault of popular culture on school culture and family culture is increasingly affecting how black males mediate their gendered identities. Schools educate in a vacuum. Schools sort children along racial, social class, and gender lines, and this contributes to inequalities in educational and occupational outcomes. In essence, public schools have never been effective in providing success for all who attend regardless of condition and circumstance. Why? Because educational leaders consistently maintain the status quo and they are not totally at fault. The training and development of school administrators have been positivistic. Educational leadership preparation programs have historically been constructed from the business model.

Kathleen Brown (2004) argues in her article, "Leadership for Social Justice and Equity: Weaving a Transformative Framework and Pedagogy," that the primary goal of educational leadership preparation programs should be to develop "critically reflective" administrators with the foundation "for both critical inquiry and self-reflection" (p. 91). She offers the following:

> Critical inquiry involves the conscious consideration of the moral and ethical implications and consequences of schooling practices on students. Self-reflection adds the dimension of deep examination of personal assumptions, values, and beliefs. Critical reflection merges the two terms and involves the examination of personal and professional belief systems, as well as the deliberate consideration of the ethical implications and effect[s] of such practices. (p. 91)

Educational leaders who negotiate these processes will understand the student resistance and disengagement. These leaders understand their own practices and biases as potential barriers to student success. They acknowledge and negotiate their biases as part of the daily decision-making process. This is the first step in developing transformational learning communities that affirm the multiple ways of learning and lived experiences students bring to the school community.

Resistance Is Futile

While the dominant themes of education are often subjected to student resistance, such resistance is most prevalent among young black males. Many black males resist "playing" the "school game." They deceive teachers, refuse to complete homework, smoke and sell "dope" in school bathrooms, delay the beginning of classes, and wear clothing and use language that is often offensive to adults. "These oppositional practices have been lived out and elaborated upon over the years, and constitute core cultural elements in the urban Black community today" (Weis, 1988, p. 185). According to Majors (1992) European Americans often view the lifestyle and culture of inner city black males as threatening, aggressive, and intimidating. Majors (1992) argues the nature of inner city black males as "cool pose," that is, he is characterized as "being cool," "with the program," and "in the house."

A dilemma of the inner city black male is his desire to exhibit masculinity; he is too often grounded in "masking strategies" that require him to deny and suppress his feelings. He is highly attractive; he is perceived and perceives himself as the epitome of control, strength, and pride. However, even in his "charismatic, suave, debonair, entertaining" persona, he presents himself as a "mysterious challenge" (Majors 1992, p. 2). How do teachers who work in multiethnic suburban schools view "students of color," particularly black males? How do white teachers view "young African American male teachers?" Do they critically reflect upon their positionality and dominant worldview when they interact with young white male youth who identify with hip-hop culture and other subversive youth cultures? Are young female youth viewed differently, particularly those who identify with subversive forms of youth culture?

The black male image continues to be commodified, copied, and created for mass consumption. Currently black masculinity is rooted in masculine hero worship in the case of rappers and as naturalized and commodified bodies in the case of athletes. The combination of the two has yielded a new public enemy number one, a sadistic and masochistic heterosexist black masculine cyborg; devoid of emotion, thought, and remorse. Discursively these new black male representations bring together the criminal, the police, and the media as one packaged object for consumption. The stigmatization of African Americans continues to be embraced by all members of American society white and black alike. The stories of Michael Vick, Tank Johnson, Kwame Kilpatrick, and O. J. Simpson, just to name a few, remind us the challenges we face in countering the negative imagery of African Americans; particularly, black males by the media. The political disturbances and cultural representations of black masculinity in popular culture require new and different critiques.

Integration Matters offers hope in our humanity and challenges us to use the total sums of who we are to effect change. Its speaks of our core collective identity—the forces of love, spirit, and democracy—as a form of protest to bring about justice for us all. In so doing we are committed to realizing this justice by acknowledging and listening to those voices absent from the historical record, especially those who remained silent during the tumultuous times of segregation and desegregation. We must also seek to hear with purpose the voices of those who seek integration of our public schools while enduring a cultural climate of resegregation. Dantley (2007) opines:

> If democratic citizenship involves being able to confront both reality and history, then schools must become those places where the concerns and issues of contemporary times are not ignored and assumed to exist only outside the walls of the schoolhouse. Neither can theses contemporary issues be assumed to have emanated outside of some historical context and grounding. Students must be given the opportunity to confront and challenge the historical discourse that marginalizes and excludes those who don't perpetuate the traditional American historical grand narrative. (p. 174)

This requires a social and equitable justice which no longer delineates our humanity based on markers of difference, but which calls to the oneness of our condition—the ability to love, to conquer our fears, to create stones of hope out of mountains of despair. As participants in this constitutional republic, Americans must realize that to improve their economic and social conditions, they must be vigilant in the pursuit and advancement of knowledge for the sake of their democracy. Ethnicity ideology, value, race and gender, and class politics, all serve as descriptors for defining our social culture because they all interact with each other in shaping human behavior. This interaction is a complex and challenging process. For America to continue to be the land of the free, the home of the brave, her citizens must not forget they are all sisters and brothers united for the common good and that when one hurts they all hurt. If our hearts ring true, then we stand firmly and shout "*E pluribus Unum*: Out of many, one." Not for the purpose of assimilation but for the purpose of transformation should our democracy be made into one that is radical and attainable with peace as our goal.

Summary of Book by Chapters

With the aforementioned in mind, I have divided the book into eight chapters. In Chapter 1, I present a critical-historical sketch of desegregation, resegregation, integration, cultural studies, and critical pedagogy and how these frameworks can be used to inform how we view identity development and culture in the United States.

In Chapter 2, I interrogate the construction and representations of black masculinity in popular culture. While the varied images of superathlete, gangster, and ghetto superstar travel across different fields of electronic representation and social discourse, there are multiple representations of black gender identity that are absent from mediated discourses. Popular media discourse and imagery continue to focus on the black male, as "thug," "convict" and "duffle bag boy." The black male as "nurturing brother," "committed educator," "anti-racist, anti-sexist activist," and "cultural critic" are often left out of mainstream media. Black heterosexual masculinity is used in policy debates, in television news, and popular film representations to link the signs of patriotism, whiteness, family, nation, and individual responsibility; I disrupt this paradigm by queering black masculinity.

In Chapter 3, I present how the commodification of gendered identities by mainstream media further stereotypes black identities. I also interrogate how the black community is complicit in perpetuating victimization, race-baiting and anti-intellectualism particularly by those in leadership positions in black media, the black church, and the black community. I include the narratives of Raheem and members of "Leaders of the New School." Raheem and his crew powerfully speak of the issues of resistance, black masculinity, culture, and identity. There lived experiences give voice to the text.

In Chapter 4, I offer a discussion by African American educators on rap music and student resistance at Case Junior-Senior High School. These educators struggle with educating students who are second-generation hip-hoppers regardless of ethnic background; however, they are concerned with the black males and how they interface with the culture of Case.

In Chapter 5, I continue the discussion of these educators on their interaction with white colleagues and their students. They expressed their views concerning how white teachers did not consider the impact of their decisions on some students, particularly the students of color and they also discussed the many challenges they faced when interacting with white parents about what and how they taught. Their teaching authority was questioned. The administrator in the group stated that the superintendent focused more on "raising" test scores than providing resources needed for instruction.

In Chapter 6, I present not only the experiences of my colleagues, but also my own experiences while serving as the interim vice-principal of Case Junior-Senior High School. White teachers overly disciplined African American students. I also discuss my personal philosophy and professional conflict with the "zero tolerance" discipline policies adopted by the Belton School District Number 74 Board of Education.

In Chapter 7, I present the current state of education, democracy, and schooling. The national economic downturn, the last wave of horrific budget-cuts, and the present political climate are adding to the hurdles for educators particularly administrators, who must successfully educate students with less than adequate resources. These resources are not just monetary but human as well. I also discuss and provide pragmatic "Keys of Collaborative Activism" for educators, parents, and students and how these "keys" will facilitate the development of successful learning communities. In Chapter 8, I offer the reader my personal and professional narrative. This is *my* story, who I believe myself to be and, and how I navigate the multiple identities that I enact daily. Situated in the context of my own black masculinity, I present to you not just what you see on the outside, but who I am on the inside. This narrative of hope is one of activism.

· 1 ·

INTEGRATION MATTERS

We deal here with the rights of all our children, whatever their race, to an equal start in life. Those children who have been denied that right in the past deserve better than to see fences thrown up to deny them that right in the future. Our nation, I fear will be ill-served by the Court's refusal to remedy separate and unequal education, for unless our children begin to learn together, there is little hope that our people will ever learn to live together.
—*Justice Thurgood Marshall, 1974*

Instead of buying and selling you on the block, they buy and sell you with education.
—*T. L. H. April 20, 2008*

The democratic promise of public education is "at risk" of being abandoned, forgotten, and emptied of meaning.
—*Dennis Carlson and Charles P. Gause,*
Keeping the Promise: Essays on Leadership, Democracy and Education

American citizens are becoming more isolated and divided on the basis of race, class, gender, and cultural constructs. The ability to connect with individuals globally via the Internet is often cited as the reason for the current lack of human interaction. With the increase in social networking sites, as well as professional and personal socials groups, the ability to become anyone you choose to be while remaining comfortably stationed in front of your home computer is appealing. When you have the ability to order food, make purchases of your favorite products, download your favorite movies and music, pay your bills, work and attend church, from home all online, why venture out into our violent and chaotic society? Parents who are concerned about their children's safety and well-being are enrolling them in online high schools to complete their secondary education, giving young people for the first time in history the opportunity to complete their entire education online. Some deem this as progress; but I believe in the absence of people, we lose our sense of connectivity and without connectivity our humanity is lost. Computers, digital peripherals, software, and the Internet were considered to be the foundational tools to full technological integration. Without the human factor, technological integration is a fallacy. Human beings are the bridge builders to integrating technology into our society; however, as we all seek to integrate technology we must strive to integrate the multiple perspectives, ideologies, and cultures that comprise our human identity. Resisting our differences is futile; integrating them is to be human.

Integration matters require us to constantly seek opportunities to bridge differences by integrating our cultures, values, and beliefs with our daily practices. The very act of participating in rituals and events with one another provides us the opportunity to develop the habit of reflection. The habit of reflecting on our individual as well as our collective identities informs our daily practices as citizens of our society seeking to promote the common good for all instead of focusing on our individual needs. This is the foundation for our sense of democracy, "united we stand, divided we fall." This democracy hinges upon what John Dewey calls the "habits" of democratic public life. According to Carlson and Gause (2007),

> Democracy is more than a set of abstract principles of governmentality, that it is something we practice in our everyday lives, and thus something that becomes "habit" in the good sense. Public schools and colleges in this sense are "embryonic communities" of democratic public life, teaching young people the "habits" of respect for difference, freedom of expression, questioning and debate, working with others, and participating in the "making" of a democratic culture. Of course, any habits that become so taken for granted that doing things differently would be "unthinkable" would not be democratic. So the habits of everyday life in public schools and college need to be continuously made the topic of deliberate self-reflection and change. (pp. viii–ix)

The challenge we face as educators in developing and sustaining embryonic learning communities that teach young people the habits of our democracy are numerous. The competing forces of American popular culture such as the desire to seek fame and fortune via the Internet, the ability to access drugs, sex, and rock and roll virtually, and connecting with like-minded individuals for acceptance far exceed what Dewey had imagined. The ability to be reeducated and miseducated while gaining a profit, respect, and notoriety drives our young people. This is the *era of idols*. Today's youth are engaged in self-worship as a form of competition. Success is about outdoing one's peers, although your peers are the judges of your performance. How might the *era of idols*, interface with today's public schools? Digital cameras are no longer tools of education, but the tools of iniquity. Students are using them to record aggressive, violent, and nihilistic behavior, including harming self and others and then uplinking the footage to social networking sites to gain notoriety, "juice," "props," and respect.

Public School U.S.A.

The students who enter and walk the halls of today's public schools are younger than MTV, have witnessed the birth and rise of Google, Yahoo!, and the iPod, were born after the fallout of the First Gulf War, and witnessed the beginning of the Second Gulf War. They believe that casting a vote for the next American Idol is a proper form of exercising their right to vote. They have witnessed the end of the War on Drugs and the beginning of the War on Terrorism, the possible impeachment of a sitting president, and the fall of the energy corporation, Enron. According to Kitwana (2005), "members of both generation X (those born between 1965 and 1984) and the millennium generation (those born between 1985 and 2004) have inherited and created a new world when it comes to living race in America. Many of these students received their formal K-12 education in re-segregated public schools, but were the first Americans to live their lives free of de facto segregation. Both generations witnessed the possible impeachment of a sitting president, the collapse and/rebirth of the Savings and Loan Industry, the Home Mortgage Sub-prime Loan Crisis, the bankruptcy of the airline and automobile industry, the attack on the World Trade Center and two of the most horrific natural disasters of human record; The Tsunami of Indonesia and Hurricane Katrina of the United States. They have witnessed the failure of the government to protect basic human rights, the hopelessness and despair of humanity and global tragedy instantaneously via 24-hour digital mass media coverage."

The lives of students of today are filled with blogs, MySpace, Facebook, chat rooms, instant messaging, cellular phones with individualized ring tones, and the ability to go Wi-Fi through virtual portals and entry points located in various locales across America. The Internet has become the vehicle for global socialization and information. Media outlets constantly bombard us with situations and circumstances such as war, famine, disease, and greed that are detrimental to the human condition. It occurs so frequently that the American public, particularly the youth have become anesthetized to it. Students are becoming substance abusers at alarming rates, particularly as it relates to prescription drug use. There has been an increase in the "underworld" economy and recreational drugs are more prevalent in high schools than textbooks.

Separate and Inequitable

Public schools with high minority and poverty enrollments continue to inadequately prepare students of color and those in poverty. These schools are also continuing to show signs of resegregation. Orfield and Yun (1999) assert, "resegregation decisions of our present period may well have a similar impact on the next century since there is considerable evidence that the resegregated schools of the nineties are profoundly unequal" (p. 6). Thus as our country continues to grow and become home to people with multiple nationalities, cultures, faiths, and languages, the role of democratic education must be at the forefront of domestic and foreign policy because integration matters. The academic achievement divide narrowed during the 1980s but owing to shifts in population, class disparities, and school choice reform efforts, the racial and economic composition of schools in many parts of the United States today resemble that of schools pre-*Brown*. Schools with a majority of students of color and high poverty struggle to excel. Sara Melendez in her article, "From Humble Beginnings Comes Great Achievement," which can be found in *Reflections on 20 years of Minorities in Higher Education and the ACE Annual Status Report*, writes:

> Comparing figures in the 1983 report with the 2001–02 numbers, we see that whites, African Americans, and Hispanics all increased high school completion and college participation rates. However, while the gap between African Americans and whites has narrowed considerably, the gap between Hispanics and both whites and all other groups remains unacceptably high. Furthermore, both African Americans and Hispanics continue to trail behind whites and Asian Americans in rates of four-year college completion. For Hispanics, the gap is serious: 9.7 percent, compared with 29.6 percent for whites. (p. 6)

I find this continued trend disturbing. Are African American and Hispanic students trailing their white colleagues and Asians because of cultural issues? Is it because of tracking and placement? What about the curriculum? Is it possible that the schools that African American and Hispanics students attend are in segregated, urban and/or rural communities where resources are limited and expectations for success are low?

Students of color in segregated settings have low achievement scores, low high school completion rates, inadequately prepared teachers, and very limited resources to support the curriculum. Integrating black, Latino, and white students in schools with higher achievement levels, with highly qualified teachers and with an abundance of resources to support the curriculum will benefit all members of the learning community. However, black and Latino students will still be disproportionately placed in special education classes, tracked into lower-level courses and provided very few opportunities to gain access to resources that would prepare them for postsecondary education. Segregation is about power and the controlling resources. It is predicated upon identifying difference to force division based on race, class, and gender. Segregation is racial and class isolation that reifies subordination. It is a system of oppression that privileges white domination while marginalizing and disenfranchising the "other." Segregated schools may provide students with a platform to learn academic skills; however, the psychological, emotional, and spiritual damage students experience is tragic and goes unmeasured. Powell (2005) asserts:

> We...find ourselves today having to defend the principles of *Brown* against arguments that segregation has been disestablished or that its persistence is merely a matter of choice. Focusing on choice misconstrues racial separation as symmetrical, as if whites and blacks choose to be exclusive in the same fashion. Segregation, however, has historically been and remains today a reality imposed by those with power and privilege on those without. (p. 283)

Why Integration Matters?

The present role of schools continues to be that of transmitting knowledge as defined by those in power. We are far away from educating a citizenry to become active participants in our democracy. Power and how it benefits those in the majority continue to define the curriculum of American public schools. Schools are ongoing sites where the politics of culture unfolds. The raging national battle in public school curricula and policy is whether schools will serve the democratic or economic needs of our country and our flawed democracy and federalist society are currently being defined by those who have enough economic and cultural capital to speak and speak with a very loud voice: public schools in America will serve the economic needs of our country to further democracy. We continue to witness in this country the more economic, cultural, and political resources you have, the louder your voice, and our ruling elite, those in the Congress, continue to defy the will of the people. Unfortunately those who have limited sociocultural and political capital rely on the ruling elite to speak for them. They represent the voice of those who cannot speak but rarely do the ruling elite have the best interests of the voiceless at heart. I believe our American democracy is a social experiment and practice instituted through a hierarchal system of denial and oppression. If we look at the writings of Thomas Jefferson, George Washington, James Madison, and Benjamin Franklin, the American democracy we celebrate and mythologize was designed to be neither publicly participatory nor representative. It was designed for those with educational capital who were members of the ruling class and who had great wealth and opportunities for formal schooling.

As Giroux (1988) asserts, "public schooling offers limited individual mobility to members of the working class and other oppressed groups, but it is a powerful instrument for the reproduction of capitalist relations of production and the dominant legitimating ideologies of the ruling group" (p. xx). If this is to continue, people of color and those in abject poverty will suffer economic and catastrophic devastation that has yet to be witnessed by humanity. To solve medical, natural and man-made disasters, the American public educational system must be integrated ethnically, culturally, and economically. There is no greater time of criticality than now and this must be done particularly for the African American male. How might this be done? We must look to the vision of schooling.

The future vision of schooling is that of deconstructing taken-for-granted meanings and knowledge, which would allow for the recognition of multiple voices and perspectives in the construction of knowledge. In allowing for those multiple voices, schools will allow for multiple identities. Schools play an important role in identity construction. Carlson and Apple (1998) have noted the growing interests in student identity formation not only from sociologists and anthropologists, but also from postmodern academicians as post-structural and postmodern theoretical discourse become more influential. Carlson and Apple (1998) present to us the importance of understanding the postmodern conception of identity formation. "All postmodern conceptions of identity formation begin with a common, nonessentialistic conception of the self, that is, one that views the self as an historical, cultural, and discursive production that is always in the process of reconstruction. Furthermore, the self is understood to have no meaning apart from the power relations it constitutes and is constituted by, which is to say that the self is relational and defined by a web of relationships with "Others" (p. 14).

Schools Resegregation

The United States during the current time of economic expansion and globalization must embrace diversity and equality of participation in our schools. Kathleen Brown in her article, "The Educational Benefits of Diversity: The Unfinished Journey from 'Mandate' in *Brown* to 'Choice' in *Grutter and Comfort*," writes, "The U.S. Supreme Court has longed recognized that 'education...is the very foundation of good citizenship' (*Brown v. Board of Education*, 1954). Education is pivotal to sustaining our political and cultural heritage with a fundamental role in maintaining the fabric of society (*Plyler v. Doe*, 1982). To succeed as a nation and be competitive in the global marketplace, the United States must have diversity and equality of participation within its society in general, and within its educational system in particular, if the dream of one nation, indivisible, is to be realized" (pp. 325–326). I believe the very success of our nation depends on integrations matters. The *Brown* case was not the first one to challenge legally mandated segregation in the United States. A lawsuit had been filed as early as 1849 in Boston, Massachusetts. At least eleven suits were filed against segregated school systems in Kansas alone, between 1881 and 1949. The *Brown v. Board of Topeka, Kansas* suit arrived at the steps of the United States Supreme Court at a time when racial segregation was the norm in public schools across the nation and was legal or permitted in twenty-four states. The *Brown* case is significant because of its radical impact on American society, the first of its kind, and because of the scope and nature of the ruling and decision rendered by the Supreme Court. In spite of being a landmark decision of the late 20th century, its impact, fifty-four years later, is being eroded owing to resegregation.

The South is resegregating. Orfield and Yun (1999) identify several educational trends with regard to resegregation: "the racial composition of America's schools are changing, the South is re-segregating, segregation of Latino students is increasing, and black and Latino enrollment in suburban schools is increasing along with segregation within suburban communities" (p. 3). With the reversal of court-ordered desegregation by the United States Supreme Court and the

United States becoming more racially and ethnically diverse, resegregation is exacerbating educational inequity in our schools for black and Latino students. Gary Orfield and Chungmei Lee in *Historic Reversals, Accelerating Resegregation, and the Need for New Integration Strategies*, assert: "There has been no significant action to forestall or reverse the rapid increase in Latino segregation and its strong relationship to dropout rates and low test scores. Unfortunately the period of explosive Latino growth came after the civil rights era and those problems have been treated largely with test-driven reform strategies that ignore unequal school and community conditions" (p. 10).

Brown I was a landmark decision. *Brown II*, which focused on the implementation of *Brown I*, was never fully realized. Ladson-Billings (2004) speaks of the state of *Brown* and our nation and the road that lies ahead for us if we are to become one nation:

> *Brown* is more accurately characterized as *a first* step in a long, arduous process to rid the nation of its most pernicious demons racism and White supremacy. While we celebrate its potential, we must be clear about its limitations. The nation has never fully and honestly dealt with its "race" problem. Our lack of historical understanding seems to obliterate some rather daunting facts. For example, slavery existed legally in North America for almost 250 years. An apartheid-like social segregation was legally sanctioned for another hundred years. The United States as a nation is but 228 years old and existed as a slave nation longer than it has existed as a free one. The norms, customs, mores, and folkways that surround our racial ecology are not easily cast aside. Our attempt to deal with racial problems through our schools is an incomplete strategy. (p. 8)

I concur with Ladson-Billings. The way in which we deal with racism in our society, by allowing public schools to serve as a vehicle to teach tolerance and pluralism is not only an incomplete strategy, but it is also a strategy that dismisses the importance of multiethnic living communities, integrated places of worship, and the importance of persons of color in leadership roles in all walks of life in our society. Public schools are microcosms of our society. The values inherent in our communities and institutions both public and private find their way into public school classrooms. Students, teachers, administrators and those who work in public schools do not leave their beliefs, values, and ideologies outside the schoolhouse door; nor should they. This is why integration is so important and segregation maintains such a foothold on our society.

Segregation has the stain of inequity that can only be cleansed with true integration. With the resegregation of America's schools, particularly in the South, the hope of a democratic pluralistic and equitable society has been replaced with protectionism.

Integrating North Carolina

As a postintegration African American educator, I continue to witness the impact of the *Brown* decision daily. To teach practicing and aspiring school administrators in North Carolina is challenging and rewarding. So many of my students admit I am the first African American teacher they have ever had in their entire educational career. Some of my students currently teach in the same school district and schools in which they received their elementary and secondary education. One student reports she does not talk about diversity because she has no students of color in her classroom, let alone her school.

North Carolina reports approximately a 300 percent increase in the Latino/Latina population in the past ten years and the remigration of African Americans from Detroit, Chicago, and New York in search of r better schools and affordable housing explains the population growth occurring in this state (Cooper & Allen, 2006). Not everyone in North Carolina is happy about the increase in the state's population. Countless news reports and conservative newspaper editorials articulate the positions of many citizens of North Carolina. I have personally heard and was saddened by the following comments: *"We are tired of those Northerners coming down here and buying housings and raising property taxes." "I wish dem' Mexicans, Latinas; whatever you call'em go back to where they come from." "Why can't they just stay in their own country?"* I have often expressed my professional and personal opinions to individuals who make these statements by reminding them we were all immigrants at one time in our history and immigration has made the United States of America one of the greatest and wealthiest nations on earth.

North Carolina struggles to keep up with this population explosion and so do its school districts. Schools in North Carolina continue to be inadequately funded and availability of resources to meet the needs of ethnic and linguistic minority students continues to be limited. School districts with the ability to build new schools find that when schools come on line they are filled to capacity. School leaders and policymakers struggle trying to assimilate the "undocumented newcomers," as well as provide curricula and instruction to close the academic achievement divide between ethnic and linguistic minorities and their white counterparts. Resegregation often forces local, district, and state policymakers to make resegregated schools equal by redistricting and/or developing magnet school programs and global studies curricula designed to increase the presence of white students in predominantly black and Latino schools. These well-intended plans usually yield cumulating evidence of exacerbating inequality. These issues are not peculiar to North Carolina; they exist across the United States. Gary Orfield and Chungmei Lee in *Historic Reversals, Accelerating Resegregation, and the Need for New Integration Strategies* address the issues regarding America's public schools and equality:

> Although the U.S. has some of the best public schools in the world, it also has too many far weaker than those found in other advanced countries. Most of these are segregated schools which cannot get and hold highly qualified teachers and administrators, do not offer good preparation for college, and often fail to graduate even half of their students. Although we have tried many reforms, often in confusing succession, public debate has largely ignored the fact that racial and ethnic separation continues to be strikingly related to these inequalities. As the U.S. enters its last years in which it will have a majority of white students, it is betting its future on segregation. The data coming out of the No Child Left Behind tests and the state accountability systems show clear relationships between segregation and educational outcomes but this fact is rarely mentioned by policy makers. (p. 8)

African American males continue to be the lowest performing subgroup of all statewide achievement test data reported by the North Carolina Department of Public Instruction. I believe many oppressive sociocultural and political systems have been at work that continually marginalize and disenfranchise black males in the United States. Historically, separate but equal doctrine, race, discriminatory hiring practices, and class politics have prevailed; however, I cannot let my brothers off the hook. The African American community; particularly black males must realize that to love, teach, learn, lead, and empower self and others requires critical change. Critical change occurs with significant self-sacrifice, potential alienation, rejection, and at times costly consequences. We must educate our community and young people to be critical in their thinking and responsible for their actions. In doing so, we will develop citizens who seek to transform the human condition and spirit not for themselves but for all. This critical shift in thinking translates into critical action. To bring about this change we must tell our stories of triumph. In *We Real Cool: Black Men and Masculinity*, bell hooks writes: "There is not even a small body of anti-patriarchal literature speaking directly to black males about what they can do to educate themselves for critical consciousness, guiding them on the path of liberation" (p. xvi). Through this work, I strive to address this very situation.

Black Males and the Struggle for Integration

According to the United States Census Bureau, current statistics reveal there is a clear disadvantage to being born black and male in America: black males have higher rates than white males of mental disorders, unemployment, poverty, injuries, accidents, infant mortality, morbidity, AIDS, homicide and suicide, drugs and alcohol abuse, imprisonment, and criminality. Black men have poorer incomes, life expectancy, access to health care, and education. Researchers are identifying these social problems as social symptoms and are linking them to the history of oppression.

The fascination with black popular culture has re-enslaved many of our communities. The echoes of wisdom by Mary McLeod Bethune, Shirley Chisholm, W. E. B. Du Bois, Frederick Douglas, Sojourner Truth, Booker T. Washington, Barbara Jordan, Audre Lourde, Baynard Rustin, James Baldwin, and Langston Hughes can be heard in the great halls of the our communities. Juan Williams in his work *Enough: The Phony Leaders, Dead-End Movements, and Culture of Failure That Are Undermining Black America—And What We Can Do about It* asserts, "And anyone—including black leaders—who confuses black people about what it takes for their children to make progress is no friend. Over the last decades, black Americans have benefited from court decisions like *Brown vs. Board of Education*, the civil rights laws that offered some political legal protection and the development of strong political voices to advocate civil rights positions. But these things can only take black America so far. At some point, people have to take a personal accounting, turn away from any self-defeating behavior, and be sure they are doing everything in their power to put their families and their communities in a position to prosper and advance" (pp. 42–43). This requires evolutionary change.

Presently attention focused on the African American male labels him an "endangered species." A significant portion of research presents the many negative schooling outcomes, experiences, and social conditions of the African American male with less focus on the academic disparity between the African American male and his peers. The media portrayal of the African American male in sports, politics, and entertainment would have one believe that every African American male in America is aggressive, bestial, and prone to criminal activity. Information presented by news outlets un-critiqued would lead even the most politically astute consumer to believe that my brothers are shiftless, lazy, and nihilistic, and victims of their own circumstance. Little attention is given to those African American males who serve as chief executive officers of Fortune 500 companies and who serve as civic, business, political, and educational leaders who are affecting American lives daily. In *We Real Cool: Black Men and Masculinity*, scholar, writer, author and cultural critic, bell hooks poignantly presents the condition of the black man in America. She states, more than any other group of men in our society, black males are perceived as lacking in intellectual skills. Stereotyped via racism and sexism as being more body than mind, black males are far more likely to be affirmed in imperialist white-supremacist capitalist patriarchy for appearing to be dumb or as we called it growing up in the fifties, appearing to be slow (meaning not quite bright). In childhood it was obvious to everyone in our all black neighborhood that the thinking black man was perceived to be a threat by the racist world. There was no correlation made between one's ability to think, to process ideas, and level of schooling. Well-educated black men have learned to act as if they know nothing in a world where a smart black man risks punishment (p. 33).

Black males have engaged in forms of resisting hegemony that have been counterproductive, refusing to study for fear of "acting white," posturing and engaging in "cool" behavior to impress friends, and using "aggressive" vocal tones and body language to challenge authority. These behaviors are often misinterpreted and usually result in the student being referred for special educational services, suspension, or in worst-case scenarios, expulsion. Sandra Tutwiler in her essay, "How Schools Fail African American Boys" opines: "Schools and society treat African American boys as if they are society's expendable children. Fear, mistrust, and a lack of understanding has led to a set of reactions to them by school personnel and society at large that ensures an image of failure is maintained" (p. 143). I believe that these behaviors indicative of black males striving to navigate their identity within school cultures they find non-stimulating and engaging yield high levels of resistance. I have visited many schools in and outside the United States. Successful teachers of students regardless of circumstance and condition are those with engaged and inviting classrooms. Students themselves in these classrooms are the teachers. They engage their peers by questioning, inquiry, dialogue, and debate. Teachers in these learning communities facilitate the learning process by providing students with the resources, tools, strategies, and techniques to construct knowledge through their own lived experiences.

The lure of popular culture has always been a competing force in schools; however, a teacher who facilitates an engaged and inviting learning community integrates popular culture into the curriculum. She knows her students are "hooked in" and "wired to" all sorts of digital content and she uses it to provide her students with content to deconstruct and reconstruct taken-for-granted information and sources of knowledge and it is here that critical literacy and critical pedagogy interface with her leadership. Leadership for teaching and learning makes the student and subject the centers of the power and politics of schooling. The teacher who facilitates a classroom of learning understands and embraces this pedagogy that provides opportunities for students from all backgrounds, but particularly the African American male student with the space to navigate his identity through school cultures which are affirming and which yield low resistance but high achievement.

Critical Pedagogy

Public school administrators and teachers who seek to transform schools must operate from a position of understanding how critical pedagogy forces educators to critique the fundamental issues of power and its relationship to the greater societal forces that affect schools (Weis, 1988). Teaching and learning are a part of real life, and real life includes politics and people (Freire, 1970). Educational leaders must be able to use their positions to launch into the deep and ask hard questions, questions to which there are no perfect answers.

A third of African Americans have been trapped in a cycle of poverty and a poor quality of life because of inadequate educational preparation. We need a public education system that decolonizes the minds and imaginations of young people, a system in which teaching and learning for critical consciousness are the primary objectives. This is the foundation of liberatory education. Such practice moves beyond lesson delivery and focuses on constructing knowledge through questioning and critique. hooks (1994) speaks of the very nature of this practice.

> What does it mean for us to educate young, privileged, and predominantly white students to divest of white supremacy if that work is not coupled with work that seeks to intervene in and change internalized racism that assaults people of color; to share feminist thinking and practice if that work is not coupled with fierce action to share feminist thought and change sexism in all walks of life? To create a culture in which those who could occupy the colonizing location have the freedom to self-interrogate, challenge, and change while the vast majority of the colonized lack such freedom is merely to keep in place existing structures of domination. (pp. 5–6)

Teacher education programs and learning communities in general focus on privileged perceptions of the dominant culture. This is evident in many of the curriculum programs that stress "tech-prep," "groupings," and "tracking." Having spent a significant number of years in public schools in various parts of the United States in varying positions, it is my perception that a privileged white middle-class workforce continues to enter multiethnic public schools with their "own" worldview of educating the masses, with little regard for the masses' own worldview.

I have worked in settings where the perception was white teachers are "all-knowing," African American teachers have "limited knowledge," and black kids are "underachievers, but the gifted ones are exceptions." Ladson-Billings (1994) argues for "culturally relevant" teaching styles, because the desire of the African American community for a "quality" education is but yet an "elusive dream." For the "elusive dream" of a quality education to be realized, we must critique the present power structure, reflect upon that critique, and then act to bring about social transformation. Critical pedagogy is a liberating theoretical construct, which can provide the map for this journey. Critical pedagogy assist educators in critiquing issues of power and its relationship to societal forces that impact schools. It causes educators to question how and why knowledge is constructed the way it is, and how constructions of reality are legitimized by the dominant culture while others are not. We see this in educating "people of color," and "others" who are not a part of the privileged class. For example, when educating black children, often the culture of this group as a potential force for political, economic, and social development is given very little attention during the "schooling" process. Many times students are perceived to be passive recipients of knowledge transmitted by the teacher. Freire (1970) describes this didactic teaching by drawing upon the metaphor of banking

> A careful analysis of the teacher-student relationship at any level, inside or outside the school, reveals its fundamentally narrative character. This relationship involves a narrating Subject (the teacher) and patient, listening objects (the students). The contents, whether values or empirical dimensions of reality, tend in the process of being narrated to become lifeless and petrified...The teacher talks about reality as if it were motionless, static, compartmentalized, and predictable. Or else he expounds on a topic completely alien to the existential experience of the students. His task is to 'fill' the students with the contents of his narration. (p. 57)

In this construct teachers make deposits of information that the students receive and store for later retrieval and the more students work at storing these deposits but not reflect critically upon them or develop "critical consciousness," the more they are unable to intervene in the world as transformers of that world. Critical theory is a broad tradition based on the use of the critique as a method of investigation. The primary characteristic of this school of thought, which has its roots in the Frankfurt School, is that social theory regardless of whether it is reflected toward educational research, philosophy, literature, art, or business, it should play a vital role in changing the world and not heavily concerned with just recording information.

Critical Theory and the Frankfurt School

The Frankfurt School of "critical theory" was regarded by orthodox Marxists as "revisionist" partly because of its criticism of economics and crude materialism, and partly because of its eclecticism. In media theory it is important for offering the first Marxist attempt to theorize about the media (Gurevitch et al., 1982, p. 8). However, it provided no real way forward for the study of the mass media. The most notable theorists connected with the Frankfurt School were Theodor Adorno, Herbert Marcuse, and Max Horkheimer—all committed Marxists— who were associated with the Institute for Social Research, which was founded in Frankfurt in 1923 but shifted in 1933 to New York. The educational process in which African American children engage reflects European cultural and educative hegemony, the domination of one group over another with consent. The aim is to control the flow of knowledge to the dominated group and its ability to read the information. The stigmatization of African American males has been embraced by both blacks and whites. The power to critique and dismantle the dominant culture's system of promoting negative imagery of African American males through media, film, and music is beyond the ability of the oppressed group and because African Americans believe they are powerless they reify their own domination. Freire (1970) asserts it is the oppressed and not the oppressors who allow this to happen. As I "read" critical pedagogy for the African American educators who are a part of this work and me, critical pedagogy is a lens, which enables us to see clearly our past, our present, and our future. Critical pedagogy also provides tools and equips us with the ability to critique our past, reflect upon our present, and transform our future, not only as African Americans, but also as educators, change-agents, and human beings.

Critical pedagogy awakens in us as social and political actors the desire to transform our environment, institutions, and our world by becoming agents of democracy and social good for all humankind. This occurs through our understanding of not just transmitting knowledge, but by creating new knowledge. Vygotsky (1962) suggests that from the relationships of our thoughts and language new knowledge is created. This creation of new knowledge and language removes the barriers that are created from "old ways of knowing." Through this process we gain the language of possibility and the language of critique to inform our practice as educators and to facilitate learning environments in which students are empowered to create new knowledge from their lived experiences. By doing so students will understand and appreciate the true purpose of an education: to gain insight, knowledge, and critical understanding to transform your world and the world around you. Students will become cocreators of knowledge with educators by developing collegial relationships to engage in multiple readings of environments that shape our communities and institutions.

Educators who invoke critical pedagogy help others read the world and read the word (Freire & Macedo, 1987). We must be able to take the text, a collection of symbols and give them meaning. This reading can be interpretative, placing the text into context; normative, bringing ethical or moral positions to bear on the text; or analytical, viewing the text for claims or evidence. Regardless of whether the text makes an argument, it is likely to present a narrative or story. Through the language of possibility and the language of critique educators should no longer take for granted positions of power and privilege. The behavior, values, and practices that are valued by the dominant society are reflected upon critically and action is taken to transform those positions of power. This transformation can be seen in gender-equity and the absence of hierarchical power structures. Wink (1997) surmises that "cultural capital is a process of powerful practices: ways of behaving, talking, acting, thinking, moving, etc. These practices are determined unconsciously by the dominant culture and are used to promote success for specific groups in our society" (p. 34). For the transformation to occur we must experience the dialectic and then dialogue using our new language to create new "ways of knowing." We must experience conversations, listening and responding to various "voices" in the discourse. For the change to occur, there must be dialogue. Dialogue is two-way interactive sharing and visiting, which changes our context or us. As this communication takes place and goes on, discourse develops. The discourse is not just rhetoric; it is socially and culturally grounded. I consider discourse as politically centered, loaded conversations inherent in dominating power relations. Historically "people of color," Native Americans, and the "other" who operate from multiple identities, were not included in "the discourse" of education. Their voices still remain silent in various discourses, which have developed over the past century. I am problem-posing. Why are the voices of many "ethnic" groups absent from several discourses in the field of social science? Why are first-person narratives of African American educators absent from discourses on teacher education, educational leadership, and curriculum and instruction? Could there be something hidden in the process of instruction and/or the curriculum? Yes, indeed. Wink (1997) suggests that "the hidden curriculum is the unexpressed perpetuation of dominant culture through institutional processes. The hidden curriculum is covert and insidious, and only a critical lens will bring it into view. It teaches what is assumed to be important. It defines the standard for the dominant culture. Critical pedagogy asks: Whose standard? Whose culture? Whose knowledge? Whose history? Whose language? Whose perspective? Critical pedagogy seeks to make pluralism plural: standards, cultures, knowledge's, histories, languages, and perspectives" (p. 43). The hidden curriculum is supported sometimes by those it marginalizes and disenfranchises because they have not reflected critically on who they are and on their responsibility and also sometimes it is seen as a "means to an end." Educators have been taught how to transmit knowledge, but they have not been taught to reflect nor act critically. The learning community must practice critical literacy. Critical literacy is reading the world, or encoding the power structures and our role in these processes (Freire & Macedo, 1987). This critical reading includes the entire cultural, political, historical, and social context. By doing this we develop our praxis. "Praxis is the constant reciprocity of our theory and our practice. Theory building and critical reflection inform our practice and our action, and our practice and action inform our theory building and critical reflection" (Wink, 1997, p. 48). Throughout my educational experience, particularly in the early years when I was an elementary student, I was always told that I was very social, "too talkative." Many of my teachers stated that I was smart and they even labeled me "gifted." My belief was that I was supposed to be there to not only learn, but also to share my learning and knowledge with others. That was a very radical thought back in 1973. I knew that my experiences may help one of my friends in helping them to make "real" learning take place. I spent many hours in the corner, or writing lines, because, "I talked too much." I was punished at home often, because, I wanted to share the knowledge that I was receiving daily, not just from school, but also from my world. As a student and even now I believe schools are social. They contain real people with real problems who have valid concerns. Schools are not in isolation, nor are they immune to outside forces. Outside forces are brought inside daily by the members of the school community. Schools comprise competing and conflicting groups of people who desire to have their needs met regardless of condition or circumstance. These are the power and politics of teaching and learning. Teaching and learning are a part of real life, and real life includes politics and people. Schools are filled with sociocultural politics that have to be negotiated daily. How we negotiate those politics and who we empower or disenfranchise while negotiating them will determine our understanding of critical pedagogy.

Cultural Studies

Popular music has always had an impact on the lives of young people. Throughout history parents and teachers alike have strived to teach young people to arm and protect themselves against the ideological power of popular music. No period was more pronounced in this undertaking than the late 1980s and early 1990s. The censorship campaign organized by the United States government and the former vice president's wife Tipper Gore against "Gangster Rap" is unparalleled in any other time of censorship in our history. Hip-hop culture and rap music has reached global prominence and young people from all classes and ethnic backgrounds appear to identify with this genre of music. Young people today are consumed with redefining their identities. Their cultural significance is developed through the meanings they construct from the signs and symbols that comprise our world. Young people are recreating these signs and symbols into values that have meaning for individuality and collective identity. These expressions, signs, and symbols are ignored by the formal school curriculum and oftentimes are banished to the margins. This banishment continues to privilege an official school culture that forces students to identify and secure alternative resources to sustain desirable identities.

Culture is socially constructed and lived experiences translated from the meaning making of individuals, that is, how individuals view themselves daily as participants in the world around them and how they "make sense" of those daily interactions. Culture is not always directly observable; it must be understood through remnants of indirect evidence, which requires interpretation.

Culture is historically transmitted systems of symbols and patterns embodied with meaning. Culture is also the circuit of values, ideologies, and power in which multiple images, sounds, and texts are circulated and produced. Through this process identities are inhabited, constructed, and discarded. Institutions produce and constrain social practices, while agency is manifested in social and individualized constructs. The transmission of these symbols and patterns create discourses that make culture itself the object of inquiry and critical analysis (Giroux & Giroux, 2004). The communication and/or events from this process are often witnessed in the form of rituals.

Ritual is a key facet of cultural production. Rituals are forms of enacted meaning that enable us to frame, negotiate, and articulate our existence as social, cultural, and moral beings. Rituals are components of ideology that shape our perceptions of daily life and how we live.

In the national African American community in general, the concept of black culture is generally viewed and accepted as a severely limited one (Madhubuti, 1990). Madhubuti (1990) asserts that many African Americans view the concept of "culture" as an invisible entity: "To most of us, culture, as a concept, is abstract—that is, one does not actually observe culture. Yet, we all experience its manifestations, such as clothing, art, music, housing, weapons, films, literature, language, food, political, educational and social organizations and economic structures (p. 5)." Cultural studies is a transdisciplinary approach to "making-sense" of the world and it is "not based on disciplines, but focused on issues on gender, class, sexuality, national identity, colonialism, race, ethnicity, cultural popularism, textuality and critical pedagogy" (Giroux, 1995, p. 43). Cultural studies' foundation is formulated by the political and the ideological. Giroux also asserts:

> Cultural studies rejects the traditional notion of teaching as a technique or set of neutral skills and argues that teaching is a cultural practice that can only be understood through considerations of history, politics, power, and culture. Given its concern with everyday life, its pluralization of cultural communities and its emphasis on knowledge that is multidisciplinary, cultural studies is less concerned with issues of certification and testing than it is with how knowledge, texts, and cultural products are produced, circulated, and used. (p. 2)

This critique of cultural studies displays its interest in power and representation. Within and throughout the cultural studies discourse, power and representation comprise the very fabric of the construct; however, culture is the ground "on which analysis proceeds, the object of study, and the site of political critique and intervention" (Giroux, 1995). Lawrence Grossberg (1993) suggests that there are three commitments of cultural studies. "First, reality is made through human action, and consequently, contestation is a basic category. Second, the 'popular' is regarded as the 'terrain on which people live and political struggle must be carried out in the contemporary world'" (89). Finally, "cultural studies are committed to a radical contextualism which means that cultural practices cannot be reduced to or simply treated as texts" (as quoted by Henke, 2000, p. 7).

Subcultures are not isolated from the powerful; they are set in relation to the dominant cultures surrounding them (Quantz & O'Connor, 1988).

I am wielding a type of power based on positionality to yield a very different reading of the texts. I am striving to articulate the experiences of three African American female educators and one African American male educator, as well as four African American male "street educators" who are presenting controversial and unpopular rhetoric concerning their white colleagues and a formally subversive youth subculture that has undergone assimilation and commodification. These individuals also are presenting their praxis to an individual who brings his own worldview to the table. I am using the lens of cultural studies to deal emphatically and seriously with the work I have undertaken that involves the articulation and the negotiation of power as it intersects with race, class, and gender. "Power is the moving substrate of force relations, which, by virtue of their inequality, constantly engender states of power, but the latter are always local and unstable. [It] is not an institution, and not a structure; neither is it a certain strength that we are endowed with; it is the name that one attributes to a complex strategical situation in a particular society" (Foucault, 1979, p. 93). Educators and the very institution of education operate from and are constructed from social and historical relations of power. Because of this, privileged narrative spaces are constructed for some social groups (dominant culture) and a space for inequality and subordination is constructed for the "other." Foucault and Gramsci agree that power is not imposed from above, but that operations of power and their success depend on consent from below. For both Foucault and Gramsci, power is produced and reproduced in the interstices of everyday life, and for both, power is ubiquitous.

Becoming Social Justice Educators

The new millennium has arrived and schools are still faced with issues of power, race, identity, violence, and ethics. The meaning and purpose of schooling are being redefined, and the relationship between teachers and students has entered into a critical stage of renegotiating what and whose knowledge is of greater value. I believe our nation's children deserve the best education possible. Our place in global society depends on young people being able to use their knowledge, skills, and dispositions to critically identify and secure resources to create solutions to problems that are yet to be identified. Public schools in the United States must foster environments in which young people develop skills in new language acquisition, the ability to dialogue cross-culturally, and work collaboratively with people who do not identify with them. Brown (2006) asserts the following social and academic benefits of diversity to our society:

1. Enhanced student learning (i.e., diversity promotes learning for all students, classroom discussions involve more critical-thinking skills)
2. Preparation for work or further education (i.e., diversity prepares students for living and working in an increasingly diverse workforce and society)
3. Improved cross-cultural competence (i.e., diversity breaks down racial stereotypes and increases racial tolerance and understanding)
4. The creation of a set of leaders with legitimacy in the eyes of the citizenry (i.e., diversity reflects rapidly changing global demographics) (pp. 347–348).

While concurring with *Brown's* four benefits, I must also offer, the social and academic benefits of diversity move American democracy from a social experiment to lived experiences for the citizens of this country. Students better understand how competing and conflicting individuals coexist, reach consensus, and construct perspectives that affirm the value of human life with dignity, respect, and love. Access and equity are still issues for those who are not members of the dominant culture, because barriers and hierarchical power relations have not been replaced with realms of equality. Sue Books (2007) in her essay, "Devastation and Disregard: Reflections on Katrina, Child Poverty and Educational Opportunity," speaks of the powerlessness felt by many:

> As I think about the scope and depth of child poverty in this country, about the ghettoization that isolates poor blacks and immigrants in central cities, about the persistent disparities in school funding across and within states and school districts, about highly publicized "achievement gap" between white students and their black and Latino peers across the socioeconomic spectrum, about declining wages among all but the highest paid workers, and about the growing number of people coping with untreated sickness and injury because they cannot afford health insurance, I wonder, how many others have been left behind, pushed to the wrong side of the nation's vast divide between the haves and have-nots and rendered invisible by a political gaze directed elsewhere. (p. 5)

What must we do to insure not only the success of African American youth, but the success of all of America's youth? School districts, board members, teachers, administrators, parents, and students must recognize the importance of an integrated education. They must "fight for integrated education as both a basic educational goal and a 'compelling social interest' in a society going through vast racial transformation" (Brown, 2006, p. 347).

Integration matters require us to rethink racial, cultural, and gender politics in ways that foster border crossing and bridge building among and within communities to overcome issues of adversity. Together as a critically consciousness nation we will address the propensity of America's youth to not strive to gain critical knowledge to transform their lives and their communities. Integration matters require educators to confront issues on identity, sociocultural politics, and notions of resistance by being advocates of social justice (Cooper & Gause, 2007). Educators committed to social justice often confront hegemony and dominant-culture thinking. They engage in a form of pedagogy that speaks of notions of justice, compassion, and equity. Social justice educators critique taken-for-granted perspectives on power, politics, and schools so that learning communities engage in policies, procedures, and educational delivery that is equitable and culturally responsive. Schools and classrooms are places of inquiry where everyone's voice including the voice of dissent is welcomed and affirmed. Social justice educators cocreate these learning communities with all stakeholders. Their classrooms are democratic and participatory, providing an environment in which each participant feels empowered to engage in dialogue and debate, share their perspective, and above all, contribute to the development of knowledge for each member in the learning community. Social justice educators also encourage students to critique school, society and self. We believe the scrutiny of racist, sexist, classist, and homophobic practices in schools is a part of our pedagogy. We also believe that the examination of the inequities related to ability and language is included in a democratic and liberatory education. Pushing students out of their comfort zones is a central part of our instructional methodology and can be found in materials used and assignments given. Social justice educators encourage students to speak, think, and act critically while drawing upon courage, and moral and political fortitude.

The narratives, stories, biographies, autobiographies, ethnographies and auto-ethnographies of African American educators and young black males continue to be limited in academic discourse, particularly in educational leadership, policy, and teacher education. The absence of these important voices contributes to the duality in which African Americans must struggle. And because of the absence of the marginalized and silenced "other" in the literature, there are very few current first-person narratives, which articulate the issues African American educators face in educating today's youth and the actions today's young people who have been pushed out, dropped out, and/or moved out of public school classrooms must take to survive.

· 2 ·

BLACK MASCULINITY

Man of Fire-Man of Passion

No, I am not an angry black man
Although 50 years after Brown v. Board
Children of poverty and children of color are still mis-educated

No, I am not an angry black man
Although, I reside in a country that historically and
Continues to marginalize and dis-enfranchise "The Other"

No, I am not an angry black man
Although, the policies and procedures of this region
Are still rooted in White Supremacist Capitalist Patriarchy!

No, I am not an angry black man
Although, individuals who identify as Gay, Lesbian, Bi-sexual or Transgendered
Are vehemently despised and not protected by those who claim
To love each of them with the love of God

No, I am not an angry black man
Although, I am constantly reminded by some educators
Through their actions, that I don't deserve the respect often given by them
To my white colleagues

No, I am not an angry black man
Although, I am always under the "gaze" of
Suspicion, policing, interrogation, and even retribution

No, I am not an angry black man!

I am a brother who is a social activist
I am a colleague who is a critical theorist
I am a leader who believes in peace and social justice
I am an educator who views the world from multiple perspectives
I am a Same Affection Loving Soul who seeks the same
I am a friend to the friendless
A man of compassion
A guide
A light in the time of darkness
I am the reflection of the Divine Creator who has called me to
Transform the world, the human condition, the human spirit so that
We can all be who we need to be not just for self, but for you and for me.
No, I am not an angry black man
I'm just a man, a man of fire and a man of passion. (©Charles Phillip Gause)

Through the lens of critical spirituality, queer legal theory, and collaborative activism, I offer a critique which is pragmatic and hopeful and which goes beyond the historic construction of black masculinity that consistently appears in the popular imagination as the logical and legitimate object of surveillance, policing, containment, and punishment. This is why I open the chapter with my "Man of Fire-Man of Passion." I wrote it as a response to my first experience with graduate students in North Carolina. While engaging a seminar with a cohort group of practicing and aspiring school administrators enrolled in a Master of School Administration program, I continued to hear sidebar conversations challenging some of the information presented. I was sharing my mission and vision regarding educational leadership and social justice, although some students were engaged, many of them appeared to be disinterested. I thought to myself, "How could a group of adults be behaving in such disrespectful manner?" I told them that my goal was through the language of critique and possibility, to bring a level of criticality to the dialogue and discourse surrounding leadership preparation and to do so means challenging the present notions about schooling and the politics of local educational agencies. I further informed this group that I believed in developing learning communities that understood that democracy was messy, provocative, and it required the participation of all voices in the dialogue. After assisting the students in understanding the power of language, I reminded them the use of language should be purposeful and I was currently engaged in that practice during our seminar. I closed the seminar by challenging them to question the present hegemonic policies, procedures, and practices of their school communities, especially those that continue to disenfranchise and marginalize students of color, students in poverty, and students who articulate alternative gendered identities.

This was not anything unusual for me. I had presented this rhetoric often before and during class sessions with all my courses as an activity to deconstruct power relations in our language, actions, and ideologies. I wanted them to understand "what they see" may not be really "what they see." I knew my positionality and social location would contribute to some level of resistance; however, I thought the South had at least begun its great transformation, particularly after the death of Jesse Helms and Strom Thurman. I had enacted and practiced pedagogy of hope activism because I view myself as a passionate pedagogue who believes in social justice, transformational leadership, and democratic education. I thought at the time that these students wanted to transform schools and their communities; however, I was wrong.

The class comprised white and black females and males. The age representation was late twenties to early fifties and the group represented a spectrum of classroom teachers, district level personnel, and acting assistant principals. I knew a majority of the group had spent most of their academic career and personal lives in North Carolina and the southeastern part of the United States; however, I thought with the bombardment of popular culture and the plethora of educational material presented to educators through print and digital media, this group would somehow be just a little different, but they were not and I began to see several common themes from the previous classes that I had taught over the past academic year emerge. At the conclusion of class as I got into my car, I overheard a group of black and white male and female students, state "he's just an angry black man."

As I heard a loud chorus of agreement, I knew this term "angry," was not used to mean moral outrage, but it had a negative connotation. The use was rooted in racist and sexist constructs to further perpetuate the notion of a black man who shows any emotion is bestial, aggressive, and animalistic. I could not believe what I was hearing. How could they misconstrue my passion for knowledge, my spirit of activism, and my love for teaching as anger? How could a seminar on resistance, spiritual renewal, and transforming schools into vibrant and affirming learning communities be reduced to a stereotypical assertion? Why are black men who respond with passion and compassion to injustices considered to be angry?

I spoke with my colleagues about the cohort and what took place after class the previous evening. I wanted as diverse a perspective as possible, and so I presented the scenario to a group of colleagues that included an African American female, a Jewish female, and two white males. I am the only African

American male in the professoriate in the entire School of Education and my department, and so I could not gain a perspective from another black male professor who has interfaced with that group. As we discussed the many issues on this cohort, a sense of entitlement, privilege, and lack of respect for professorial authority; we discovered that the previous courses that addressed diversity, change, and difference, without such an uproar were taught by white male faculty members. Ultimately we realized many of our students never had an African American male as a professor in their entire academic career until I joined the department. Confronting issues surrounding racism, sexism, ageism, and gender identity when presented by a white male faculty member elicited a different response from that presented by a female faculty member and/or a faculty member of color. Gender, race, class, and cultural politics were at work in this cohort and I believe that to dismantle the master's house, I was going to need a different set of tools.

One of the major psychological traps preventing black males from actualizing their dreams is getting caught up in the web of dichotomous thinking that arises from polarities generated by living under white oppression: the inclusion/exclusion dilemma, acceptance versus rejection of mainstream norms and goals, gay versus straight, black versus white lifestyles, acquiescence versus assertive confrontation, macho toughness versus authentic caring, and so on. This experience forced me to put my pen to my paper and do something pragmatic, controversial, and revolutionary. I distributed and recited the poem at the next class meeting and then invited the students to investigate their own identity politics. Many of the responses were superficial. "I don't see color." "I believe in equality." "I'm not prejudiced." Inside, I chagrined at the responses. How could these practicing and aspiring school administrators not see beyond their own frame of reference? They had not engaged in a level of criticality about their own practice and they considered themselves seasoned and thoughtful educators. I was disturbed and realized that my work as a social justice educator as one who believes in education as the foundation of liberation and as a tool for engagement and empowerment, had only just begun. I thought this group of students picked by their superintendent had at least begun the process of deconstructing their own practice. During class they often informed me that they had diversity and sensitivity training. I told myself that evidently it was a session rooted in transformation; because issues of color blindness were spoken of in the class and superficial statements on what one wasn't were still at the forefront of many of their conversations. I wanted them to understand that negotiating identity politics and questioning one's practice were part of being a democratic progressive educator. Critical reflection was the essence of understanding self and others in ways beyond superficiality. The semester ended far better than it began; however, the event still haunts me at times.

Black Male Images: Tools of Liberation or Consumption

The international face of the United States of America is African American and male. The explosion of rap music, hip-hop culture, and professional sports has turned the black male image into a marketing icon designed to sell by any means necessary (Magubane, 2002).The popularity of reggae, jazz, and rap music in places such as Bosnia, China, and New Zealand testify to the global rise of the cultures of the black Diaspora. During the days of American apartheid, representations of blackness was nearly absent in American popular culture. Black characters, with the exception of the occasional maid or butler were rarely seen in television shows and movies. In less than four decades African Americans have gone from being invisible in popular culture to one of sheer dominance. Douglas Kellner (1995) in his book *Media Culture* speaks of the significance of media culture in our society:

> Our current local, national, and global situations are articulated through the texts of media culture, which is itself a contested terrain, one which competing social groups attempt to use to promote their agendas and ideologies, and which itself reproduces conflicting political discourses, often in a contradictory manner. Not just news and information, but entertainment and fiction articulate the conflicts, fears, hopes, and dreams of individuals and groups confronting a turbulent and uncertain world. The concrete struggles of each society are played out in the texts of media culture, especially in the commercial media of the culture industries which produce texts that must resonate with people's concerns if they are to be popular and profitable. Culture has never been more important and never before have we had such a need for serious scrutiny of contemporary culture. (p. 20)

The marketing and commodification of celebrities, particularly black celebrities and their images are so important to advertising in this digital age. One of the distinguishing features of late-capitalist culture has been the fusing of American culture's latent and persisting desire for blackness with consumerist desire.

The political disturbances and cultural rearticulations of the black male image as presented by the media require a critique that moves beyond the hypersexualized heterosexual menace to society. In *Scripting the Black Masculine*

Body: Identity, Discourse, and the Racial Politics in Popular Media, Ronald L. Jackson II asserts: "With the emergence of new media transducing racialized information from multiple popular cultural constituencies and mass-mediated news sources, and through the steady climb of hate group prosyletization via the Internet, Black bodies are being socially reconstituted and redefined on a daily basis" (p. 5). While the varied images of superathlete, gangster, and ghetto superstar travel across different fields of electronic representation and social discourse, there are multiple representations of black gender identity that are absent from mediated discourses. Black heterosexual masculinity is used in policy debates, in television news, and popular film representations to link the signs of patriotism, whiteness, family, nation, and individual responsibility.

Gender is fluid and not a static concept. Our human behaviors and their interpretation by those who witness them speak of how gender is constructed, enacted, performed, and contextualized. To be male or female is to engage in and read a pattern of behaviors for the production of gender. Masculinity and black masculinity in particular, is not a compilation of lifestyles; although popular culture seeks to construct black masculinity from a pattern of consumption. Black masculinity is constituted and constructed in relation to other gender identities. These constructions are based on how those relations interface with social structures. Gender and masculinity are performed on the basis of the circumstances and people that surround us and how we view the way in which we are viewed. Commercial hip-hop and its construction of black masculinity create environments that nurture aggressive behaviors we see portrayed in music videos and hear in the lyrics of many heavily rotated songs. The action of these heavy rotations serves as a vehicle for the continuation of the construction of black masculinity in popular space as a way to reify negative constructed identities.

Rux (2003) using an interpretation of Fanon's (1986) dream reality/dream identity, speaks of the social construction of gender. Rux (2003) asserts African Americans, the oppressed, continue to live in the dream of identity, the dream that (in reality) the oppressed are, in fact, Negro, Colored, Black, Minority, Afro or African American, Hispanic, Oriental, Dykes, Bitches, Hos, and Niggaz. All are accepted as real identities. The acceptance of these identities further compels a performance of these identities, whether compliant or rebellious. Juan Williams in his work *Enough: The Phony Leaders, Dead-End Movements, and Culture of Failure That Are Undermining Black America—and What We Can Do about It* offers this: In March 2006, the *New York Times* reported on its front page that a "huge pool of poorly educated black men are becoming ever more disconnected from mainstreamed society and to a far greater degree than comparable white or Hispanic men" (p. 23).

Black males in America, a systematically oppressed and depressed group, must no longer accept nor perform these identities. Discursively located outside the margins, representations of African American males who are contributing legally to the American economy by serving as power brokers in Fortune 500 companies, rearing children in same-gender multiracial households, and providing financial, cultural, human, and social resources to their communities do not serve as the symbolic basis for fueling and sustaining panic about crime, the nuclear family, and middle-class security while displacing attention from the economy, racism, sexism, and homophobia. Contemporary expressions of black masculinity work symbolically in a number of directions at once; these expressions challenge and disturb racial and class constructions of blackness; they also rewrite and destroy the patriarchal and heterosexual basis of masculine privilege (and domination) on the basis of gender and sexuality. The contemporary images and expressions of black masculinity I offer work to disturb dominant white representations of black masculinity. These images also stand in conflict with definitions and images of masculinity within blackness. This is found most notably in constructions of black masculinity produced by the middle-class wing of the echo boomers and those produced by black men who negotiate and navigate gender/transgressing sexualities/identities. So how did we end up in this situation?

In her insightful book, *We Real Cool: Black Men and Masculinity*, bell hooks writes:

> Without implying that black women and men lived in gender utopia, I am suggesting that black sex roles, and particularly the role of men, have been more complex and problematized in black life than is believed. This was especially the case when all black people lived in segregated neighborhoods. Racial integration has had a profound impact on black gender roles. It has helped to promote a climate wherein most black women and men accept sexist notions of gender roles. Unfortunately, many changes have occurred in the way black people think about gender, yet the shift from one standpoint to another has not been fully documented. For example: To what extent did the civil rights movement, with its definition of freedom as having equal opportunity with whites, sanctioned looking at white gender roles as a norm black people should imitate? Why has there been so little positive interest shown in the alternative lifestyles of black men? In every segregated black community in the United States there are adult black men married, unmarried, gay, straight, living in households where they do not assert patriarchal domination and yet live fulfilled lives, where they are not sitting around worried about castration. Again it must be emphasized that the black men who

are most worried about castration and emasculation are those who have completely absorbed white-supremacist patriarchal definitions of masculinity. (pp. 9–10).

The current construction/representation of the black male brings together the dominant institutions of (white) masculine power and authority—criminal justice system, the police, and the news media—to protect (white) Americans from harm. Working this heavily surveyed and heavily illuminated public arena, the figure of the menacing black male is the object of adolescent intrigue, fascination, and commodification. By drawing on deeply felt moral panic about crime, violence, gangs, and drugs, numerous black entertainers; namely, athletes and rap artists have rewritten the historic tropes of black masculinity from provider and protector to pusher and pimp. This corrosive nihilistic construction of maleness reifies notions of (hyper)sexuality, insensitivity, and criminality that serve as the new tropes of fascination and fear for the dominant culture.

The cultural effects of these images are as complex as they are troubling. The complex cluster of self-representations embodied in images of the black male as rap artist, athlete, and movie star is complicit in racist depictions of black males as incompetent, oversexed, and uncivil—ultimately a perceived threat to middle-class notions of white womanhood, family, and patriotism. Self-representations of black male youth who construct their identities based on these mediated images rely on definitions of manhood that are deeply dependent on traditional notions of heterosexuality, authenticity, and sexism. Black heterosexual male youth who employ these representations see themselves as soldiers in a war for their own place in American society. These soldiers believe, in doing battle, they must threaten and challenge the white man's (liberal and conservative) conceptions of public civility, private morality, and individual responsibility. Through this performative act of black masculinity these youth become casualties of their own war.

Writing about the plight of the black male in the 2006 *Black Enterprise* essay "Can Young Black Men Be Saved?," Matthew Scott describes the condition of black males in America: "The statistics have reached near pandemic proportions. Several reports released at the start of 2006 highlighted a litany of corrosive trends: 50% of all black males drop out of high school; 72% of black male high school dropouts were unemployed in 2004; and by the time they reach their mid-30s, 60% of black male high school dropouts had spent some time in jail." I often ask the very same question, can young black men be saved?

Pleading the Blood: My God, My God Why Has Thou Forsaken Me!

I remember hearing my grandmother say, "in times like these you have to rely on your faith. You sometimes have to fall down on your needs and pray. You can't get up, you pray and wait and da' Lord will give you an answer. Once you got your answer, you get up and leave them burdens right down there. Move on give God the glory and continue on your journey." The question "Can young black men be saved?" needs no answer. But of course, they *can* be saved. Many are saved. They are living and leading productive lives. They are transforming their communities locally and globally, contributing to their homes, schools, synagogues, families, churches, and civic organizations daily. It is the power of deception that leads many to believe young black males are lost and headed for a path of destruction.

The words of Jesus Christ during his crucifixion reverberate within the consciousness of my being. The mainstream media and in many academic texts the black male is often castigated and castrated. His manhood is stripped from his humanity and his dignity is flogged from his flesh. It is only upon the rock of his faith that he finds shimmers of light and glimpses of hope. Regardless of how we are represented, I know the grace of God and the belief in a power greater than me will sustain not just me, but all "brothas" (black men) if we just plead the blood. Baldwin speaks of this rite, one in which I practiced as a "minister of the gospel," one that brought me to Baldwin (because we have many similar commonalities in our life histories); I thought pleading the blood would deliver me from my sexuality, from my downtrodden spirit of loneliness, and abandonment. Pleading the blood made me more aware of my faith in the Divine Creator. Here's Baldwin's description:

> When the sinner fell on his face before the altar, the soul of the sinner then found itself locked in battle with Satan: or, in the place of Jacob, wrestling with the angel. All of the forces of Hell rushed to claim the soul which has just been astonished by the light of the love of God. The soul in torment turned this way and that, yearning, equally for the light and the darkness: yearning, out of agony, for reconciliation—and for rest...Only the saints who had passed through this fire had the power to intercede, to "plead the blood," to bring the embattled and mortally endangered soul "through." The pleading of the blood was a plea to whosoever had loved us enough to spill his blood for us that he might sprinkle the soul with his love once more, to give us power over Satan, and the love and courage to live out our days. (as cited in hooks, 2004, p. 159)

Historically, spirituality has been a very important part of African American life in the United States. Brought to this country in chains, surviving the middle passage by relying on multiple systems of faith for safe passage, African Americans' life was centered on the practice of faith. This was our way of making sense of the events that were transpiring in our lives. It was a way of navigating the terrain of torture, despair, and senseless hope for redemption. Dantley (2000) asserts the following:

> Spirituality is that part of life and community through which we make meaning and understanding of the world. The spirit also informs our sense of resistance. What this suggests is that inherent in the resistance motif, which we believe is the spiritual impetus to create projects and agendas that transcends present realities of domestication and oppression. In fact, it is the spirit that informs our exogamous relationship to a transformed future rather than our being wed to the hegemony of the present. (p. 1)

Organizational religion is not spirituality. Spirituality is not capitalistic in nature nor does it seek to become an economic empire. Currently in our society we have megachurches that have the very appearance of Fortune 500 companies. Some of these entities speak of spirituality; however, spirituality goes beyond rhetoric. Spirituality is the nexus of belief made into action. At the core of how we view the world and engage in our daily interactions is this notion of faith and belief. Hudak (2007) presents the understanding of Huebner's (1998) essay, "Education and Spirituality" that speaks of an understanding of spirituality, religion, and faith with which I concur.

> One knows of that presence, that "moreness," when known resources fail and somehow we go beyond what we were and are and become something different, somehow new...it is this very "moreness," that can be identified with the "spirit" and the "spiritual"...Spirit is that which transcends the known, the expected, even the ego and the self. It is the source of hope...One who acknowledges that "moreness" can be said to dwell faithfully in the world...Through the presence of the "other" my participation in the transcendent becomes visible—the future is open if I will give up the self that is the current me and become other than I am. (as cited in Hudak, 2007, p. 346)

I believe the very essence of spirituality is found at the core of understanding "self" is powerless and we must become more than we believe ourselves to be. To know more of self and the world we inhabit by faith is the dimension of spirituality that goes beyond religion. Religion and spirituality both reside in dimensions of "faith and knowing"; however, it is what we know but what we are unable to articulate about our faith that goes beyond religion. Religion resides in knowledge, while spirituality resides in faith.

Black Masculinity

The historical evolution of the gender identity of African American males presents many problems for analysts due, in large part, to the quality and paucity of the remaining data that have been spared by the ravages of the legacy of capture, importation, and enslavement. It is clear, nevertheless, that at the level of values, attitudes, and behaviors, distinct characteristics of African American males can be discerned. What does it mean to be male and black in America? What informs the construction of black masculinity in our society? The construction of race is the precursor to understanding what it means to be black and male in America; however, it is the intersectionality of race, class, and gender that informs the totality of our being. To be a black male or an African American male in America is inextricably tied to the history of servitude, slavery, and sex within and between the races in our society.

Earlier research has shown that while many elements within the values, attitudes, and behaviors of white and black males are shared, the total configuration differs in quantity, quality, and their relationships to one other. This can be partially attributed to the legacy of African culture and significant causal factors derived from the dialectic of development of African American slavery and its Jim Crow aftermath, and, more recently, the social dynamics of black urban life. Of singular importance in this regard is the evolving male role as African American males themselves perceive it, against that which the larger, white society perceives.

Gender may have little to do with an individual's actual biological sex or sexual orientation as it is based on the sociocultural dynamics of what is defined as male or female (Case, 1995; Eskridge, 2000; Franke, 1995; Miller, 1995; Somerville, 2000; Terry, 1999; Valdes, 1995; Yoshino, 2002). "Gender is an ongoing, life-long series of evolving performances. Sex is chromosomal" (Lugg, 2007, p. 120). Chafetz (1974) presents in descriptive terms seven areas of masculinity. They are as follows:

1. Physical—virile, athletic, strong, brave. Unconcerned about appearance and aging;
2. Functional—breadwinner, provider for family as much as mate;

3. Sexual—sexually aggressive, experienced. Single status acceptable;
4. Emotional—unemotional, stoic, *boys don't cry;*
5. Intellectual—logical, intellectual, rational, objective, practical;
6. Interpersonal—leader, dominating; disciplinarian; independent, free, individualistic; demanding;
7. Other personal characteristics—success-oriented, ambitious, aggressive, proud, egotistical; moral, trustworthy; decisive, competitive, uninhibited, adventurous. (pp. 35–36)

Those scholars, who pinpoint the black male dilemma as deriving basically from the gap between the ideal male gender role for the American society and the actual ability of black males to realize it, miss the mark. Throughout American history, black males were not expected to be able to fulfill the ideal male gender role. Indeed, it was made abundantly clear that severe repercussions would follow if they made serious and persistent efforts to do so. Exercising power, at the economic, political, social, and cultural level, was not only not expected, but it was also fervently opposed. Indeed, this was the source for innumerable violent conflicts, notably lynching, pogrom-like invasions of the African American communities, and lesser forms of repression (Booker, 1997).

Black males and females of every period were quite aware of these iron ceilings placed on their advancement and of the restrictions that bound their every movement. For this reason, these barriers were regarded as a fact of black life, a clearly observable injustice, and this premise was embodied in the historically molded gender role values that emerged within Africa America. Thus, notions of the proper methods to respond to systematic injustice were and are an integral element of the evolving African American masculinity (Weatherspoon, 1998).

The dialectic of development for white males was historically linked to the underdevelopment of African American males. Slavery, reconstruction, Jim Crow, and other forms of exploitation served to transfer resources from blacks to whites. While there are some parallels between the social construction of white masculinity and that of blacks, it is notable that in almost every instance of, for example, war, technological change, or migratory movement, the lived experiences, perceptions, and the responses of black and white males to these challenges were distinct. In particular, the African American male experience with war has left a significant imprint on their masculine attitudes and behavior.

From the American Revolution, when some took advantage of Lord Dunmore's offer of liberty upon enlistment with the British, through the Spanish-American War when black heroism seemed unappreciated outside of the black community, to the Persian Gulf War, when returning veterans were greeted by mysterious illnesses, and unemployment. Disillusionment, bitterness and, contrastingly, a new determination to smash the remaining obstacles to free travel, full employment, and full respect for African Americans, have characterized the mood of returning black soldiers (Booker, 1997).

This historical oppositional cultural current within black male America continues to play a role and it can be seen in the diminished enthusiasm of black males for certain aspects of the mainstream American culture including the arenas of conventional business and politics. In the national African American community in general, the concept of black culture is generally viewed and accepted as a severely limited one (Madhubuti, 1990).

When educating black children, the culture of this group as a potential force for political, economic, and social development is given very little attention during the "schooling" process. The educational process in which African American children engage reflects European cultural and educative hegemony. Madhubuti (1990) asserts that many African Americans view the concept of "culture" as an invisible entity: "To most of us, culture, as a concept, is abstract—that is, one does not actually observe culture. Yet, we all experience its manifestations, such as clothing, art, music, housing, weapons, films, literature, language, food, political, educational and social organizations and economic structures" (p. 5).

Compensating for feelings of insecurity in a Eurocentric world has led the African American male particularly the youth to redefine what it means to be a man in the present world. For most, this includes risk taking, machismo, aggressive social skills, and sexual promiscuity. To be bad is to be cool and to be cool is a sign of power, strength, and protection. The latest brawl occurring in the NBA (National Basketball Association) is evidence of the black male's cultural signature, his cool. It is sometimes the only source of pride, dignity, and worth in the absence of the outward status symbols of materialism and title that mark success in American culture. His status rides on his ability to communicate through human encounters, the most important information about himself: his coolness, power and strength. The identity of coolness is so prized that preserving it becomes an end in itself. (Majors & Billson, 1992)

The consumption of these images reifies the construction of hegemonic heteronormative black masculinity. To not fight is a sign of weakness and effeminacy.

To not protect one's turf makes you less of a woman to be talked about across the airwaves and relegated to homophobic domination. This is evident in the latest lyrics in rotation on today's hip-hop stations. For the black male, to sexually dominate his opponent metaphorically and figuratively speaks of the absence of his heteronormative black masculinity, his maleness. These noted mannerisms include physical posturing, style of dress, dialect, walk, greeting behaviors, and how one is accessorized—in diamonds, platinum, and cars—further situates the construction of black masculinity and identity within the realm of commodification and consumption of image. The black male is socialized to view every white man as a potential enemy, and every symbol of the dominant system as a potential threat. Because of this, he is reluctant to expose his innermost feelings. Playing it cool becomes the mask of choice. Cool pose is a well-developed and creative art; it also exacts a stiff price in repressed feelings and suppressed energy.

African Americans and African American males, in particular, have resisted domination since slavery. African American males historically have rejected exclusion and marginalization. Genovese (1974) explains that enslaved Africans developed a culture of resistance to the institution of slavery and demonstrated their opposition through their language and communication patterns, their work rhythms, and their frequent running away from their burden of slavery (quoted in Kreisberg, 1992, p. 17). "These oppositional practices have been lived out and elaborated upon over the years, and constitute core cultural elements in the urban Black community today" (Weis, 1988, p. 185). This has been demonstrated consistently in our schools. The behaviors of black males are resistant forces. Many resist and disengage from "playing" the "school game." They find school not to be congruent with their own lived experiences and life goals. School is not viewed as a way to achieve the desire to make money, live large, drive a nice car, and enjoy life especially in the urban centers of our nation. Schools are filled with white female authority figures with no desire to understand who these students are, what they want to achieve, and who the communities which they inhabit are. So students who disengage from the educative process engage in the following behaviors: they deceive teachers, refuse to complete homework, smoke and sell "dope" in school bathrooms, delay the beginning of classes, and wear clothing and use language that is often offensive to adults. I consider the patterns of consistent inappropriate behaviors as the culture of resistance, which is evidenced by the destructive behaviors pervading black communities. Those behaviors are nihilistic in nature. West (1993) asserts, "nihilism…is far more, the lived experience of coping with a life of horrifying meaninglessness, hopelessness, and (most important) lovelessness" (pp. 22–23).

F. D. Weatherspoon in his *African-American Males and the Law: Cases and Materials*, has provided the following statistics that reveal the catastrophic levels of despair inherent in the lives of black men.

- One in four black men in the United States in the age group 20–29 is under the control of the criminal justice system–in prison or jail, on probation or parole.
- African-American males presently represent 38 percent of all individuals arrested for a drug violation.
- African-American males represent almost 40 percent of individuals on death row.
- More African-American males are incarcerated than enrolled in college.
- On any given day, African-American males are at least eight times more likely to be in prison than white males.
- African-American males receive longer sentences than white males who commit similar crimes.
- The homicide rate among African-American males is 125.2 deaths per 100,000 within the 24–44-age range, whereas the homicide rate for white males is 14.2 per 100,000.
- African-American males have a lower life expectancy than all other groups.
- African-American males are disproportionately suspended from school.
- African-American males have the highest dropout rate in elementary, secondary school as well as in college, if they go at all.
- African-American males with college degrees are three times more likely to be unemployed compared to whites.
- African-American males have the highest level of unemployment. (p. x)

Combating these statistics will require the African American community to engage in systemic transformational change that holds all members of the community accountable for their actions. This change will seek to re-create the spirit of unity as a form of collective work ethic for black men will come into own their rights as citizens of this democracy. This change will emphasize the development of critical consciousness and awareness as tools for engaging the educative process, and by doing so students will construct their visions of self with purpose and see their lived experiences as a part of constructing new ways of knowing to navigate society. Black males will radicalize the way in which they construct, enact, and perform their gendered identities. They will cease to consume images that reify aggressive heteronormative behaviors as forms of "true masculinity" and develop cognitive, spiritual, and emotional awareness in identifying and constructing new masculinities. They will seek help for and treat their pain in discovering the beauty of their creation.

Male Development and Masculinity

Dr. Naim Akbar (1982, 1992), a well respected black male psychologist, asserts that "maleness" is a mentality that operates with the same principles as biology, that is, it is a determined biological fact, which is in no way subject to choice. Akbar (1982, 1992) further suggests this mentality is dictated by appetite and physical determinants and guided by instincts, urges, and desires, and feelings. He continues to assert that the "male mentality" is predicated on a sexist and objectified perception of manhood and predominates only in males who are not willing to take the prerogatives and responsibilities of "real manhood." On the basis of this premise, Akbar believes, for black males to transform into black "men" (that is, responsible, productive citizens), their culture and orientation must be understood. According to Majors and Billson (1992), European Americans often view the lifestyle and culture of inner city black males as threatening, aggressive, and intimidating. These researchers view the nature of inner city black males as "cool pose," that is, he (the black male) is characterized as "being cool," "with the program," and "in the house." Majors and Billson (1992) defines this inner city black male disposition as

> [a] [d]istinctive coping mechanism that serves to counter, at least in part, the dangers that black males encounter on a daily basis. As a performance, cool pose is designed to render the black male visible and to empower him; it eases the worry and pain of blocked opportunities.... Cool pose is constructed from attitudes and actions that become firmly entrenched in the black male's psyche as he adopts a façade to ward off the anxiety of second-class status. It provides a mask that suggests competence, high self-esteem, control, and inner strength. It also hides self-doubt, insecurity, and inner turmoil. (p. 5)

A dilemma of the inner city black male is his desire to exhibit masculinity; he is too often grounded in "masking strategies" that require him to deny and suppress his feelings. He is highly attractive; he is perceived and perceives himself as the epitome of control, strength, and pride. However, even in his "charismatic, suave, debonair, entertaining" persona, he presents himself as a "mysterious challenge" (Majors & Billson, 1992, p. 2). The only way for black males to transcend the hegemonic construction of their masculinity and overcome these masking strategies is to seek new constructions by using the historical narratives of their brothers and sisters to construct new narratives of liberation. This requires a critical understanding of the spiritual self. African Americans must engage in critical spirituality, a process that undertakes, "critical self-reflection, deconstructive interpretation, performative creativity, and transformative action" (Dantley, 2007, p. 160).

Writing this text is critical spirituality engagement. I am practicing critical self-reflection by revising by practice as an educational leader and teacher. I am engaging in deconstructive interpretation by reading and rereading the research, narratives, and life stories of those interviewed. The use of poetry, multiple voices, and storytelling is the essence of performative creativity of this writing and the transformative action lies in bringing the many stories, events, and critiques to the reader. A process filled with anguish, pain, laughter, beauty and love, the result speaks of a new construction identity, queer black masculinity. I rely upon Queer Legal Theory presented by Valdes (1995) and Lugg (2007) to move toward a new way of understanding the construction of black masculinity because of the various issues surrounding the intersections of race, class, and gender and identity construction. According to Lugg (2007),

> Queer Legal Theory springs from the intersection of several strains of progressive thought in legal theory. It draws on Feminist Legal Theory's commitment to disestablishing patriarchy, Critical Race Theory's dedication to unmasking the deep racist structures within U.S. society and life, Critical Legal Theory's examination of how class structure are perpetuated and reinforced, and Gay and Lesbian Legal Theory's understanding how heteronormativity (the notion that the entire world is non-queer, or that it should be) is reproduced, while queer identity and individuals are eliminated. (p. 124. Internal citations omitted)

Given the history of slavery, racism, sexism, and homophobia in our country, I believe beginning with Queer Legal Theory also speaks of how I see myself as a same-gender-loving black male academic who seeks to disrupt taken-for-granted assumptions of gender and identity. Queer Legal Theory presents many different ways "to be," and therefore queering black masculinity is not only a professional project, but a personal one as well.

Queering Black Masculinity

I believe queer legal theory is important in answering questions of how black males see themselves juxtaposed with the African American community and the larger white society. I believe queer legal theory speaks of issues of race, class, gender, heteronormativity, patriarchy, white supremacy, and gender essentialism. These issues have historically, presently and will continue to have a profound impact on black male identity development unless a project of queering black masculinity is engaged. I begin the journey with this work. According to the expert on the subject, Francisco Valdes,

> "Queer" as a legal theory can and should help to signify inclusiveness and diversity. As culturally (and politically) reclaimed, the term's elasticity can and should accommodate all identities grouped into or within sexual minority categories, including the bisexual and the trans/bi-gendered. Using Queer cultural politics and studies as a substantive point of departure, Queer legal theory can be positioned as a race-inclusiveness enterprise, a class-inconclusive enterprise, a sex-inclusive enterprise, and a gender-inclusive enterprise as well as a sexual orientation-inclusive enterprise. Thus, Queer legal theory, perhaps even more so than Queer consciousness and Queer activism to date, must convey a sense of political resolution that this Project seeks to invoke: reflecting the gains and challenges of sexual minorities since the Stonewall Riots, Queer legal theory must connote an activist and egalitarian sense of resistance to all forms of subordination, and it also must denote a sense of unfinished purpose and mission. (1995, pp. 353–354. Internal citations omitted)

According to White and Cones (1999, p. 67), "in contemporary America, the distorted images of Black masculinity projected by the media and social scientists are an ongoing phenomenon." African American males are typecast as entertainers, clowns, and superathletes. As I sit down to compose this piece with the thought of making a difference as a teacher/researcher/leader-activist, I cannot help but reflect on how my masculinity (black masculinity[1]) has been constructed. I realize that I do not want to play the game that has been set by the heteronormative order (Koschoreck, 2003), but I also realize that this order has influenced my personal and professional choices. Am I possibly looking for validation of African "ways of knowing" (Asante, 1987)? Asante (1987) argues:

> African methods seek to legitimize expression, public discourse, feeling, myth-making, and emotion as acceptable avenues of inquiry. Unlike European paradigms, Afrocentrism seeks out transcendence—that is, the quality of exceeding ordinary and literal experience. (as cited in Watkins, 1993, p. 332)

There is a full range of gender expressions witnessed by all students, teachers, and administrators in today's public schools; however, given the power of the media, the only representation often presented of black males is the duffle bag boy—drug runner and money carrier; the thug—an aggressive no-holds-barred bad boy; and the convict—a prison lifer, always in and out of jail. The underlying messages in these images are ones of heteronormativity, homophobia, and patriarchy. The constructions of aggressive male identities are still prevalent because tolerance and not affirmation of the "other" continues to be the accepted norm in our society and schools are microcosmic representations of our larger society. The affirmation of queering masculinities by society as a whole and by school leadership would expand male-dominated constructions of maleness beyond the heteronormative. Queering masculine characteristics would move beyond typically viewed/accepted "male" behaviors and embrace behaviors of all members of the learning community regardless of sexually identified, gender-perceived, and biologically confirmed positionalities. The political disturbances and cultural representations of black masculinity in popular culture require new and different reading strategies and contextualizations. Currently black masculinity is rooted in masculine hero worship in the case of rappers and as naturalized and commodified bodies in the case of athletes. The combination of the two has yielded a new public enemy number one, a sadistic and masochistic heterosexist black masculine cyborg, devoid of emotion, thought, and remorse. Discursively these new black male representations bring together the criminal, the police, and the media as one packaged object for consumption. The stigmatization of African Americans continues to be embraced by all members of American society, white and black alike. What situations does black masculinity create for those brothers who refuse to play that game? Who decides the rules?

Schooling Black Males

According to Joseph (1996), Walker (1993), and Warfield-Coppock (1992), the public educational system has been dysfunctional and genocidal in its education and socialization of African American youth. The American public education system is defined as a white middle-class institution, tailored for the white middle class and not germane to the life of African Americans. This thought is supported by the lack of effort to incorporate the achievements and experiences of African Americans in the school curriculum, which sends a negative message to young black students about the importance of their educational development.

Is the failing of the black male one of the consequences society's failure to highlight the achievements of African Americans? Instead of fostering achievement, public schools reify the perceptions of the dominant culture with regard to the expressiveness of young black males (Harris, 1995; Lee, 1992; Majors & Billson, 1992; Mincy, 1994; Ogbu & Wilson, 1990). The representation of the black male continues to be constructed out of popular culture mediated discourses, and educational leaders are complicit in how they use this imagery to label youth. I have witnessed teachers and administrators from diverse backgrounds on several occasions single out black males as the source of trouble and a menace to classroom communities across the United States. Many of these young men are not given the chance to showcase their abilities owing to reputations earned from preceding years in schools. And because of their dress and cultural expression black males are disciplined, suspended, and expelled from school owing to the consumption and construction of popular identities. Schools are the primary locations in which youth construct their identities and learn how to consume them. If you want to be popular or just be considered "normal," you have to wear the "in" clothes, listen to the right music, and have the right digital gadgets to communicate with your friends. Because schooling is such a substantial process in identity formation, educational leaders must exercise courage in making educational decisions that promote social justice.

The American public education system has a secondary effect on the socialization of adolescent black males, however (Warfield-Coppock, 1992). Mincy (1994), Taylor (1990), and Taylor, Casten, Flukinger, Roberts, & Fulmore (1994) join Willis (1990) in suggesting that for the black male to succeed in this world, acquiring an education is very important. Specifically, high school is acknowledged as a central organizing experience for young black males. During this period, young black males are socialized by interactions between the black male, the adult administration/faculty, and fellow high school students. According to Brookins (1996), Gill (1992), Harris (1995), Joseph (1996), Kunjufu (1990), Mincy (1994), Walker and Sutherland (1993), and Willis (1990), public school records indicate that a disproportionate number of young black males are placed in a special education curriculum or remedial courses. Several authors agree that the overabundance of black males in special education, remedial academic tracks, and excessive disciplinary referrals are due to the low academic expectations of teachers and administrators in public schools. Poor academic performance and excessive discipline problems are attributed to the boredom that some young black males experience from a perceived irrelevance of the educational curriculum. It has been suggested that Black Male Educational Academies should improve the academic achievement of young black males through an Afrocentric curriculum that is taught by African American male instructors (Biggs, 1992; Detroit's, 1994; Gill, 1992; Impact, 1992; Lee, 1982; Lometey, 1992; Midgette et al., 1993; Wilson, 1991). The philosophy of an all-black-male academy is supported by President Bush's America 2000 Education Plan that called for 535 new American schools to be developed throughout the nation. Midgette (1993) listed the advantages of the Black Male Academies as (1) advocates of excellence that promote the development of the young black male; (2) achievement beyond sports in the subjects of math, language arts, and computer science; (3) expansion of the graduation ratio of young black males with the encouragement of vocation schools and college; (4) teaching young black males self-responsibility, self-love and appreciation of the human experience from an Afrocentric point of view and; (5) promotion of the family unity through parental involvement in academic and extracurricular activities.

Paul Robeson, Malcom X, and Marcus Garvey are the names of Black Male Academies in Detroit, Michigan (Detroit's, 1994). In Milwaukee, Wisconsin, the Kuumba Academy was formed to prepare black students to meet the expectations of the 21st century (MacCaskill, 1997). In Chicago, Hales Franciscan High School is an independent Black Male Academy that boasts of a hundred percent college acceptance rate for the classes of 1996 and 1997 (personal communication, 12/22/97).

Moving toward a New Identity

These solutions are the initial steps to counteract the nihilism that exists among young African Americans; I believe this is a start; however, it will take an integration of radical consciousness, critical spirituality, and a deep love of self and the community before young African American males can begin the journey to wholeness. According to Scott (2006), the Black Enterprise Board of Economists devised eight solutions that should be implemented to transform the condition of the black male in America:

- Create a philanthropic network.
- Increase mentoring and job shadowing opportunities.
- Restore Summer Youth Employment Programs.
- Actively campaign for early childhood education and school reform.

- Attack public policies that have an adverse effect on black males.
- Collaborate with other groups with common interests.

The aforementioned solutions should be coupled with those suggested by Gordon (2006) that all leaders and government officials should engage:

- Invest in child and parental development.
- Implement federal support at all levels of education.
- Ensure an education in which students truly amass knowledge and preparedness for the next level of schooling and life.
- Develop a universal, well-rounded, and comprehensive curriculum.
- Adequately train and compensate professional staff that teach in responsible ratios of adults to children and are trustworthy and culturally sensitive.
- Guarantee that all children have access to appropriate and sufficient facilities, curriculum resources, and materials. (p. 38)

How we view ourselves as men whose lineages are found in the Black Diaspora will dictate who we are, what we do with our lives, and how we impact our communities and society. I am not in the process of becoming, but I am, a spiritual brother who brings a level of criticality and understanding in making sense of our world. Life is a gift to be shared with one another as a form of love for our humanity. Life is often considered a game and if this is to be a thought in the mind of brethren, we must empower ourselves to create new games with new rules that honor the multiple identities we construct. We must engage in forms of resistance that build up our self-esteem, self-concept, and self-worth. We must most use the pain we feel to move to higher places of understanding and acceptance of our frailties and fears. Only then will we overcome our silence, and leave our existence on the margins to allow our passion to become our activism. As we move along the path of our journey we will understand the expressions of our gender are fluid and plural. The moment of transformation is when we love unconditionally, weep openly, and seek to feel the beauty of our weaknesses and strengths as human beings and not as men devoid of emotion. I offer you this prayer of renewal and faith:

> *Oh, Divine Creator of all things, we, beseech and honor your presence in our lives this day. The dreams of who we are as black males are no longer shattered by the "unscripted reality" that exists in our schools and society. Who we are is not predicated by the faceless identity the media has created for us. We are yet African American males whose lives of love, lest we*

forget, are interwoven with the intersections of our race, class, gender, and political selves. Our new masculinities rupture the institutions constructed to oppress our identities; our family, our schools, and our churches. This love for self and others is no longer situated in institutionalized oppressive practices. We have overcome with your hands of grace and mercy. We are liberated men who remain committed to transforming our lives and communities through anti-oppressive practices with the gifts of love and understanding. We do not forget, you the Divine Creator of all things and giver of life. We know we were created each of us within a "divine image of love," and for that we are grateful. We thank you for all things and for you who transverses our presence in unity, peace, oneness and love. Amen.

Note

1. Black masculinity is situated with a racial construct. It is tied to the historical and political implications of being black in America.

· 3 ·

FROM PREACHERS, PUSHERS, AND PIMPS TO HOOCHIES, HEIFERS, AND W(HO)RES: LEADERS OF THE NEW SCHOOL

Brother Denied

We no longer hold you up above the heavens in which the gods
Drink their nectar

We no longer pay you homage for the ancestry and kinship
That is rightfully yours

Our eyes no longer look at you with love and compassion
That often greets those of royalty

The smell of dirt and shiftlessness
Tickle our noses because of the disdain for whom
And what you represent

Our waiting has been in vain
For your rise to the position of
Lover, authority and head of household

The births that welcomed you have ceased to occur
Why?
You kill that which is born from you
By neglecting the spirits which spoke of your glory and of your coming
We hide from you

You
Who they hate but we embrace
You who we long love

To end your terror
Our love is your love
Yet you will not receive
Freedom from self is what you need

Why?
We know not, yet
You are the one
The denied brother
Brother denied (©C. P. Gause, 2007)

The African American community has long endured the fall and rise of black men. Some were anointed black leaders and spokesmen for the entire community and others were self-appointed. We saw those who were gifted preachers, professionals, and political leaders in the civil economy, as well as those who were gifted preachers, pushers, and pimps in the underworld economy. I don't have to name them. We are reminded daily who they are by a host of "news" shows, political pundits, and bloggers. We see them daily on our streets, in our schools, and in our churches. The continuing importance of religion and the role of the church in black politics and leadership are well documented. Survey-based research from many scholars through the late 20th century speaks of the role of black churches as incubators of political activism. The black church served as a vehicle for race-group identity development, a point of building solidarity, and a place of mobilization for resources and political leadership. As we enter the early 21st century, the scope of the black church and her leadership has changed. Black leadership is no longer mobilized through churches; other locations, such as the Internet, college campuses, and community activist organizations have developed. Many of today's black youth are not active church members, because they have witnessed the hypocrisy of black leadership. Many have witnessed the message of prosperity as a form of depriving their single mothers of resources needed for the family. They have listened to messages of hope grounded in waiting on the Lord to deliver them while their pastors build large homes, drive fancy cars, and wear the best clothes even as they have little or nothing in their homes. The call and response of the preacher's rhetoric to our need to be seen as victims reverberate through the hallowed halls of our communities. These men profess to be Christians, pastors, church leaders, and men of faith, but their interpretation of Christ's Gospel is often one of civility and not rooted in progressive interpretation. Michael Dantley, a leading researcher in critical spirituality, who happens to be an educational leader and pastor of a very large congregation in the Midwest, believes a progressive interpretation of the Christian faith causes the believer to be pragmatic.

> Spirituality grounded in a progressive interpretation of the Christian faith is one that motivates the believer to bring about radical change in society and culture. For many, spirituality linked with a traditional religious expression, emphasizes docility and acquiescence to the structures and rituals of the dominant society. It is claimed by some that Christian spirituality is best demonstrated by compliance with the status quo and blind acceptance of the authority stemming from established cultural institutions. (Dantley, 2005, p. 130)

I concur with Dantley's critique of those who profess Christianity, but yet their interpretation of their faith facilitates a response of docility. The essence of Christian is to be a follower of Jesus Christ and he was not docile. Christ's life was pragmatic and controversial. I believe we must critique the leadership of our faith organizations because many encourage blind-faith leadership from their congregations. The leadership of such congregations reminds us who we are as a collective, with regard to gender and racial politics and never speaks of our individual and collective identities as forces of power and truth in our society. I want to believe what I hear from their voices; however, they operate from an outdated basis of "group think." "Prominent leaders like Al Sharpton and Jesse Jackson, neither of whom has ever won an election or held political office, have—through the force of their personalities and rhetoric, and the limitations of their ideas and strategies—slowed the emergence of any new model of national black political leadership" (Williams, 2006, p. 47). I am a beneficiary and a child of the civil rights revolution. This revolution included the passage of the Civil Rights Act of 1964, the Voting Rights Act of 1965, and the Fair Housing Act of 1968. Their impact on black America has been unprecedented. The fight to achieve these milestones was facilitated and brokered by black leadership, both male and female. The premise of these laws was the removal of the legal basis for racial domination by whites. As a collective, these acts of legislation were just as profound as the landmark *Brown v. Board* decision of 1954 by the United States Supreme Court. Black people and their leadership did gain cultural, social, and political capital; however, over the past forty years since the inception of the civil rights revolution, black leadership has succumbed to the temptations of white capitalism.

Many of the black leaders have become capitalists, believing the greatest path for change is to become giants in America's economy. Because of this shift, the black community continues to be impoverished. I respect the ideology and philosophy of the leaders of the civil rights revolution; however, I came of age during the first wave of the information age. I was taught to believe that information is power and how we use it can be more powerful than we can imagine. The information about the African American community of today is not empowering. It is filled with hate and despair. Schools are resegregating and/or never have achieved full integration; communities are suffering from economic blight; and the business of the black church focuses now on becoming bigger but not better. Despair is everywhere. My mother and father reared us to not succumb to this despair but to use the power in our faith and ourselves to transform our condition. It is here that our hope lies. I was taught that the black community is neither monolithic nor homogenous. It is filled with individuals across the Diaspora and it was up to me to define my identity. The black community includes individuals with roots across the globe. We are multiracial, multiethnic, and multilingual. Our political affiliations range from ultraconservative to neoliberal and independent. Our faith systems are rooted in all known religions and those of us who live and worship in the United States have more church denominations to consider than the number of ice cream flavors found in the dairy case of local grocery stores. Black people in America continue to be victimized by leaders who relive the civil rights movement as the only movement of transformation and liberation in our society.

Black Leadership

In 2004 at the Democratic National Convention in Boston, Rev. Al Sharpton, the self-appointed black leader from New York City who ran for the party's nomination, responded to a speech given by President Bush at the urban league by asking, fifty years after the *Brown* decision, if quality education for all children is at the heart of what he called "the promise of America," why do we as a people continue to establish and maintain communities and leadership that do no good for the people, but only present superficial rhetoric to make us feel good? Black leaders have always risen to the occasion in the past, and in far more desperate situations. Where are our talented leaders now? Many of them are heading global corporations, governmental agencies, and religious organizations. They have left the charge for civil rights to integrate into mainstream society and hope to make changes. I believe the presence of many black leaders has brought about major changes in domestic and foreign policies, as well as legislation and regulations that govern our daily lives; however, some may be complicit in perpetuating negative constructions of what it means to be black. Heads of corporations do make decisions on products we consume, the cost and safety of those products, and how the manufacturing of those products will be regulated. Does making profit and keeping the shareholders happy outweigh our moral responsibility to insure that corporations do not engage in practices that can be destructive to a group of people? If we look at just one industry, the media industry, we may have our answer.

There are some in the black community who engage in social transformation; however, there are large portions of our community who engage in sociocultural politics that has yielded poor schools for our youth, persistent high rates of unemployment, and a sentiment of government entitlement that is generational in nature. I have met four generations of one family who receive public assistance, in the form of food stamps, subsidized housing, and vouchers to pay for their utilities. The members of this family are ambulatory and have the ability to be gainfully employed; however, the majority of them are employed by the underground economy. Money in the African American community and having lots of it speak volumes to many African American youth, male and female. How one acquires excessive amounts of money; particularly if it is through the deadly drug economy, is often celebrated. To be a duffle bag boy and/or hustler gains much respect in many urban ghettos. Writing about the practice of hustling in *Look Out, Whitey,* Julius Lester (as noted by hooks, 2004) presents the following:

> Today resistance manifests itself in what whites can only see as the "social ills" of the ghetto, i.e. crime, high school dropouts, unemployment, etc. In actuality, many blacks have consciously rebelled against the system and dropped out. After all, why waste your life working at a job you hate, getting paid next to nothing, when you make more money with half the effort. So, a new class is created, the hustler who gambles, runs numbers, pushes drugs, lives off women, and does anything to avoid going to "meet the man" five days a week, year in and year out. It is dangerous, rough, and a none too beautiful life, but it has some compensation: A modicum of self-respect and the respect of a good segment if the community gained. (p. 19)

The African American community continues to consume and perpetuate the negative imagery that pervades the "public sphere" by encouraging nihilistic and anti-intellectual behavior that can be viewed via video and gaming technology, Web portals, video streaming, television, and other forms of print and digital media. Go to any high school in the United States on any given day and you will see this evidenced. School administrators continue to struggle with negotiating the elements and influence of popular culture on the daily lives of students. Popular culture cannot be controlled, policed maybe, but not controlled. Nor should it be, for I believe we have to give students the tools to negotiate culture, navigate identity, and resist any media they choose not to consume. However difficult, it *can* be done. I share my thoughts about how it can be done in the following paragraphs.

During the course of my educational career, particularly in the past five years, African American educators and white teachers have discussed the achievement gap among white, black, and Hispanic students at great length. Reading circles, attendance at professional meetings, and critical analyses of the topic have all been undertaken to better meet the needs of the students. Further conversations have centered on how to get parents and civic and community leaders involved in the schools and with specific populations. I realized one day that we were leaving the key component out of the conversations, the students. During my last year as a school administrator, I did an informal survey by asking students I saw throughout the day, who they would like to see in their schools. Interestingly enough, white students often talked about individuals who represented career professionals, Hispanic students often mentioned career professionals and individuals who had businesses in the community. Black students for the most part often spoke of entertainers, namely rap stars and professional athletes. After spending nearly two weeks asking the same question and getting the same answers, I brought together a group of black students who were considered leaders in the school but who also had the same type of answers and asked them why they only wanted rap stars and professional athletes to come to their school. The answers focused on the fame and fortune often associated with these individuals and how they are always in the spotlight. I then began a conversation with this group by talking about how the media portrayed life. I invited them to do a critical analysis of the images shown on television and the messages that were communicated. These students took the essence of leadership to the next level. I realized that we have not lost our talented tenth in the black community. The talented tenth have grown exponentially and with guidance will transform their communities. The following is a summary of our findings:

African Americans continue to be demonized subhuman species by mainstream media outlets. We are often portrayed as

- Welfare queens
- Whores
- Heifers

- Hoochies
- Public housing tenants
- Rapists
- Murders
- Spouse abusers
- Lying preachers
- Drug dealer or pushers
- Pimps
- Prostitutes

We often appear in various media outlets as individuals

- Who are anti-intellectual,
- Who do not vote,
- Who are overly sexualized,
- Who are aggressive,
- Who are often substance abusers.

The news media often bombards the "airwaves" with negative statistics and images of African American families. They contribute the negativism to weaknesses within our community structure.

- Female-headed households
- No work ethics
- Poor work ethics
- Underclass values
- Criminality
- Uneducated
- Victimization

At the conclusion of the activity, I asked the students how they felt about what they found, and they shared the difficulty in accepting how everything on television is skewed and biased. The students also began thinking about their own futures and did some additional research and discovered:

Although African American children may score lower on standardized tests than their white counterparts they have

- Higher educational aspirations
- Higher occupational aspirations

- Creative ability
- Stamina and athletic prowess

Since the students empowered themselves to be critical thinkers, I wanted to know what they were going to do next and they shared the following:

Stand up and claim our rightful place in society as

- Heirs
- Nubian princes
- Nubian princess
- Business executives
- Doctors
- Engineers
- Musicians
- Entrepreneurs
- Great husbands
- Great wives
- Committed same-sex partners
- Great children
- Dreamers

Black Values Postintegration

Scholars point to a shift in class values in black life once integration was upon us. There have been many movements: political, social, and cultural. We have the opportunity to live anywhere we choose, practice any profession we like, and vacation among the rich and famous. We have purchasing power that includes owning major corporations. We sit on the boards of Fortune 500 companies and serve as chief executive officers. We invest, develop, market, and distribute products to all sectors of society. From tennis shoes to bottled water we are behind and in front of the products many Americans consume. Why do many of our communities still suffer in abject poverty? Why do our young people wear this notion of a "hard life" as a badge of honor? In this *era of idols*, why do our young people consume and enact the gangster image, the pimp lifestyle, and objectify their bodies as tools for profit? Black male youth today would rather be a duffle bag boy (i.e., drug runner and money carrier), thug (i.e., an aggressive no-holds-barred bad boy), or convict (i.e., a lifer in terms of prison, in and out of jail) instead of a gainfully employed, educated member of our democratic society. African American females continue to be objectified in rap videos and through rap lyrics. Hip-hop once the counternarrative to dominant culture has been co-opted to become a tool of capitalism. The images from the Blaxploitation films of the 1970s are being repackaged and sold as images to construct new black identities and masculinities with great reward. "It's Hard out Here for a Pimp," won an Academy Award in 2005 for Best Original Song. The song was written for the movie *Hustle & Flow*, which featured a pimp's journey in becoming a rap artist. The song was written by Three 6 Mafia, a hip-hop group from Memphis, Tennessee. Three 6 Mafia became the first hip-hop group to win and perform their song at the Oscars.

W. E. B. Du Bois, in his book *The Soul of Black Folk*, wrote: "while it is a great truth to say that the Negro must strive and strive mightily to help himself, it is equally true that unless his striving be not simply seconded but rather aroused and encouraged by... [the white majority] he cannot hope for great success." Du Bois added that the burden of lifting formal slaves to equal status in American life belonged to the whole nation (p. 360). I don't think W. E. B. Du Bois envisioned the recognition of a hip-hop group and their music by the dominant white motion picture establishment as reaching the pillar of equal status in America. I would think his thoughts would be, "we are still 'bucking and cooning for Massa.'" The new value of the post–civil rights revolution for African Americans is "I have to get mine by any means necessary... it's all about the Benjamin's." Money is the focus and how one gets it is of little concern.

The idea that money was the marker of success regardless of how one earned it changed the dynamics in black communities. Education took a back seat to achieving financial independence because of the many other opportunities, legal and illegal, that were made available to the new integrated class. Black males had never been paid a living wage before integration, although their brute labor had helped build the foundation of advanced capitalism in this society; therefore, black males were uniquely positioned to accept the devaluation of the work ethic. Alternative work arenas were nothing new to the black male; however, when opportunities for fame and fortune presented themselves as forms of entertainment, the black man wanted to cash in on them. Black males began to enter the mainstream world of sports and along with that came fame. The world of professional sports became a viable alternative work arena for many black men who did not want to work in dead-end jobs with menial pay. The use of black males in sports industry has been likened to a new form of slave labor. The black male body once used for brute force, and field and factory labor has been transformed into a biological machine for the world of competitive sports. At one time black men used their new-found profession to bring political and social awareness to the state of black America; however, over time, fame and fortune became the center of many African American sports figures' lives. Pushing against racial boundaries took a back seat to being the best and having the most. The advantages of being a black male in professional sports have been overshadowed by aggressive behaviors and criminal activities often linked to the sportsmen. Much of this is often attributed to materialist greed rooted in asserting one's patriarchal manhood.

Realizing that the odds are stacked against them, young black males continue to disengage from formal schooling processes to engage in the underground economy. Instead of resisting the nihilistic messages of mass media, young black males continue to immerse themselves in black masculinity that is patriarchal, misogynistic, and destructive. The consumption of mediated images that send out the message that mainstream work is irrelevant, money is god, and being the thug means the person who prevails, takes precedence over acquiring knowledge to transform and liberate their minds, bodies, and souls. The educational process in which African American children engage is hegemonic at its best and catastrophic at its worst and it reflects European cultural and educative hegemony. A good example of this is how the stigmatization of African American males and females has been embraced not only by European Americans, but also by African Americans as well. The dominant culture continues to perpetuate negative imagery of African Americans through media, film, and music, and self-appointed African American leaders are complicit in this undertaking as well.

While conducting research on black masculinity in one of the most impoverished neighborhoods of Cincinnati, Ohio, Over-the-Rhine, I found that the local politicians use this community to reify negative images of the black male for political power. In *The Ghetto Sophisticates: Performing Black Masculinity, Saving Lost Souls, and Serving as Leaders of the New School* I offer this critique:

> Media representations of poor black males...served as the symbolic basis for fueling and sustaining panics about crime, the nuclear family, and middle-class security while they displaced attention from the economy, racism, sexism, and homophobia. This figure of black masculinity consistently appears in the popular imagination as the logical and legitimate object of surveillance and policing, containment and punishment. Discursively this black male body brings together the dominant institutions of (white) masculine power and authority—criminal justice system, the police, and the news media—to protect (white) Americans from harm (p. 24).

The assault on black males by the predominantly white Cincinnati police force and the plight of Over-the-Rhine got national coverage when riots broke out after the police gunned down Timothy Thomas, an unarmed young black male who was allegedly being chased for parking violations (Gause, 2005a).

Delpit (1995) reminds us of the status quo in our society of young black males:

> We live in a society that nurtures and maintains stereotypes: we are all bombarded daily, for instance, with the portrayal of the young black male as monster. When we see a group of young black men, we lock our car doors, cross to the other side of the street, or clutch our handbags. We are constantly told of the one out of four black men who is involved in the prison system—but what about the three out of four who are not? (p. xiii)

Social practices that influenced racial dualism early in American history continue even today: the segregation of black and Latino communities, the discriminatory and regressive allocation of unemployment, miseducation of the underclass, and the absence of health care and living wages for the poor. These systems of domination have been constant for generations of black men, from the 1940s to the present hip-hop generation.

Race, Class, and Gender Politics

Communities in the southeastern part of the United States are experiencing an alarming increase in segregated schools, the expansion of nationally and internationally recognized African American and Hispanic gangs, and the loss of jobs and hope in their communities. While this is happening, African American leaders will not agree upon the best avenues for addressing these problems. W. E. B. Du Bois and Booker T. Washington had distinct philosophical differences but were able to reach an agreement on what is best for black America. Racial and class politics, I believe, are ingrained in the psyche of black America just as much as hypertension and heart disease.

Du Bois and Washington agreed on three points, thrift, patience and industrial training for the American Negro, and binding together in oneness to make the dreams of the Negro in America a reality. These points are often overlooked when discussing their debate. The great debate between Washington and Du Bois is always and represented by a distinct difference between the two classes—"the high yellow" black bourgeoisie and the dark skin working man. These issues are still common in black America today; however, they are overshadowed by the competitiveness within the black community.

The desire to work and build as a collective community has been replaced with the following perspective: "I got to get mine, before you get yours, because there isn't enough to go around." Class struggles are more divisive now than ever before due to the perception that resources are limited. The notion of "we shall overcome" has been lost owing to capitalism and globalization. Black political power that once defined the civil rights movement has now been replaced with meritocracy and nepotism. Black political power of yesterday believed in serving the people and repairing the damage of racist politics that neglected our neighborhoods and schools. The black political power of today exercises the right to serve self and special interest groups, forget about the constituency. Black political, spiritual, and civic leadership has forgotten the promise to serve the needs of black people; providing access to adequate healthcare, living wages, professional careers, affordable housing, thriving neighborhoods, economic security, and an education that leaves no child behind. We have become victimized by those who knew the cost of victimization. We have been preached to by preachers who push a social gospel of prosperity while "pimping" the human, material, and economic resources of the congregation, metaphorically, figuratively, and in some cases literally. We allow ourselves to be victimized by waiting instead of speaking the truth to power and placing our faith in action. Jerry Watts (1994) reminds us of the price of victimhood:

> The victim status is an inherently unequal relationship, one premised on the fact that the victimized is necessary for the existence of the victimizer. The victimizer is able to enjoy the life he or she lives in part because of his or her exploitation of the victimized. As a result, the best moral posture one can expect from a victimizer locked into a victim status relationship with the victimized is paternalism. Through paternalism, the victimized can often receive material benefits and economic improvement. Paternalism cannot grant the subjugated emancipation. (p. 17)

We have fled thriving communities to flock to the megachurches for personal fame and fortune espousing, "God wants you to prosper as your soul prospers," but yet our souls are dying with the sickness of despair. We continue to be in bondage and often are held captive by self-appointed and self-anointed leadership. We as black people must rise up and allow the transforming message of Christ's Gospel move us to a place of self-determination and self-worth beyond the paternalism inherent in our religious dogma. God not only delivered Daniel but He also has delivered us all from the physical chains and shackles of servitude, but what about our minds? We are no longer victims of "the man"; we have been left to our own devices. Black people, particularly black males, need to break free from the self-imposed chains of spiritual, physical, and psychological slavery. The acceptance of being a victim continues to emasculate and subjugate the black male's identity. Because of his victimhood, he cannot recognize his manhood as his manhood is shrouded in paternalism.

As a licensed minister of the Gospel who received degrees from secular and Christian universities, I was never ordained owing to the homophobic values of the black church. "Don't ask, don't tell" was long prevalent in the black church before it became a policy of the Clinton administration. I have attended and served many churches across many denominations. I was reared in the Black Progressive Baptist middle-class church from a very young age. I "found the Lord" in the holiness of the church and spent many years, seeking answers to life's problems through the practice of my faith. I have been a member of multiracial and multigendered congregations, as well as the only black member in an all-white church. On my journey, I questioned why there was so much suffering in the world. Why do people of all colors, faiths, and backgrounds refuse to worship together? Why, must I suffer because I am black man with multiple identities? Along the way, I received many answers to my personal questions and met people who were suffering as well. The struggles of brothers and sisters from all backgrounds were painful to witness; however, those of my fellow black brethren were at times unbearable. I decided to venture out and listen to their stories to see whether there were commonalities so that I could better serve in my role as a social justice educator. I wanted to hear from other "lost souls." What I offer you next is a journey into the lived experiences of four black males. These stories speak of the issues I have raised on black leadership, the perpetuation of negative mediated images of African Americans, and the power of a capitalistic and consumer-oriented society. I have changed the names of the individuals for anonymity and confidentiality purposes. The gaps, silences, and pauses in the text are based on their conversations and interactions with me as a brother, researcher, and friend. Because of my background and experiences I was allowed access to people, places, and events beyond the scope and role of a researcher. I was open and honest about my interactions and sought to build a relationship and bond with those I encountered. At times, my life was endangered, but I felt protected by my faith and by my newfound friends. Interestingly enough, my friends wanted their stories told and celebrated the idea of being valued far more than what they could produce on the street, in the bed room, and for "da man." Their lived experiences became my lived experiences.

Lost Souls

Visiting several "hoods" and "ghettos" in many cities across the United States as a student and semiprofessional I saw many distressed communities. I saw individuals without adequate food, clothing, or shelter. Many of them did not have the education to gain access to these basic life-sustaining resources. I often wondered what I could do to make a difference in the lives of people who were in such need. I figured maybe a career in social services would be the path I should take and so I began a five-year journey working with youth who were in the custody of various state human service agencies. While doing so, I realized that before, during, and after school hours, the majority of the individuals out on the streets were African American males between the ages of thirteen and twenty-five. Why I did not see this before baffled me. Could it be that I was now working with that particular age group? Maybe I was using my critical eye for the first time. While traveling and visiting friends, regardless of the place, urban or rural, I witnessed the presence of black males during all times of the day and night hanging out in front of local stores, near schools, and in various neighborhoods. I found this to be fascinating and I questioned how this phenomenon existed in so many places.

While riding the metro in one particular city, I was struck by the look on the face of one young black brother. He appeared to be approximately fifteen years of age, his pants were extremely baggy, and he wore a red "hoodie" (hooded sweatshirt) with a very long T-shirt underneath. He had on a pair of black leather Timberland boots unlaced with a matching red and black baseball cap. I was so fascinated by the lack of emotion I saw from this young man. He had a face of stone. He was stoic and stared ahead without blinking an eye. This fifteen-year-old boy carried the face of a seventy-year-old man. I got up and moved to the seat across from him. He did not move nor acknowledge my presence. The bus continued for another fifteen minutes; then he signaled the driver to get off. Right before the next stop, I introduced myself and asked him if I could talk to him for a few minutes. He said, *"Yo, get off at my stop and I'll give you a few minutes, then I gotta go meet my homies."*

I disembarked from the bus and followed the young man into a fast-food chain. I introduced myself again:

> CP: *What's up? I'm C. P. and I teach at Miami.*
>
> Young Black Male: *I'm RJ and I saw you looking at me on the bus, so what do you want?*
>
> CP: *I am a former teacher and school administrator and I wanted to ask you why you look so hard and filled with despair.*

RJ:	*Why you want to know that for? You da' police, I gotta go.*
CP:	*No, I am not the police, I just wanted to find out why on a school day, you aren't at school and why you look like there is no hope in this world.*
RJ:	*Why, don't you follow me down the block to my spot and you will see a lot of brothers on the corner just hanging out and not in school, alright?*
CP:	*Cool dude, no problem.*

So I followed RJ down to his spot about a mile from the bus stop and about a mile from the main street into a neighborhood that I had never seen before. There were red brick brownstones, gray apartment buildings, and two-family houses up and down both sides of the street. I saw three neighborhood corner stores, one laundry center, and two bars opposite each another. Just as he said, there had to be about eight guys on the street in front of one of the corner stores. When I walked up with him, one guy flashed a gun. RJ told him that I was cool and I just wanted to ask a couple of questions. I spent about two hours that day talking with these young men. Several spoke candidly of their time in juvenile detention center, county jail, and prison. They talked about going to public school but said that they often ended up at the district's alternative school. Some spoke of memorable times in middle and high school, playing in football and basketball teams, participating in student council, the marching band, and debate clubs. My central question to each of them was simple.

What happened to make you decide to spend the majority of your time in the streets and not in school?
Many answered:

Young Black Males:	*"School ain't for me," "I ask 'da' teacher a question, and get ignored." "I get mad and try to control my temper, but get pushed over the edge." "Half of those teachers don't know nothing anyway, they want respect but they don't give respect."*
RJ:	*I got tired of being told, I was nothing and I wasn't going to ever amount to anything. I grew up hearing enough of that from my father, who wasn't there all the time and from my mom, who was too busy fucking a different man every week, to pay the rent.*
Young Black Males:	*We weren't learning anything anyway. All we did was take tests, do worksheets and copy sentences out of the book. When the tests came back, the teachers would always complain about the scores and say we weren't on level, hell we couldn't be on level cause they weren't*

> *teaching us a damn thing anyway, so we just decided one day to up and leave.*
>
> RJ: *I could make more money staying out of school than I could by staying in and plus it was a waste of time. Cut the noise for a minute, here comes Raheem.*

I discovered Raheem was one of the biggest and youngest dope boys in Over-the-Rhine on that day hanging out with Red and his friends. Raheem was considered a "Baller" (had lots of money) and "Shot Caller" (chief decision maker for his peer group). He drove around in a chromed out Cadillac Escalade, "Iced" down with the latest platinum and diamond jewelry, and wore designer suits. He only wore hip-hop "gear" on the weekend because Monday to Friday were considered days for conducting business. He was sophisticated and savvy in conducting business affairs and made more money from the "underground economy," in one month than I did as a principal in a year.

> RJ: *Yo', What's shaken, Raheem?*
>
> Raheem: *Nothing popping off just yet, Yo' RJ, who's your friend?*

As, I was about to speak, RJ grabbed my arm and told me not to say a damn word, because Raheem was talking to him. For the first time RJ was nervous.

> RJ: *A dude that's cool like that. I met him on the bus. He is some teacher at Miami and wanted to know about why brothers like us was hanging out on the street instead of being in school.*
>
> Raheem: *Didn't you tell him you are in school? In fact, didn't you tell him you are a member of the "Leaders of the New School" and you are giving and receiving education every day?*
>
> RJ: *No, Raheem! I figured you are our Teacher and it should be you who have that conversation with CP.*
>
> Raheem: *So, the cat's name is C. P.? What does it stand for?*

I then took RJ's hand off my arm and walked up to Raheem's Cadillac and said:

> CP: *It stands for Crazy Person, that's what"*
>
> Raheem: *You sure have to be damn crazy to get off the bus and follow RJ to my part of the city. RJ is one of my best and most respected soldiers, so evidently you alright.*
>
> RJ: *Master-teacher Raheem, he cool, but he ain't alright until you say he is alright.*

Raheem pointed at me and told me to get in the SUV. He wanted to take me on a ride and interview me so that he could better understand this project I was working on. I looked at RJ and he assured me it was okay. He said, "If you wasn't cool Raheem would have me shoot you." So I got in the car and that began a friendship unlike no other. Over the next year, I was able to meet and become a part of Raheem's "inner circle." They called themselves, "Leaders of the New School," which is the name of a rap group that was popular in the 1990s. The rap group was from Uniondale, New York and Busta Rhymes, a well-known hip-hop artist was its famous member. The rap group LONS (Leaders of the New School) became very popular with the underground hit, "Case of the P.T.A.," which speaks of their high school antics and the trouble they experienced while in school. I thought it was interesting that Raheem and his crew would assume this name, but for them it had a very different meaning, one which spoke of the power of cash, money, and women. Raheem was the captain, and RJ, Black, and Tiger were his soldiers. I think Raheem did this because he saw himself as a businessman and believed that I functioned as his "counsel." As I continued to develop a friendship with Raheem, I realized that his concept of masculinity was definitely constructed out of the images he consumed from rap videos, the lack of a father as a child, the black church, social relationships that were developed while in school, and from his gang, "Leaders of the New School."

Raheem and His Gang Befriend Me

Raheem: *G-man you are really cool for an old cat (older gentlemen). I mean you having been a principal and still understand what young heads like me are going through; I wished I could have been at your school.*

CP: *Raheem, I treated all of my students like they were my own children. I keep up with the latest music and styles of dress, in fact sometimes I like to wear my "Tims" and the latest hip-hop gear. I sort of devoted my life to helping people, especially young people.*

Black: *It's mighty bold of you to hang out down here in da hood. You know people think you da police, but we tell them you cool with us.*

RJ: *The day you got off the bus to interview me, I figured you wanted something.*

He and Tiger looked at me with smiles on their faces. I did not focus on their looks, but I got the feeling they were checking me out, sort of cruising me up and down.

Tiger: *I figured RJ was going to have us jump you and take your cash and credit cards. I figured it was a setup, that's why I flashed my gun.*

RJ: *Raheem, man I like that suit you got on. Where did you get it?*

Tiger: *Damn RJ, you can't tell that man is wearing a Hugo Boss?*

I was somewhat surprised; Raheem was wearing a Hugo Boss suit and Tiger knew it off the cuff.

> Raheem: *Thanks soldiers. You know I got to represent the cause. It's hard out here, but I want you three to succeed and do things right, not the right thing. Doing the right thing will get you a few dollars, but doing things right will keep money in your pocket at all times and that is the name of the game. You see those preachers, always in fine cars, nice clothes and with good-looking ladies, that's because they aren't doing the right thing. They are doing things right. The same for the pushers and the pimps, they are keeping their business to themselves and that's how we do it. Keep your business to yourself. If you keep your business to yourself, you will always stay in business; but if you share your wealth share, it among the "Leaders of the New School." We are all we got.*
>
> Tiger: *Raheem, you right about that, we are all we got.*
>
> Black: *You know I got your back Raheem, you been like a father to me and an uncle to my kids.*
>
> RJ: *You have been looking out for me Raheem since I came into this game. I will always be loyal.*

Raheem looked at them and gave each one of them five one-hundred dollar bills and then focused his attention on me.

> Raheem: *Man, with all them (expletive) degrees you have, you should be working in a big company or running your own business. Hey, maybe one day, I will open up something and you could run it for me.*
>
> CP: *Raheem, well man, I don't know about that. You are still dealing with some stuff that I think is a little shady. You make a lot of trips across the city, you keep weird hours, and you are always loaded with money and trying to buy me stuff. I think you are engaged in the underground economy and I can't participate in that world.*
>
> Raheem: *G-man, you are cool and I just like that fact that you shoot some knowledge to me to help me understand myself as a young black brother. You, the first dog, I met who don't want nothing from anybody, including me. You also the first dog I know who understand the streets and ain't afraid of coming down here to help at anytime of the night.*

After, listening to Raheem, Black, Tiger, and RJ, I realized that while in school they saw themselves at or near the bottom in academic standings. Their perceptions of themselves were based on their schooling experiences and how their teachers refused to see them as individuals worthy of love and respect. Their teachers also did not seek to build relationships with them nor did they spend time nurturing the gifts they possessed. As black males saw the streets as an economic opportunity on a daily basis, school would have to offer examples of success and the results of delayed gratification. Owing to frustration and what they perceived as injustices, Raheem, Black, Tiger, and RJ viewed school as a deterrent to achieving financial stability and so they dropped out. Interestingly enough, they knew sooner or later they would be pushed out (Gause, 2005a; Harper, 1996; Tutwiler, 2007). The negative pathological labels used to identify them as "permanent underclass," "at-risk," "culturally deficient," and "troublemakers" marginalized and banished them to the borders of the schooling process. As outliers Raheem, Black, Tiger, and RJ as so many other black males in our school became the oil for the school to prison pipeline the black gold of our society used for the further expansion of the industrial prison complex economy that has become such a part of American rural communities.

Raheem and his soldiers do not lack the intellectual ability or aptitude to be successful in school. They possessed exceptional computational and communication skills and the ability to reason far beyond what they were told of their academic abilities. The hegemonic testing data schools relied on that reproduces the stratification of class in American society were not accurate predictors of achievement or ability. The mantra of teachers lamenting to youth, "get an education, so you can get a good job and be successful in life," does not hold true. Raheem, Black, Tiger, and RJ were considered successful, had great jobs (in their minds), and were indeed educated. Because Raheem is the leader of this group and considered to be their Master Teacher, the group decides Raheem should be the focal point of the narrative. I spent time individually with Black and Tiger witnessing their daily interactions and lives, but they insisted Raheem should be the focus because his story was their story. Before sharing Raheem's perspectives I would like to share a little of Black's and Tiger's narratives. Some of RJ's narrative is told through Black's narrative. I decided not to do an extensive individual narrative with RJ. I just listened to his conversations and observed his interactions with the other members of the group.

A Conversation with Black

      CP: *Tell me who you are, what you believe and how you deal with day-to-day life.*
  Black: *Well, where do I begin? Let's see. My name is black, actually my real name is Roderick, but they call me "Black" because of the color of my skin. When I was born my skin was so black my mom wanted to name me Ebony, but my dad said no, because Ebony was a girl's name. So they named me after my no good father*

and since he ain't no damn good, I don't go by Roderick, everyone calls me Black. Even when I was in school if someone called me by Roderick, I wouldn't answer. The teachers would call my mom and she would always tell them, he don't answer to Roderick, he answers to Black so that's what you need to call him. The girls are always after me because of my black skin and my white teeth.

CP: *How old are you and do you have any brothers and sisters?*

Black: I am 21-years old and I have one brother and three sisters. My brother is the oldest and I am the last child. We are stair stepped. My brother is 25, my sisters are 24, 23, 22 and I'm 21. My mother had us when she was young. She was only 15 when she had my brother so that makes her 40 now. By the time she was 20 she had five kids. My grandmother helped raise us, because my daddy was 21 when he got my mother pregnant and he went off to the military. He had to sneak in the hospital to see me because my grandmother said if she saw him again she was going to prosecute him for rape.

CP: *So how hard was it for you then and now?*

Black: My life is good. I hustle and make money. I wanted to finish my education and go to school but it wasn't working out for me. I grew up going to church with my grandmother and I really liked the church, but I didn't have the best of clothes and stuff, so the kids picked on me. Some parents wouldn't let their kids play with me, they said I was from across the tracks and poor. I used to hang out with the white kids in school. I had a few cool white friends and I would hang out with them in middle school. By 9th grade everything changed. We got to high school and everybody went their own way. So that's when I met Raheem and Tiger. We kicked it after school a lot playing street hoops, then we got introduced to the game. Well, actually Raheem got introduced first, by his uncle, then he brought us in, hell, the money was more than I had ever seen so I just jumped in full speed ahead. I did finish my GED last year, Raheem made me and Tiger go back after he finished his, we just trying to make sure RJ gets his. We protect RJ, he ain't got no family. We all he got, so he stays with me and Tiger in an apartment in the hood near the store, he brought you the day we met you.

CP: *What happened to RJ's family?*

Black: Don't mention this to no one. RJ is the nephew of Raheem's uncle. He would be Raheem's cousin, but nobody on the street knows this. RJ was sent from down South to stay up here with us. His dad was killed in a turf battle between rival drug gangs in the South. His mom had a mental breakdown over the situation when he was only a baby, so Raheem's uncle is his people; but Raheem treats RJ like a son, so everybody believes Raheem is RJ's father. On the streets no one ask any questions. For protection RJ stays with Tiger and me and to keep Raheem's wife from acting like black mommas act, RJ sees Raheem on the weekends and in the middle of the week on Wednesdays. If the gangs down South get wind of this then there will be hell to pay. I let my girl home-school RJ since she is a teacher and all. This way he can get his GED and not have to deal with knuckleheads at school. RJ is really smart and hustlers on the street want to take advantage of his skills.

This is a portion of Black's narrative. He shared moments of anger, pain, and frustration with being black in our society. He talked about being chased by the police for no reason. He admits he has done things in the past, but on that particular day he had nothing on him and he was just walking to the store to get something to drink. The day of this interview his girlfriend was about to go into labor. She was a senior in college when they met. She graduated and now teaches elementary school and has been on Black's case about "doing the right thing and not always doing things right." Black dropped me off at the bar to meet Tiger for a drink and headed off to the hospital.

Tiger Talks Openly with Me

As I walked into the bar, I noticed Tiger sitting near the back on a barstool with a glass in one hand and his cell phone in the other. He had a strange look on his face and did not seem to want to talk to me. I waved at him and turned around to head out of the door, but he beckoned me over, and pointed at the stool next to him. I sat down. He was drinking his usual—a Jack Daniels and Coke. He muted his cell phone, told the bartender to pour me a shot of Absolute vodka with a Corona as a throwback, said "hello," and told me to give him a few more minutes. I did not realize he paid that much attention to what I drink. We had only been out for drinks a couple of times, he, Raheem, Black, and I. RJ did not go with us when we visited bars because he was only fifteen. The bartender brought me my drinks, I reached in my pocket to pay and he said, "*Tiger has already paid for your drinks, as long as you come to this bar with or without him, your bar tab has already been paid?*" I was speechless. Whenever we hung out, I made it a point to pay for my own food and drinks, but I have noticed lately now whenever I am with the group somebody has already paid for the meals. I leave a tip for the service equal to my portion of the check. Tiger got off his cell phone and motioned me to a booth closer to the front of the bar. We exchanged greetings again and then I asked him a few questions.

CP:	*Tell me who you are, what you believe and how you deal with day-to-day life.*
Tiger:	*I am 21- years old and the oldest of four. There are four of us in all, one girl and three boys. The girl was born after me. My real name is William, but everyone knows me by Tiger. I think Black already told you he, Raheem, and I met in 9th grade. I liked school. I was popular with other students and teachers. Creative Writing was my favorite class and my English teacher loved all of my short stories and poems. One of my short stories won a competition. I just got tired of not looking like I belong. I had the brains but I didn't have the clothes; although I worked and dressed the part,*

> it was hard keeping up with that image. So Black, Raheem, and I took a couple of classes and even got in trouble together to keep our group tight. Everybody wanted to be like us or a part of our group, but we wouldn't have it. We started hanging out then and been together ever since. I was on the phone with my mom when you walked in, she is not doing too well. She has high blood pressure and diabetes. I stay on her about taking care of herself but sometimes she has a mind of her own. What else do you want to know?

CP: *Tell me about you and your life.*

Tiger: *Well, I think you know Black and I went back to school for our GEDs last year and we got them. Raheem pushed us to do it after he got his. My goal in life is to be a successful businessman. I want to establish a business that serves the public, make my own money and set my own hours. I have worked at fast-food restaurants, for distribution companies and I also cooked at a university up until recently. I believe in working. I know Raheem, Black, and RJ like to hustle and I am in the game but on the periphery. I don't like jail nor having a negative image. I have to make my mom proud and be an example for my brothers. They are RJ's age and they have already spent time in the juvenile detention center. I want them to learn from their mistakes and my mistakes to do right by my mom. I have a nephew. My sister's son already knows about the streets from his father and what happen to him so I am trying to be an example for him as well. I want to leave this city one day and live in a place that doesn't remind me of all the hard times we had, I had growing up. We were poor, dirt poor. I watch my mom raise four kids by herself and as the oldest, I oftentimes had to help her. I know what it feels like to wear clothes from the "free store." Standing in line, watching your friends on their way to school while you are waiting for the "free store" to open in order to get the best stuff. Then getting to school late with a note from your mom excusing your tardiness, but everybody saw you waiting at the free store two hours before school started. I know what it feels like to have to do my homework by daylight because once it got dark we had no electricity. Couldn't afford electricity half of the time. When my mom worked we did alright but she got sick and had to go on public assistance. My mom wasn't like other mothers in the neighborhood, selling her food stamps and welfare check for beer, cigarettes, or marijuana. She took care of her kids. Her kids have always been important to her and under no circumstances was she not going to take care of them.*

I was very intrigued by how open Tiger was in sharing his story. At times it was very moving. He wept as he told the story about his mother and the "free" story. It was quite evident he was a victim of extreme poverty, but he had a determination to do something with his life outside of the "underground" economy that I had not seen in the other young men.

Raheem called and told Tiger where to bring me to meet him and so after one more drink we left. On our way to meeting Raheem, Tiger told me a few more things about his life and who he was. He shared with me things the group did not know. I felt a kinship with him. We both had witnessed extreme poverty in our lives and we were different from what we were on the inside than we were on the outside. We both vowed that regardless of where we ended up on life's journey, we would remain forever connected.

Raheem Discusses Being a Man

CP: *Tell me who you are, what you believe and how you deal with day-to-day life.*

Raheem: *G-man, I'm a man and in these streets only men survive. I put these boys on some of that knowledge you shoot to me, because I realize that I'm going to need some skills to survive out here. That's why I went back and got my GED and that's why I made Black and Tiger go back. You see, "Luda" (Ludacris, a rap artist) and them boys in that latest "joint" (video), man dim Spinners (Rims for tires), are sweet. That's what "Leaders of the New School" are out here trying to do. We are trying to make as much paper (money). I ain't got no daddy, and I want more for my kids. I didn't have a father to provide for me and my sisters, but I provide for mine. When we go to church, the preacher always talking about taking care of the family, well that's what I'm doing. Maybe it's wrong, but this is my way, and all you see on these streets is people surviving the best way they know how. Maybe I will open up some business. Maybe a laundry for the community, a corner store, and a liquor store would be the ticket? I'm trying to clean this money up and do the right thing for the community. After I finished my GED I realized I needed to do something with all of this money to bring about some changes and to make sure Black, Tiger, and RJ have some legit to do, especially RJ.*

Raheem Discusses School and Dropping Out

Yo, G-man, I used to like school. When I got to middle school that's where it all began for me. I got tired of those teachers, the white ones and black ones, always dragging the brother. I used to come in you know, with the latest street gear, and I wasn't carrying no books. I talked to the honeys. I knew my work, but I was cool, so I didn't want nobody to know I was smart at least in some of my subjects. I just got tired having to prove myself and what I knew. I had one black teacher that was cool. Ms. Taylor stayed on me, but in a way my mom did. She would talk to me in a cool, but hard manner. She didn't play. I did my work but she never made a big deal out of it, cause she expected me to do it and when I didn't do it, she didn't holler and stuff she just smiled and told me she would talk with me after class. Man, those other teachers, when, I didn't have no work, they put me out of class. So I roamed the halls.

I dropped out of school near the end of 9th grade. I think Black and Tiger told you the story. I was trying to sling packages in them streets (sell drugs) and just wanted *to make some ends (money). I didn't have a father and mom worked 12 hours a day to keep a roof over our heads. So, I figured it was easy for me to help out and get my own stuff (personal needs and clothes). I hung out all night with the boys on the block and did my thing. My attendance was poor and half those tests they gave us, didn't measure what we knew, because those teachers didn't teach us a damn thing. Plus, I was too tired to take them anyway, so I figured wasn't any need to keep going and really didn't want to be there. I had one teacher, he was black and the track coach. Mr. Johnson tried to get me to go out for track. I knew he was trying to help me. I came out once, but I told him I wasn't running. He talked to me about being disciplined, but Yo! I wasn't hearing that (expletive).*

Throughout our informal conversations, I encouraged Raheem to invest in the community. He opened several businesses, sponsored several athletic teams, and underwrote educational opportunities for several young people in the community. Spending time observing and becoming friends with these young men, I realized they were not just "drug dealers," "hoodlums," nor "gangsters"; they were "ghetto sophisticates" who were out to save lost souls and serve as leaders of the new school. And because they believed there was no salvation in their schools, in their homes, nor even in their churches, they looked for salvation among their peers. Salvation can be found in one's faith and in one's self. Raheem's critique of the black church and corruption is not far off the mark.

The corruption in the "underground economy" could be seen everywhere in our society. But for African Americans for corruption to be located in one of its most sacred institutions, the black church was problematic. The following is an example of how problematic the issue of corruption is for black Christians. The nation's largest black church organization, the national Baptist convention's leader, Rev. Henry J. Lyons entered into illegal deals with corporations that want to gain black churchgoers' business. He gained over four million dollars from these deals and was later convicted of racketeering and grand theft. He pleaded guilty to bank fraud and tax evasion. Rev. Lyons used the money to buy jewelry, extravagant vacations, waterfront property for his mistress, and other luxury items. After Lyon's conviction the acceptance of political corruption and deceit was quite evident; many black American leaders came to his defense by comparing him to other corrupt white ministers and argued that church leaders of all colors had problems. These black leaders completely failed to consider the critical role the church played in black American life, and why it was such a betrayal of vulnerable people in need of honest leaders—poor and working-class black people who put their trust and their dollars into churches. After accepting his resignation the board of the National Baptist Convention voted to continue paying Rev. Lyons his $100,000 salary for five years, which was the length of his prison sentence (Williams, 2006).

Raheem, Black, Tiger, and RJ are striving to live an American dream but have come to realize it really is the American nightmare. To be black and male in America renders one defenseless against the horrors and atrocities inherent in a white, paternalistic, racist, classist, and sexist society. They have come to realize the safe havens of the public school and black church only exist when oppressive practices are overcome by those who lead them. This is why they themselves have developed their own community of learning and salvation. The "Leaders of the New School" as they call themselves have forged a bond of commitment to one another to survive in America. They realize the love they have for one another is stronger than the love we as educators have for the students and subjects we teach. We are bound by words, they are bound by deeds.

· 4 ·

RAP, RACE, AND RESISTANCE

We confine discussions about race in America to the "problems" black people pose for whites, rather than consider what this way of viewing black people reveals about us a nation.
—*Cornel West, 1994, Race Matters*

Bellowing deep from within
I listen to his voice as it echoes through the spirit
Channeling thoughts of innocence
Before time was time
Between the intersections of eternity
I gaze upon the thought of his very being
As the lyrical musings flow from his lips
His Rap speaks not lies but truth
Truth of my race and our resistance
—*C. P. Gause, ©2008 "Voiceless Spirit"*

As we head into the 21st century, rap music/hip-hop is in the earth-wide sound stream, the child of soul, R & B and rock n roll, the by product of the strategic marketing of Big Business, ready to pulse out to the millions on the wild, wild web. It's difficult to stop a cultural revolution that bridges people together.
—*Chuck D, "The Sound of Our Young World"*

Personal Reflection

The second Friday of October 1979, I can remember being in the gym of W. A. Perry Middle School, which is located in Columbia, South Carolina; dancing at the first "sock hop" of the year. It was my eighth grade year and the final year for middle school and all of us were excited. The student body of W.A. Perry numbered approximately 600 students during those days, and only 20% of the student population was white.

My elementary school, Arden was 50% white and 50% African American. It was located one block from my house and I had the privilege of walking to school with white and black kids every day; however, W. A. Perry was different. It was located across the street from Jaggers-Terrace, a subsidized housing complex located six miles away from my neighborhood. Riding the school bus was a big thing and for the first time, I had the opportunity to leave my neighborhood to attend school, boy was I excited. W.A. Perry a suburban majority African American middle school, at that time, was the place that I first heard rap music played at a school. I was so used to square-dancing in elementary school I couldn't believe my ears.

The D.J. played "Sugar Hill Gang's Rapper's Delight." I knew that I heard the song previously; in fact it was during the summer of that same year in Long Island, New York in the basement of my Aunt Isoline's house. My cousin, Gary was an aspiring "rapper" and DJ. I can remember Gary having headphones on his head and moving his hands across those albums, it was as if he was in another world. Aunt Isoline would call his name; I would have to hit him on his arm to get his attention. He wouldn't let you touch his turntable but you could listen to his music. I could not believe the song made it "down south" to Columbia, South Carolina. As the lyrics flowed through the towering speakers, my friends sat in awe as I repeated the lines simultaneously along with the record (there were no CDs at the time). Little did I realize that moment would be so profound that I would be sitting here 22 years later writing about it (figuratively, literally, and prophetically). Personal Journal (June 2001)

A Lesson in Rap: Gary Speaks!

Gary: *Rap was about having house parties in the Boogie-down Bronx. Sometime parties were thrown in the parks with loudspeakers. The "shorties" and "honeys" would come around the block and across the way to hear the music and see these dudes spin their records. I was well on my way to becoming one of the world's most famous DJs but hey that's life.*

CP: *You served your country well, retired military with one of the highest honors awarded to a soldier, you run the post office, nice big house, with an in-ground swimming pool, a beautiful wife, two beautiful daughters and nice cars to drive. You made it big and you still DJ. What more do you want?*

Gary: *Well you know some dreams never die.*

Rap: The Beginning

Kool Herc eventually hired someone to "MC" these parties. This person would talk to the crowd between the songs to keep the party going. This was the beginning of "rapping." DJ Hollywood, one of the early MCs at Kool Herc's parties would use rhyming verses in his rap. One of these included the words "hip-hop" "which much later were used interchangeably to define the music of rap and the culture of those who attended Kool Herc's parties (Africana.com, 1999)."

Afrika Bambaata was another early figure in the rap/hip-hop world. He participated in many early "battles," or competitions between DJs and MCs. In addition to rapping, these battles were decided on who had the more interesting collection of beats to play. Afrika Bambatta's breaks were drawn from many genres, including rock, rhythm & blues, mambo, German disco, and calypso. This aspect of hip-hop, incorporating "found sounds" (which can include recorded samples of music by other groups in addition to voices or ambient sounds) has led to lawsuits when the groups involved failed to credit their sources. Another early hip-hop innovator was DJ Grandmaster Flash. He extended Kool Herc's break-beat deejaying by precueing records to match the songs. This meant there was a smoother transition between songs. Indeed many of the recordings in the discography identify the number of beats per minute for each song, enabling a DJ to match songs on this basis. Grand Wizard Theodore developed another important part of hip-hop music, scratching. This technique involves moving a record back and forth underneath the needle, and creating a scratching and percussive sound. This technique has led some to claim that hip-hop has led to the emergence of the DJ as musician, and to call the turntable used in this way a percussion instrument.

With globalization, mediated digital culture, and a more diverse population, cultural studies as a discipline has enormous possibilities for assisting educators to rethink ways of knowing and interfacing with America's youth. Today's youth are more connected than their parents and foreparents ever were to popular culture media. The explosion of the digital information age has given the youth of America an opportunity not only to access various media, but also to become architects and creators of media for a global audience. With homegrown Web sites, blogs, and music videos on the World Wide Web at their fingertips, today's youth have redefined how media are produced and absorbed. Many have gained instantaneous fame with their peers wanting to idol-worship them. This *era of idols* has left many educators pondering how to teach youth who are more technologically astute than their teachers. However, many youth of color are technologically challenged, given their limited access to computers outside of their school experience. This lack of access also contributes to youth of color maintaining a position of consumers instead of producers of digital media. Many youth of color still use the Internet as a tool for researching their favorite rap artists and viewing the latest fashions and dance styles of newly released hip-hop videos.

As an African American educator who witnessed the beginning of the hip-hop movement, I felt the hip-hop culture could provide opportunities for informing K-12 curricula. I believed the oral traditions many of the artists drew from would motivate students to gain more knowledge about the beauty and pageantry inherent in their ancestry. I began to informally question many of my colleagues from diverse backgrounds about their understanding and experiences with the hip-hop generation—"those young African Americans born between 1965 and 1984 who came of age in the eighties and nineties and who share a specific set of values and attitudes" (Kitwana, 2005, p. 4). As a member of this group and as an educator, I really wanted to know what my colleagues believed about this generation. Many were troubled by the lyrics and posturing seen in rap videos. They often spoke of not understanding what was being said over the beats of the music and felt it was unintelligible noise making. Some were emphatic about the negative impact the music on students and believed there was little or no value in the music; however, students across all walks of life thought otherwise. Hip-hop emerged out of the performance spectacles of rap music that began in the mid- to late-1970s, but its roots are much older (indeed, hip-hop's use of music from other genres is reflected in Renaissance parody masses). What is hip-hop? Hip-hop is rap music, graffiti art, urban dance styles, language, and fashion. It is black and Hispanic youth at their finest, and to most African American youth, hip-hop is "a way of life." Because hip-hop culture encompasses fashion, attitude, and style, it becomes a genuine subculture, and for many, even a way of life.

Rose (1991) asserts:

> Stylistic continuities were sustained by internal cross-fertilization between rapping, break dancing, and graffiti writing. Some graffiti writers, such as black American Phase 2, Haitian Jean-Michel Basquiat, Futura, and black American Fab Five Freddy produced rap records. Other writers drew murals that celebrated favorite rap songs (e.g., Futura's mural "The Breaks" was a whole car mural that paid homage to Kurtis Blow's rap of the same name). Break- dancers, DJs, and rappers wore graffiti-painted jackets and tee shirts. DJ Kool Herc was a graffiti writer and dancer first before he began

playing records. Hip-hop events featured break-dancers, rappers, and DJs as triple-bill entertainment. Graffiti writers drew murals for DJ's stage platforms and designed posters and flyers to advertise hip hop events. (p. 35)

Hip-hop is an art form that co-opts and commodifies various cultural artifacts in the production of a new medium for consumption. Hip-hop is the blending of various genres of music to create new sounds for recording and creating new productions. Fashions become blended cultural refabrications of yesteryear with futuristic blends for a wearable work of art. Attitude, performance, dance, body movement, multimedia imagery, fashion, and sound are incorporated into the spectacle for the purpose of entertainment and capitalistic gain. Hip-hop is the vehicle of consumerism and it dominates all forms popular culture. It has gone beyond the elements of every isolated genre of music from the classics to rock and roll. Rock and roll was considered by many the contribution of white youth to American society. Many black youth feel as if rap music and Hip Hop culture is their contribution to the world. Rap is the familiar soundtrack to postmodern "techno" culture, advertising, film and television, and digital and multimedia culture as well. As it breaks down the boundaries between musical styles and genres, absorbing every conceivable type of music, rap crosses the national borders of the world becoming a key component of global culture.

Elements of Hip-Hop and Cultural Identity

Rap music and hip-hop culture are considered the vehicles for turning wannabe stars into big- time acts overnight. They are also considered as a legal form of the drug trade. Huge sums of money can be made from one hit song. One song can be edited and repackaged as a single, jingle, dance remix, and corporate theme generating millions of dollars for media companies, artists, and record executives throughout the recording industry. Hip-hop is now considered a trillion-dollar global entertainment industry. Many major corporations, such as Coca-Cola, Pepsi-Cola, and Anheuser-Busch use rap music and hip-hop spectacle to advertise their products. Rap music is used as the background for Cadillac, Mercedes-Benz, and GMC advertisements. Elements of hip-hop culture are readily seen on all network programming on television and every sporting event capitalizes on that genre of music to sell sportswear items. As viruses have the ability to affect every part of the human body, so has rap. Rap presently permeates every cellular membrane of our culture.

Rap is thus not only music to dance and party to, but also a potent form of cultural identity. It has become a powerful vehicle for cultural and political expression, serving as the "CNN of black people" (Chuck D), or upping the high-tech ante, as their "satellite communication system" (Heavy D). It is an informational medium to tune into, one that describes the rage of African Americans facing growing oppression, declining opportunities for advancement, changing moods on the streets, and everyday life as a matter of sheer survival. It has become a cultural virus, circulating its images, sounds, and attitude throughout the culture and body politic. Together, these forms provide a vivid hip-hop spectacle, providing style, identity, politics, and a way of life for individuals throughout the world. Indeed, rap embodies a postmodern aesthetic, absorbing every conceivable musical style Rhythm & Blues, funk, soul, reggae, techno, pop, and house, while migrating to every national culture, local scene, and realm of culture. In turn, hip-hop and rap have influenced all other musical styles and cultures, involving a breaking down of boundaries between music, image, spectacle, and everyday life.

Hip-hop culture can be viewed as postmodern based upon this very notion of the "peculiar" splitting of time. African Americans have cause for not having much faith in the "progressive" time, since for more than four hundred years, white males benefited from this economic progress. There has been a persistent hunger and thirst for a future filled with promises of wealth and opportunity. The yearning for success in the African American community has often been met with the tragic awareness of the presence of past oppressions. Resisting the awareness of past oppressions by the black community leaves its citizens with moments of déjà vu; living in the present, but yet reeling from the tumultuous past. This "spatial rift" or "split in time" is connected to the "double consciousness" articulated by W. E. B. Du Bois. African Americans have sought to build from a full sense of authenticity and to exist in a nation in which the symbolic structures of race and identity are the markers of oppression. Continually being placed in the position of the "other" disrupts the African American citizen's ability to transcend the chains of enslavement and envision themselves as a liberated people. Ferguson (2000) presents:

> For African Americans, "race" as an identity and as a nexus of identification has never been theorized or experienced as a simple, unitary, decontextualized subject position. At the beginning of the twentieth century—long before the poststructuralist discovery of the socially invented, multiply positioned, nature of "self"—W. E. B. Du Bois was describing the African American experience of self as unstable and dualistic. Blacks identified both as Americans, as "citizens," and as a racially subordinated minority that

was excluded politically and socially. This "double consciousness," as he described it, has served as the matrix for identification as "black" culturally and politically, grounding a culture of resistance and struggle against denial of the full rights of "citizens" because of "race." (p. 205)

Rappers and hip-hop participants were once considered outliers of mainstream society. They were the grassroots reporters of the real economic conditions in urban centers of America. During the golden years of Reagonomics, drugs and poverty lay at the center of black life in our metropolitan cities. Those who suffered from these conditions were on the margins of society and were considered as the "other." In being "true" to themselves, "true" to their "hood," and "true" to their "peoples," "keeping it real" became the vantage point for the production of a powerful critique of the social order and it fostered a representation that contested the order as it stood. Before its co-optation, rap music and hip-hop culture had been the essence of that contestation, and rappers occupied a position central to the production of counterhegemonic discourses. These forms of contestation were not just found in words but habits of being and in the way one lived as well (hooks, 1990). According to Dimitriadis (2001), hip-hop began as a situated cultural practice, one dependent on a whole series of artistic activities or competencies:

> Dance, music, and graffiti were all equally important in helping to sustain the event. Like many African musics and popular dance musics, early hip hop cannot be understood as aural text alone but must be approached and appreciated as multitiered event, in particular contexts of consumption and production. (p. 16)

Hip-hop also had an impact on the continuing production of recordings in the LP format. Without this format, hip-hop DJs were unable to do scratching, which was an important aspect of the music. However, presently the development of compact disc players that function like LP turntables and virtual digital computer software has allowed the music to evolve in forms that did not exist ten years ago. The direct result, for better or for worse, has been the invasion of misogynistic lyrics in popular culture. The glorification of sex, violence, and gangster lifestyles can be seen twenty-four hours a day, seven days a week on the Internet and cable television. Far from its roots, rap music and hip-hop have become sexist, racist, and violent. There are some hip-hop musicians who focus on issues of social inequity, drug abuse, and nihilism; however, much of their work is underground and not played on commercialized radio.

Rap and Hip-Hop: Evolutionarily Speaking!

Rap developed as an outlet for inner city youth to describe their social and economic hardships. (Dyson, 1997) It was their stories of "ghetto life." Rap was heard throughout the 1970s in parks across New York City on "boot-leg" homemade "reel-to-reel" and TDK cassette tapes. These "ghetto-youth" stories were not taken seriously until the release of Run DMC's album *Raising Hell*, which became a triple-platinum hit (three million units sold) in 1987. This album became the "hook" for white consumers. It combined elements of rock music with rap.

Rap music in the early 1980s was mostly dance and party music. Run-DMC and Grandmaster Flash and the Furious Five were the early mainstream pioneers of rap music. Another of these early figures, Kool Herc, immigrated to the United States from Jamaica and settled in the Bronx with his sound system that he called "the Herculords." Kool Herc focused on rhythm and blues and funk records. Another of Kool Herc's innovations was to play only the "break," or the musical material between the verses of a song, repeating that break again and again. He did this using two turntables mounted with the same record. This came to be called "break-beat deejaying." People began to perform "strange, acrobatic twisting dance routines" to these episodes that came to be called "break dances."

The knowledge from which rappers draw is not only derived from their day-to-day experience, but also from the entire recorded tradition of African American music, as well as other musical genres. Hip-hop constitutes itself as knowledge, complete with its own discursive forms, citing its own tradition(s). Hip-hop is a powerful cultural movement that shapes and forms multiple identities. These identities are performed in various rituals and modes of resistance with a vernacular founded in black-signifying oral traditions. Rap is an African American tradition that follows the footsteps of signifying, playing the dozens, toasting, and boasting. This is why it is not unusual to see battling, challenging, and disrespecting of other rap artists among rappers; these are forms of competition and ways of gaining respect.

I believe as many other researchers that rap is an extension of African American oral communication and storytelling traditions. These cultural forms of storytelling were found in Africa and maintained by the village "griot" or "oral historian." As written records historically were not maintained, the "griot" maintained the village history by sharing it orally with all villagers. Rap at its inception was a form of mediation and not the competition we witness these days daily on the airwaves and in rap videos. It was also considered a form of storytelling. Rappers shared the history of local urban ghettos with their young protégés.

Hip-hop has crossed lines of class, race, and, gender it is increasingly clear that it has become a global art form capable of mobilizing diverse disenfranchised groups. Yet hip-hop, even as it makes politicized incursions into the dominant culture, is founded on the verbal play of signification; in this sense it does not exclude the foolish or even the absurd from its modes of resistance. As Spencer (1991) has observed, both rappers and scholars partake of a discursive universe in which skill at appropriating the fragments of a rapidly changing world with verbal grace and dexterity is constituted as knowledge, and given value. Despite the fact that audiences today are more diverse in terms of race, class, and region, hip-hop continues to be viewed as a particular style of music by the casual listener and even some scholars. Rap, once primarily the voice of young black males, has become the voice of multiethnic, multilingual nationals across the globe. I believe this is the reason rap has been commodified by mainstream media and has become the vehicle for consumerism in institutions of the dominant culture.

The rap artists, who once questioned tactics used by law enforcement and considered them oppressive practices against black males, glorify the images of the black males' encounters with the police to gain respect. Clips of being wrestled to the ground and shot by the police are used in rap videos to sell CDs. A growing volume of research undertaken on the "plight of the African American male," has reduced him to animalistic terms, the "endangered species." However, those scholars, who pinpoint the black male dilemma as deriving from the gap existing between the "ideal" male gender role for the overall American society and the actual ability of black males to realize it, miss the mark completely. Rap music has been complicit in perpetuating this dilemma.

Rap Music and the Black Male

Throughout American history, black males were not expected to be able to fulfill the ideal male gender role. Indeed, it was made abundantly clear that severe repercussions would follow if they made serious and persistent efforts to do so. Exercising power, at the economic, political, social, and cultural levels, was not expected and fervently opposed. Indeed, this was the source of innumerable violent conflicts, notably lynching, pogrom-like invasions of the African American communities, and lesser forms of repression (Booker, 1997).

Black males and females of every period were quite aware of these iron ceilings placed on their advancement and of the restrictions that bound their every movement. For this reason, these barriers were regarded as a fact of black life, a clearly observable injustice, and this premise was embodied in the historically molded gender role values that emerged in African Americans. Thus, notions of the proper methods to respond to systematic injustice were and are an integral element of the evolving African American masculinity, which are evident in hip-hop culture.

This figure of black masculinity marks the racial and cultural boundaries of a counterhegemonic blackness, which stands for the black nation, the black family, and the authentic black (male) self as represented by various mediated images of rappers and their families (personal and business). Cash Money Millionaires, Wu-Tang, and No-Limit Records headed by Master P, all represent themselves as musical families, which are kindred spirits of the Mob Boss Italian Crime families of yesteryear.

The rap and hip-hop artists of the 1980s and 1990s such as Sean Combs (Puff Daddy) and O'Shea Jackson (Ice Cube) are particularly emblematic of the complex social relations (race, class, sexual) and cultural politics surrounding the self-construction and representation of the black masculinity in the public sphere. Many of our African American youth, especially boys, embody the personas of these "rappers." They begin to "perform" who they are in opposition to the dominant school culture. These artists, like their contemporaries, enacted a black identity (masculinity) that not only challenged whiteness but also exiled it to the cultural margins of blackness. Through their work blackness becomes a powerful symbol of masculinity/identity.

Rap music, in its brief history, has been coded as the "voice" of the urban African American male whose desire is to express his manhood and disrupt society. Hip-hop culture and rap music as art forms began as contemporary forms of African American expression and have emerged as an articulation of a culturally specific art form in a dominant cultural context. Tricia Rose, one of the premier academic researchers of rap music and hip-hop culture, speaks of the "sociologically based crime discourse" inherent in "the political economy of rap" (Rose, 1991, p. 277). Rose asserts much of the opposition to rap and hip-hop culture is grounded in fear:

> Young African Americans are positioned in fundamentally antagonistic relationships to the institutions that most prominently frame and constrain their lives. The public

school system, the police, and the popular media perceive and construct them as a dangerous internal element in urban America—an element that if allowed to roam freely will threaten the social order, an element that must be policed. The social construction of rap and rap-related violence is fundamentally linked to the social discourse on Black containment and fears of a Black planet. (p. 279)

Rap music's popularity and global impact or hybridity finds itself not as a subversive youth subculture, but as a former counterhegemonic musical medium with counternarratives, which have been commodified by the dominant culture. This being so, it continues to be marginalized by "organized educational spaces" and this marginalization in turn continues to privilege an official or "high" culture over "pop" culture.

Jason Nichols, in his thesis "The Realist Nigga: Constructions of Black Masculinity within Rap Music" speaks of the expressions of black masculinity in rap music and hip-hop. He opines, "Over the past 30 years, hip hop, particularly rap music, has continually gained the admiration of young people worldwide. However, media attention to commercial rap music has focused on one type of performative black masculinity, which is expressed through violence and aggressive posturing." The large-scale commodification of hip-hop culture has popularized this version of black masculinity and it continues to reify the dominant culture's belief that black males are hypersexualized and animalistic. The hypermasculine façade presented here is neither unique nor new to hip-hop or our society. The expression of black masculinity through commercial hip-hop is devoid of vulnerability. Many famous rap artists and rap groups speak of their invincibility. The importance of an examination of black masculinity as expressed through mainstream hip-hop is self-evident. Hip-hop is an extremely popular youth culture that is now a worldwide phenomenon. For many, hip-hop may be the only exposure to black American males they witness in their culture; therefore, hip-hop culture could be the international ambassador for African American manhood. Understanding gender and race cannot take place unless it is done in the historical and sociocultural contexts.

Hip-Hop and the Public Sphere

Rap music and hip-hop culture are alternative and counter–public spheres that were subversive in their beginnings, but have been commodified by the dominant culture, becoming "tools of capitalism." Hip-hop in its earliest forms once considered a subversive youth culture with counternarratives to the dominant culture has become a multitrillion-dollar global industry. Not only has the music industry been transformed by this culture, but the fashion industry has been as well. The voice of black and Latino males surrounded by poverty with only the drumming of beats as a public outlet has become the foundation of institutionalized consumerism where the profits of a CD are more important than the immoral decadent messages digitized on a fifty-cent disc. Tracks of music are the public sirens of our moral ineptitude. Vulgar and sexually inappropriate images and rhythms captivate youth who then decide to emulate what they hear and witness, never realizing that it is a performance, a spectacle of the public sphere.

Western culture has defined a privileged canon as a body of literature and ideas that is seen as true and good. This canon has ignored or marginalized the voices and ideas of those with little or no power. The writing and thinking of the oppressed and poor are not generally viewed as having equal worth with the voices of the dominant culture. The infamous Chuck D, formerly of the politically charged rap group Public Enemy, notes that "people of color" have used "hip-hop" culture and "rapping" to allow "their" voices to be heard. Although hip-hop has been commodified, it continues to border on being marginalized in its purest form. It is seen by the dominant culture as a cultural phenomenon that impedes educational growth and achievement and schools are the "agents of reproduction" for the dominant culture. Thus, it is not surprising that hip-hop culture continues to be discouraged in many school districts and schools across the United States.

Rappers are the "others"; however, they communicate that they are "representing" their people. They enter the public sphere not speaking for themselves, but for their "peoples." This is often debated by scholars and rappers alike; however, we must take note that with their bold use of language, style, and dress, and the creative use of "image" and "spectacle" to enter "the scene," we find ourselves listening to their message and then we respond with our own.

Elements of rap music have been traced back to African "griots" and the African American poets of the 1960s. Public storytelling has always been intricately linked to the black community. Preachers and teachers were the "griots" of the early and mid-20th century and rap artists became the "griots" of the late 20th and early 21st centuries. The voice of black urban youth has now emerged as the voice of the global village. I began this chapter discussing my questioning educators from multiple backgrounds about their understanding and perceptions of rap music and hip-hop culture in today's schools. I would like to continue by presenting the narratives of four African American post–civil rights educators who teach the children of the hip-hop generation. To learn more about these educators and how I conducted research on this topic, please visit the appendices found at the end of the text.

African American Teachers Rap on Rap

We open with Crystal, the only African American math educator at Case Junior-Senior High School.

Crystal shares her feelings about how Rap music was different when she grew up:

> The skating rink was where I first heard rap music in the early 80s. During that time it was fun to listen to and the messages were all about having a good time. It was about dancing, skating, and "break dancing." You know, the female group Salt & Pepa, it was all about them. There were no lyrics about shooting, promiscuous sex, and pimping. My girlfriends and I would listen to the music and do our little group dances. Not the kind of dancing they are doing now, the suggestive stuff. It wasn't about that. We were kids, doing kid things. The boys would be "break dancing" with their Kango hats and Adidas outfits. Wow, those were the days. The stuff now is just horrible. Young girls are allowing themselves to be displayed in ways that are indescribable.

Crystal continues by discussing the differences she finds now and how the students are so consumed with rap music and hip-hop and how they do not realize that it is just entertainment:

> The stuff those kids are listening to is a just mess. They eat, sleep, and breathe rap music and hip-hop. It's like a religion, in fact, for some of them I believe it is their religion. They have their rituals, their icons, their own language, and they treat those "rappers" like gods. They see what they believe and they believe what they see. The images of those "gangsta rappers," they take to heart. These students don't realize that it is about money. Those rappers perform, make their money, and go home to their wives and families. Those rappers are not O.G.s (original gangsters) they are performers and that's entertainment not real life, and trying to convince them otherwise is often futile.

Doug the only African American male educator who serves as the 7th grade social studies teacher shares his thoughts and views. He also expounds on some of the same salient issues concerning growing up in the rap age. He presents his perspective on hip-hop culture and how he viewed himself as a participant in and consumer of the culture:

> Wearing my big thick gold chains, my Adidas, and listening to Run-DMC was definitely my thing. I participated in the culture heavily; however I realized that it was just the culture. The realness was my enjoyment and hanging out with my friends, playing the "boom box."

> I still went to church with my family, did my homework, and aspired to be a professional. As an adult, I listen to some of the music and I like some of what I hear, but I am critical of some of the lyrics and I share my thoughts with the students I teach. My boys and I definitely participated in the early days but it did not become a way of life for me like it is for our students today.

Christina, the only African American educator in the English department at Case Junior-Senior High School, shares her perspective on growing up in the age of rap and hip-hop; however, because she is Christian and she loves old rhythm and blues she is not fond of rap.

> Being a child of God, I don't care too much for rap music played on mainstream radio. It's too sensationalized and it doesn't represent who I am or my beliefs. I have heard some good Christian rap artists; however, I love old rhythm and blues. I told my students that many rap songs sample old R & B. They didn't believe, so I brought in the originals of it some of Mary J. Blige's remakes. They could not believe it and then they started questioning me about other artists and I was glad. I made some progress with them and started on a process of thinking more critically. They wanted to know the type of music and artists I listened to, so I shared many of the greats, like the Temptations, Teddy Pendergrass, The O'Jays, Smokey Robinson, Patti LaBelle, and Aretha Franklin. I also told them I love Gospel music and suggested some songs and spirituals they should add to their playlists.

Christina also states she does not like rap music and hip-hop culture because of its negative portrayal of women, sex, and the misogyny.

> I cannot believe the rap videos and the sex it portrays. Many of the artists in the videos treat women like objects and possessions. The rappers utilize terms that I can't even bring myself to say to identify women. I asked my students about those issues and they clearly do not see anything wrong with the way they are portrayed by rappers. In fact many of them aspire to be female rappers and live the lives they see portrayed by them on rap videos. The girls already wear fake hair, get their nails done, have gold jewelry draping from their neck, and some even allow boys to use those same terms in the videos to identify them. I constantly remind the young ladies I teach the importance of loving themselves and taking care of themselves. I also talk to the young men as well. I often ask them if they would want some young man calling their daughters those very same names. I share with them the struggles our race has to endure and that they only contribute to the struggle instead of overcoming the struggle.

Victoria, the principal of Case Junior-Senior High School, who began her teaching career in the early 1970s, discusses how she has witnessed the evolution of rap from its inception.

> Rap music began well after I started my teaching career. I was still reeling from the Age of Aquarius and Disco. When I finally heard rap I thought it was just great party music, in fact

> my girlfriends and I would listen to Kurtis Blow, Grandmaster Flash, and a few others. My taste changed for it when it moved from party music and social consciousness to gangster rap. I stopped listening to the stuff for awhile. When my son, Lexicon, became a teenager I started listening to it again to check out what he was enjoying. This was in the late 1980s through the 1990s. It was stuff I didn't recognize. The disrespect and rappers challenging one another to battles seemed so foreign to what I heard in the beginning. The social consciousness was gone replaced by sex, money, and controlling women. I witnessed the transformation of rap from dance music through all of its "growing pains" to its present form, which is beyond gangster. Rap presently is purely about perpetuating a lifestyle of consumption. As our students would say, "get yo drink on, yo sex on, and bling bling."

Victoria also presented her perspective as a mother:

> My son, Lexicon listened to some of it, but he really wasn't consumed by it like our students are. I knew I would have to limit some of the CDs he brought; however he really was more selective than I would have been. His music focus was more or less on rock. He also was more into studying Karate and sports than music, maybe that is why he was so selective. He really saw hip-hop as a culture outside of himself. He didn't identify with the style of dress nor latest dance steps. As time progressed he stopped buying the music altogether.

Victoria shared her perspective on hip-hop and schools:

> I think here at Case or any other school, the hip-hop culture has to be recognized as "where students are coming from" and acknowledged as something that is meaningful to the student. I don't know that it can be utilized as a tool of resistance for change only if the person (administrator, teacher) could be very creative. I think it is important for students to know that there is a dominant culture and that school is responsible for teaching them how to transform that culture. What students know and value is important and it should be incorporated into the educational process.

A Shift in Consciousness

During the mid-1980s Public Enemy transformed the rap genre into a political machine with the release of their albums, *It Takes a Nation of Millions to Hold Us Back, Fear of a Black Planet,* and *Apocalypse 91.* Public Enemy ushered in a new wave of black consciousness with their artistic expression and with the release of *The Enemy Strikes Back* not only made did black youth take notice, white youth joined in as well. With Public Enemy's success, other groups started to follow suit, notably N.W.A. (Niggas with Attitudes), the West Coast counterpart of Public Enemy.

Early in the history of N.W.A., its main rapper Ice Cube largely influenced the group. Like Public Enemy, N.W.A. used their music to attack oppressive government forces. N.W.A.'s song "Fuck the Police" and Public Enemy's "Fight the Power," were both viewed as antigovernment songs, and local law enforcement agents and the FBI investigated both groups. N.W.A. upon Ice Cube's departure moved toward gangster and hustler lyrics.

Doug also stated that early rap was politically charged and explained show his students did not understand that until he explained it to them:

> I remember when Fight the Power by Public Enemy came out and all the politically charged messages that was on the album It Takes a Nation of Millions to Hold Us Back, since I teach 7th grade social studies, I strive to incorporate some "political conscious" themes into some of the lessons, particularly those about us (African Americans). My students did not have a clue what Fight the Power meant, I brought the music into a lesson and explained how Public Enemy was critiquing the establishment and the issues we as black people were seeing in our communities, high unemployment, poverty, inequities in schools, and unfair housing practices. Some of the students began to respond and stated these were same issues many of their parents were facing now.

Doug also communicated that he took the lesson one step further by discussing the responsibility of African American males to transform the world:

> I also discussed with them their moral and social responsibility to become educated and liberated to transform their world. I particularly focused on my "little brothers" in the room. I want our African American males to know and understand what it is to be a black male, one who is responsible and productive. Many of them do not see this in their communities. I am often told that I am the only black male they see and to be their teacher is great. I am also reminded I am the only black male in the entire school. I know I am a role model for these kids and I don't take my responsibility lightly.

Crystal also expounds on how rap music was politically charged and on the black family.

> I remember Fight the Power by Public Enemy and I knew it was a message for the masses. What happened to that kind of rap music? I believe it still exists, however the law of supply and demand is still in operation. If these kids purchased the music, which deals with, social issues and knowledge, then the other "stuff" would not be so popular. Many of the rap artists are being played by the record companies. They see a few pennies on the dollar from the CD while the record companies are making the real money. It's another form of being enslaved.

Christina discusses how she tries to get her students to understand that rap music evolved out of the African American oral tradition of "storytelling"; and that it was a way to keep a record of a village's history, which has political implications.

> Because I teach Senior English we are involved in reading lots of literature and the writing process. When they began to complain about writing stories I explained to them that rap lyrics

are actually oral stories. One of my students can really "rap" but he has trouble writing, except for those "rhymes." I encourage him to orally tell his stories and then write them down. I explained to all of my students about the African "griot," the person in the village who kept the oral history of the people and how it was communicated orally down the generations.

Victoria expresses the view that the black consciousness and social injustices that ushered in rap music to the mainstream by Public Enemy were lost and the potential political power that rap music once possessed no longer existed.

Being a child during the 1960s I witnessed the civil rights movement and the political unrest. I also saw the power that music possessed during the times of social unrest. The singing of Negro spirituals was a way to communicate our faith and moral outrage without resorting to violence. It was a way to exercise power while holding peaceful demonstrations. The very act itself was an expression of the power we knew we had as black people. Rap during the Public Enemy days had that power, but the more youth became angry and enraged with the issues they were facing the power of the message was lost. The late 1980s were times of social unrest as well but black youth refused to utilize the tactics of peaceful demonstration to gain what they wanted. They viewed those ways of demonstrating as that of their parents and they believed the result of those times yielded the assassination of great leadership and the empowering of the white establishment. You had Ronald Reagan, his foreign and domestic policies. Reagonomics was something to contend with for the poor, particularly within the African American communities. Young people saw the rich get richer and the poor became poorer and they finally revolted and wanted to get what they rightly believed was theirs.

In 1992, the group officially disbanded and Ice Cube, Dr. Dre, and Easy E.—all former members of N.W.A.—later became the icons of gangster rap. The term "gangster rap" coined by the media to describe the criminality of one element of rap music in the early history of the genre consists of two words that are diametrically opposed. Before the commodification and co-optation of the genre, most gangsters were not artistically inclined enough to be recording artists, and rap artists—though some had criminal records—were by no means what one would consider gangsters; however that is no longer true. Many rap artists today are living the lives they are rapping about. Many are under the custody and control of the criminal justice system and many have committed heinous crimes against humanity.

Doug continues by sharing his perspective on how rap emerged into "gangsta-rap" from dance and party music and also shares that he talks to his students about the music industry. He conveys that he wants his students to understand it's about work and making money and those who survive and remain on top are those who "sell" those images.

When gangster rap came about with Ice T, Ice Cube, 2Pac and Snoop Dog, I knew it was still music, and not a way of life. I realized the difference and that those guys were doing a job. Just

> like I went to work every day, performing rap, making music, and creating an image, to sell was their job. My students don't understand that it's all about making a living, that these artists are actually "pawns" in the hands of record executives and that they must generate and create images that will sell. I tell my students about Tupac (2Pac) and Biggie (Notorious B.I.G.) and how they "believed in the life they created, and created a life they believed." Because of this "division of consciousness" they paid the ultimate price, their lives. Yes, the music lives on, however the record executives are collecting the "Benjamins," not them.

Victoria points out how students buy into an image that is not a part of their real world.

> Being the principal of Case Junior-Senior High, I know all of our students and I emphasize all of them, the Appalachians, the African Americans, the Whites, and even the exchange students, all enjoy rap music. It's the music of youth; however our African American students, particularly the male students are espousing a lifestyle that is portrayed in hip-hop culture which they themselves do not experience. All of our African American students do not come from single-parent homes, many of them may receive some form of government-sponsored assistance, however none of them are "gangsters"; however that is the image many of them like to portray. It is a form of representing, as they would say, so that they can "fit in," be "cool," and a part of a group identity.

Christina discusses how students, particularly black students, would dialogue about having careers as rap stars versus other careers. She also presents how students would discuss lyrics being stolen by white rappers and other rappers:

> When students come into the room I am open to listening to their views. They ask me questions about life, who they should date, and what I think about the latest fashions. I know many of them consider me like a mother so we have open discussions. Many of my students have excellent writing ability and I encourage them as seniors to really set their goals on selecting rewarding professions for their careers. What I find interesting is those who play sports or who are in the National Honor Society still want to be "rappers." I talk to them about other careers, however the "rap game" has replaced the "sports game" as the career of choice. I talk to them about making realistic career choices and even in the rap game there are careers behind the one standing in front with the microphone. I told them about Eminem as an example. They hate Eminem; the students believe his lyrics are stolen even after being told repeatedly rappers use other writers and that Dr. Dre who happens to be a top rap producer is producing Eminem.

Crystal also discusses how her students see rap as a means to an end:

> One of my best African American male math students, who has a 3.7 grade point average, is focusing on a rap career. He was a star football player last year and quit the team. I am concerned how this musical art form is leading so many of our kids to give up on realistic dreams. I tried to dissuade him by showing him the statistical average for becoming a college

football player with the opportunity of earning a college degree versus becoming a famous rap artist and the law of averages showed the college career path even with sports as a way to obtain his degree was the best decision. Of course, he got the math, but that didn't change his mind.

Doug continues along the same lines:

I tell my students to hold on to their "pie in the sky" dreams; however they must have an "earthly" one as well. Two of my 7th grade African American male students, practice their rap lyrics after school on a daily basis. I want them to see themselves as having the ability to achieve anything, but I want them to realize that academics are important. I think our students are so bombarded with images regarding entertainment as the path to fame and fortune they don't realize those who make it at that level are few and far between. I believe that is why our presence is so important. They need to see Victoria as the principal, a black female over a school that is predominantly white and supervising 80 white folk. They need to see Crystal, a black female chair of the math department. They need to see Christina, a sister teaching English who loves the classics including Shakespeare and I want them to see me. So they will know that all brothers who have dreadlocks are not dope dealers and gangsters.

These four educators use their perspective on rap music to speak of how race is used in context, subtext, and pretext by students and the media. According to Dyson (1997), "race as context helps us to understand the facts of race and racism in our society. Race as subtext helps us to understand the forms of race and racism in our culture. And race as a pretext helps us to understand the function of race and racism in America." (p. 33). Of course these categories are neither fixed nor absolute, but socially constructed, given the historical location and meaning affixed to multiple societal events. Several authors recognize hip-hop street culture as specific to the expressiveness of young black males (Brookins, 1996; De La Cancela, 1993; Gordon, 1995; Harris, 1995; Hill, 1992; Jones, 1989; Lee, 1996; Majors & Billson, 1992; McCollum, 1997; Mincy, 1994; Ogbu & Wilson, 1990; White & Parham, 1990; Wilson, 1991). These coping strategies have been used to ensure the survival of black males in an oppressive white society. Because of the long separation and confinement that African Americans have experienced from the rest of American society, their economic and social problems seem to remain distinct from the white community. This form of expressiveness is exhibited through young black male's style of dress, disposition, slang, and syncopated walk. Suppressed emotions other than anger, support from peers, denials of vulnerability, disdain for feminine qualities, and a predominant focus on heterosexuality are also characteristics of young black male expressiveness, specifically used to define black masculinities. All this is articulated in rap music and hip-hop culture. With its extreme sexuality and violence, rap bursts through all boundaries of propriety, good taste, and decorum, creating genuine shock effects of the sort described by Walter Benjamin (1969), who argued that in a media-saturated world, art must shock its audiences to get their attention. Rap often goes to extremes, over the edge, into that tabooed region of excess that threatens the protectors of law and order, morality, and taste. The rap spectacle is thus potentially highly subversive and in its more extreme forms enacts a Dionysian subversion of boundaries, entering a realm of anarchy, lawlessness, and chaos. Rap is thus at once a formidable form of musical expression, a subcultural means of opposition, a cultural idiom of counterhegemonic anger and rebellion, and an indicator that existing societies are structured according to a system of differences between dominant and subordinate classes, groups, races, and genders. Exploding false homogenization and humanism, rap music is an anthem of postmodern marginality and conflict, a vivid articulation of the extent to which difference and opposition are structuring principles of contemporary society, and a reminder of the growing differences between the haves and the have-nots. It is the thorn on the rose of media culture that pricks its audiences into awareness of the shadow side and underclass of American society. It is a frequently embarrassing reminder that all is not well in the home of the brave and the land of the free. Rap vividly reminds us that the red, white, and blue of the flag are not yet signifiers of a multicultural society in which the colors of the rainbow complement each other and harmonize rather than clash. Yet rap can further a destructive type of identity politics, promoting a binary opposition between white and black, cops and gangsters, men and women, straight and gay, that stigmatizes one of the terms of the binary. However, with its heavy emphasis on color, rap music calls attention to the importance of racial difference and focuses attention on whiteness as well as blackness. Rap thus troubles and problematizes the system of racial difference whereby blackness is marginalized, silenced, and excluded from the cultural dialogue, and whiteness is assumed as the norm and the normal. Rap can force white audiences to reflect on their own racial construction, on the ways in which the whites oppress the blacks, on the ways that their own subject positions are constructed in opposition to an "other" who is often presented in a negative light. Rap is thus a significant part of the postmodern adventure that forces an increasingly multicultural and multiracial society to become aware of its differences and to learn to live with otherness and dissimilarity.

· 5 ·

STILL SHOUTING, BUT NOT WITH MY VOICE

High in the tower, where I sit above the loud complaining of the human sea, I know many souls that toss and whirl pass, but none there are that intrigue me more than the Souls of White Folk.
—*W. E. B. Du Bois, Souls of White Folk*

The social assignment of Black bodies to an underclass is a historical conundrum that has multiple origins, two of which are the institutions of slavery and the mass media.
—*Ronald L. Jackson, Scripting the Black Masculine Body*

Undoubtedly, unless we accept discomfort as part of the process of reaching a deeper understanding and exploration of what is doable, possible, or necessary, then we perpetuate the status quo.
—*Leila Villaverde, Beyond Generic Democracy*

The use of the black body as a tool continues to be seen in its commodification for consumption by the entertainment industry including sports and film. The representations of the black males' physical prowess by popular culture reside in their abilities to play football, basketball, and/or baseball, as well as their uncanny ability to complete repetitive dance steps with style and grace. Digital imagery revealing their ability to think on a critical level is often overshadowed by criminalizing activities. Randall Jackson, author of *Scripting the Black Masculine Body: Identity, Discourse, and Radical Politics in Popular Media* writes, "Brought here in chains, Blacks and particularly Black bodies, in what we now know as the United States, never had the chance to be valued, celebrated, or even considered a citizen until 1863, well over 300 years after the first African slaves arrived in the New World. They were property or possession whose foreign and physical bodies were literally considered tools for labor and procreation that were evacuated of thought and culture. It was practically unimportant whether they could think beyond accomplishing a series of menial tasks demanded of them" (p. 14).

This attitude continues to prevail and pervade our public schools. I have visited many schools in which the curriculum has been "dumbed-down" because teachers perceived that the little African American kids cannot master the material; this perception is based on some preconceived notion of the language that they bring from home, the notion that they come from impoverished backgrounds, and/or on the way in which they relate to the adults in the school building who do not look like them. One in five of the schoolchildren in the United States comes from families in poverty. Jeffries (1997) believes desegregation brought white and black teachers together but it created some unsettling issues: "[M]any white teachers are unprepared to cope with the realities within the African American community. In addition, school systems are not hiring and retaining teachers who could most successfully address this problem. Indeed, higher education is failing to adequately prepare the teachers who are currently entering the classroom, and fewer African American are being trained in education at the university for public work" (p. 112). Because of these unsettling issues, racial inequalities are presently reproduced in our schools through institutional practices and cultural representations of racial difference.

The rate at which children of poverty leave school ill-prepared for adult life is alarming. Special programs, that is , Chapter/Title One and special education reform efforts, have yielded few results; children of poverty continue to experience failure disproportionate to their counterparts in their early school years and these well-intentioned efforts to give them support may even compound the problems. Sarles (1993) emphatically states: "Teaching is, among other things, getting people to play with their already formulated ideas and theories about the world. While they may add knowledge or possibly even think entirely *new* thoughts, much of learning is re-conceptualization of ideas, observations, lines of thought, conclusions and questions" (p. 108).

As a transformational teacher leader, I believe education is our praxis of freedom (hooks, 1994). This allows for my practice to be informed by the notions of democracy; particularly the freedom of voice. I view teaching, learning, and education as beyond the frame of economics. Teaching is a political and liberatory practice filled with experimentation of power, command of subject, and the ability to awaken a student's desire for knowledge. Because I believe the personal is political and because I view my role as a teacher/activist, my perspective on democracy cannot be delinked from the work in which I engage. I envision democracy as the interconnections that lie in the quest for knowledge while we navigate the manifestations of our destinies.

Teaching is fascinating. Every human being possesses the desire to explore the world around them. Teaching is liberating because one is not constrained to one particular path of inquiry or investigation. The teacher has at his or her disposal multiple tools and resources to guide students along the journey of discovery, not only of a subject but also of one's self. According to hooks (1994), "teaching is a performative act. And it is that aspect of our work that offers the space for change, invention, spontaneous shifts, that can serve as a catalyst drawing out the unique elements in each classroom" (p. 11). Many African American educators believe this form of teaching hooks speaks about was lost during the process of desegregation. The youth today are being instructed by white middle-class women who have no sense of who students are. African American educator and researcher Joanne Chesley (2007) poignantly reminds us of this in her essay, "Student Engagement and Academic Achievement: A Promising Connection." She argues the following:

> All too often the impact of the school's climate, the demeanor of the teachers, and the attitude of the community toward the students are ignored, resulting in achievement lags, disenfranchisement, and worst yet—school dropout. Some of this understanding that once was there for Black children (who make up the largest percentage of students experiencing school failure in the United States), was lost with the integration of schools. Black teachers in Black schools encouraged students to join a club, sign up for a sport, or compete in a math competition. They expected them to be well rounded. The principal expected them to attend student functions. The teachers knew the community; they knew the parents. They found it easy to comfort and provide assurance to a student who was new to the school or one who was just shy. That teacher took it upon herself or himself to help that student to blossom, and this was done through the social and the academic. The landmark *Brown v. Board of Education* decision, though not intentionally, resulted in several negative impacts for Black children—all having to do with their sense of affiliation and pride in the schools in which they would end up. Very few white students were asked to move to a Black school to make a huge

> cultural adjustment. Those that did, were generally "experiments"—a small number of volunteers, whose parents agreed to let them model "the right thing to do" for other white citizens. Black students however, lost the benefit of 38,000 Black teachers who were not only teachers to these students, but surrogate parents, counselors, disciplinarians, and advocates for these children. (p. 186)

Ferguson (2000) asserts: "Institutional practices continue to marginalize or exclude African Americans in the economy and society through the exercise of rules and purportedly objective standards by which individuals who may consider themselves racially unbiased" (p. 19). This is evident through high-stake accountability measures, such as standardized testing. We witness it with the resegregation of public schools across America, particularly in the southeastern part of the United States and through the handling of natural disasters by the government when areas affected are predominantly populated by those in poverty and "people of color." Individuals who are not members of the dominant culture live with this reality daily. When they question the powerbrokers of the dominating culture, doubts whether there is a problem or not and or whether the member of the minority group is playing the victim and/or the race card are raised.

For white people, being white is "natural" and "normal." They often operate from a position of whiteness; they fail to see that making statements such as, "I don't see color," is a very white thing to say. Whiteness as an entity is constructed by its relationship to blackness. The most commonly accepted view of race today in America is "color-blindness" (Frankenberg, 1993). Although this view is widely accepted, I believe that to dismiss color is to dismiss the physicality of the individual, as well as the historical, cultural, and political contexts in which their identities are constructed.

> Through its relationship with blackness, whiteness configured itself as different, as not enslaved, as powerful, as aligned with destiny...Such representations affirm the superiority and power of whiteness—again, its rationality, productivity, and orderliness vis-à-vis the chaos, laziness, and primitiveness of Africans and other non-Whites...Through its relation with Africanism, Whites gained knowledge of themselves as the racial barometer by which other groups were measured. (Kincheloe, 1999 as cited by Givens, p. 159)

Creating safe spaces to question and interrogate our institutions is vital to understand our humanity. The process of discovering one another's identities, ideologies, and "isms" should be inviting and engaging. Schools should be central to that process, providing adults to serve as "guides" and facilitators of the process. Schools should not be filled with persons young or old who engage in behaviors that seek to destroy the "will" of the individual. Teaching is the soul of our democracy.

Race and Its Place at Case

There are two cultural stigmatizations of the African American male represented in the United States today: one represents him as a criminal, and the other depicts him as a dangerous species. Russell, Wilson, and Hall (1992) remind white America what every African American has come to know as truth in our society—that skin color still matters and white America refuses to admit it. They assert:

> Being Black affects the way a person walks and talks, his or her values, culture, and history, how that person relates to others and how they relate to him or her. It is governed by one's early social experience, and history and politics, conscious input and labeling and the genetic accident that dictates external appearance. Skin color appears to affect identity, but in complex and seemingly unpredictable ways. (p. 62)

"African American boys' demeanors are misunderstood by White middle-class teachers. Furthermore, teachers often view African American boys as defiant, aggressive, and intimidating. It is difficult to care and nurture under a specter of unfamiliarity, fear, and/or mistrust" (Tutwiler, 2007, p. 147).

Crystal is concerned that many of the students who come to her are not ready for advanced math. The majority of them are black students who have been taught by white teachers who do not challenge because they have low expectations of students who they believe come from economically deprived backgrounds:

> *I am so tired of these teachers (white) passing these students along with substandard math skills. I ask the students about their performance the previous year and most of them give me information revealing they have not been challenged. They complain the teachers last year wanted to go over basic math facts and give them worksheets that were for elementary students. Some of the students tell me that Ms. Jones did not believe they could do high level math and wanted to place them in a basic tech-prep math track. They often complain they start out doing the work but by the second or third week of school, they are receiving the same worksheets, so they give up. Students who come from poor backgrounds may not have money, but they are not below average. I have spoken to many of my colleagues regarding this; however, they go back to outdated student records to support their belief, that the black students can't do the work. I am so frustrated by them and their practices, I could just scream. I have lobbied for many of them to be retested but to no avail; the teachers refuse to cooperate.*

Crystal continues to say that many of the teachers at Case are "paycheck" teachers. They are only there to collect a check. They really don't care about all the kids, but only the ones who need very little instruction. The gifted and above average students usually get all the attention.

> They (white teachers) don't really want to work. They do just enough to get by. A few of them are committed; the rest of them complain how bad the kids are, how ill-prepared they are and how disrespectful the students can be. See, I don't play that. The students may come in with their pants hanging down and humming some new rap tune, but I tell them to pull their pants up and get busy. They (white teachers) really want to teach the gifted and above average kids, it's easy for them to handle them, because they are self-motivated. Many of the kids complain about their classrooms. They know the teachers that care about them and those who just come put in a day's work. Teaching requires building relationships with students and going beyond the union contract.

Doug also shares his perspective on the "paycheck" teachers:

> As long as they are getting the money and putting out little effort, they will continue to do so. They (white teachers) really have preconceived notions about our children. They have low expectations, and really believe that our students cannot learn or don't have the desire to learn. I see right through them and they know it, because many of them I have known for many years, because I grew up in Belton School District Number 74. They (white teachers) put on a front. A few of them really care about educating all students and our students, but not many. The kids know it as well, in fact they will tell you which teachers really care about them learning and the ones that don't.

Doug continues:

> From their earliest years in school, these children find themselves at a disadvantage in the pursuit of learning, jobs, or personal fulfillment. I believe the logocentric rationality of governance of public education and the lack of educators to discover the role of "identity and cultural politics" are the reasons for the growing number of students who are identified as "at-risk" in public schools. There will be no shortcut in restructuring schools for the 21st century, but the "fruits of our labor" will be harvested for a lifetime.

Christina discusses how the white teachers allow the students to play games with them. She also informs us how if the students are poor and having a hard time, the white teachers like to identify them as "disadvantaged."

> I get tired of hearing the following, "you know they are disadvantaged." These kids are going to come into my room and work. They may be experiencing hardships but that builds character and perseverance. Those teachers allow the students to sleep in class, leave class when they want and do anything and everything besides their work. It's a game these kids like to play,

but not on me. They know when they come to my class, they must be ready to engage in the learning process. If they don't have paper, I give them paper. If they don't have writing utensil, I give them a writing utensil. They know I don't take any stuff from them and I tell them they have to do twice as much just to get their foot in the door. Being disadvantaged economically is not a handicap academically. I just hope these teachers will realize this and do more for our students.

Christina, Crystal, Doug, and Victoria echoed the same thoughts:

These students are black and maybe poor, but they can learn. They have to be held to higher expectations. Because many of these youth are experiencing some difficulties at home does not mean they are not able to learn. Many of them come from challenging experiences, but they are present and desire to participate in the educational process. We have to be committed to inspire them to achieve for some of them the impossible.

Victoria as the principal speaks of the struggle of the "establishment," mainly faculty and staff (many of whom are members of the local community) along with the local community to understand that the change in demographics does not have to reinforce their historical perceptions of African Americans who are in poverty:

The school faculty and staff whenever we discuss any issues concerning behavior and learning, constantly interject that because the "low income" housing is entering the community we are attracting all of the "bad" kids from inner-city school districts. They continue to make statements like; "absent fathers, drugs, gang-activity, and below average ability" are why we are having these problems at Case. However when you bring up issues concerning "cultural differences," the first thing they (white teachers and white administrator) say is "no, I am not a racist, no I am not prejudiced, I don't see color." I tell them constantly they must recognize the difference each child brings into the classroom; this is what makes them unique and special. I try to get the faculty to stop engaging in deficit thinking and look at the potential all youth bring to the learning environment.

Doug also discusses the issues of "cultural differences" and how the impact of the shooting of an "unarmed black male" by a white police officer in the neighboring metropolitan city opened the door to a discussion of issues of racism and how the faculty not one day did respond during a faculty meeting:

I often openly discuss issues our students have to contend with, particularly our African American males. When the shooting took place in Metropolitan, of the unarmed African American male, our students were very upset and many of the white students began to talk about how the white teachers treat the black students differently. In faculty meeting I brought this up and also gave an example of how during basketball season, I have to tell the black students to go straight home, walk together and if the Belton School District Number

> 74 *police department follows them or stops them, be kind, courteous and do whatever they say. The faculty was silent. No one openly said anything, however one of the white teachers, whose ethics are questionable, mumbled, "I can't believe they endure that." I believe this faculty really needs training on cultural differences and how to utilize them to affirm our students, not silence them and treat them differently.*

As Heifetz (1993) suggests, to progress toward developing a solution to these problems, there must be a shift in the individual's attitudes, values, and behavior. All individuals who interact with schools, namely, the parent community, the student community, the faculty and staff, the district community, and the civic community, have to be willing to involve themselves in the restructuring process.

Christina points out that everyone involved in the educational process at Case including the white parents have a particular attitude toward anything that is not like them and they challenge whatever is outside of their frame of reference:

> *The teachers, parents, and administration of this district all have been a part of this system for so long and they are not accustomed to thinking in any other way. The white parents questioned my educational decisions in regards to their child's progress during parent-teacher conferences and I know it's because I am an African American. It's like they don't trust what I am telling them. When I ask my English department colleagues and other colleagues in the school do they get the same response, they (white teachers), says "No!" I have been here for six years and it never fails, every year I get the same type of response. It may be from different parents of different students, but the common thread is all of them are white. Black parents trust what I say and take it as the authority in regards to their children, but the white parents always question my educational authority in terms of how I teach and how I assess their (child).*

Schools should be communities of learners. Sergiovanni (1989) asserts that schools should not only be communities of learners, but also centers of inquiry, aesthetically pleasing, idea-based, and self-managing with emphasis on moral connections. This is not evident at Case Junior-Senior High School. The various differences in education philosophies prevent the development of a "centrality of language," the ability to "empower students," and inhibit the development of Case becoming a "center of inquiry."

Victoria discusses how, the district's educational mission is not congruent with the needs of the "students of color" nor is it actualized or visibly seen in action by the faculty and staff. She also states there are some exceptions, and those exceptions happen to be the African American teachers, one teacher from Pakistan, and two white female educators:

> *All faculty members do not actualize the district's mission of "providing a quality education for all students within a caring and disciplined environment." Also discipline is focused upon more so than the students' "well being" or instruction. It amazes me how many of the teachers want to "control" and exert "force" over the students. At times this environment is so stressful, because they (white teachers) are not focusing on instruction. Some of them are, but by and large, many of them are not. They are still treating the students like they have no knowledge and that they are passive learners. The home economics teacher, whose roots are in Pakistan, actively engages the students in learning, and the intervention teachers also actively engage the students. There are a few exceptions, however many of the teachers are still teaching based on philosophies they learned twenty to thirty years ago. They (white) spend so much of their time "controlling" they forget about teaching. They believe that "controlling" is teaching, however it is not. I constantly redirect the teachers and students to our building mission, "a place of learning and a place of respect," hoping that teachers will respect the students and allow them to construct the knowledge and actively engage in the instructional process, however they focus so much of their attention on the "respect" issue.*

Crystal continues in the same vein. She also presents the "notion" of African Americans who have middle-class values but who lose their "blackness."

> *I often hear the students say, they (white) teachers don't respect us. The students also discuss how only the white administrator does not respect them, and prior to the arrival of the interim vice-principal, the black male administrator "bought into" the whole notion of discipline from the white perspective. The students did not like Mr. Stevens and I had my doubts about him, as well; he was not a people person, and he looked like one of us (African American), however he was not one of us.*

These educators began to discuss the students who were "at-risk" of school failure and/or dropping out of school altogether and how the district has failed those students. They question Mr. Stevens's motives for suspending so many African American male students. They believe he struggles with the "duality" that Du Bois (1903) articulates.

Black Educators Transforming Lives: From "At-Risk" to "At-Potential"

According to Slavin (1989), a student described as "at-risk" is one who is in danger of failing to complete his or her education with an adequate level of skills. School reform efforts have historically focused on "correcting" students who show deficiencies in basic skills. Risk factors include low achievement, retention in grade, behavior problems, poor attendance, low socioeconomic status, and attending schools with large numbers of poor students. Each of these factors is closely associated with the dropout rate; by the time students are in third grade, we can use these factors to predict with remarkable accuracy which students will drop out of school and which will stay to complete their education.

African American students at Case Junior-Senior High School are "at-risk." The rate of poverty, suspension, and academic failure is representative of the national statistics in those same areas. However, these four African American educators, Christina, Crystal, Doug, and Victoria are making a difference. If all the white educators espoused the same philosophies of effective teaching, the students of Case Junior-Senior High School would possibly experience high academic success.

African American educators have a broader conception of their role. The importance that the African American community attaches to the education profession is to be noted and it can be seen in various literary works. The education profession "ushered in" the "black middle class." Historically it is noted that whereas African American women were encouraged to become teachers, African American males who did not enter the "service" industry became preachers.

> Effective black teachers accept responsibility for nurturing their students' prerequisite skills and knowledge needed for success in school. They explicitly teach and model personal values—patience, persistence, and responsibility to self and others—that can serve as a foundation for current as well as future learning. They foster the development of student attitudes and interests, motivation—aspiration, self-confidence, and leadership skills. They are also aware of the structural inequalities in society and their practice evidences a "hidden curriculum" of self-determination designed to help students cope with the exigencies of living in a society, which perpetuates institutional racism while professing rhetoric of equal opportunity. (Foster, 1994, p. 233)

Doug believes that many of the white teachers are so caught up in their own concerns that they don't take the time to develop relationships with the black students, especially the black males. He also states, "Often you hear them shouting or yelling at our kids":

> *They (white teachers) don't care about these black kids, especially the black boys. They can't teach them because they are afraid of them, and they are afraid of them because they don't*

> understand them. They won't take the time to get to know them or try to identify with them. They are so caught into this I got to teach them something, which they forget, these kids know a whole lot more than some of them. You can hear them shouting at them sometimes. I thought about the fact, "I am shouting, but not with my voice."

The need for teachers to establish meaningful relationships with students has long been understood as a necessity for creating, inviting, and engaging learning communities.

Victoria speaks of her responsibility as an educational leader to develop teacher leaders:

> As a transformative educational leader, it is my duty to develop our corps of teachers into teacher leaders who will seek to create meaningful learning experiences with all of our students. I want them to create inviting learning communities where the content comes to life to our students and the process of inquiry and discovery becomes a time of excitement. We have to engage students by utilizing all of our resources and also by allowing them to have a voice. Students must drive the curriculum by bringing in their own lived experiences. We have talented students here at Case and I want them to utilize those talents as part of the learning process. So I often have to find new ways to do professional development for our teachers. The union contract is very specific regarding their time and professional development, but I get them to come over to my side and think about how to bring life into their classrooms.

Although today's teachers are entering schools where they are challenged to make connections with students having communication patterns, belief systems and values, and perspectives on adult-child relationships different from their own, they must seek ways to understand the dynamics operating within their classrooms that involve the broader cultural implications of the intersections of race, class, and/or gender.

Doug speaks of the notion of the power of racism and what has been accomplished since desegregation:

> Many of our students have no clue regarding the civil rights movement. As a history teacher, I bring the facts and stories to them. My desire is for them to leave with a sense of commitment to the struggle our people have had to endure. I want them to know the legacy of slavery and the post–civil rights revolutions. I want them to understand through the halls of history black people experienced great bloodshed. The tragedy of slavery was a costly one, but yet they have the opportunity to receive a free public school education and begin the path of enlightenment for themselves.

The African American faculty of Case realizes many of their students are at a disadvantage in the American society because of their race. They believe students of color must develop the knowledge, skills, and dispositions to negotiate their identities while navigating racial politics. As post–civil rights educators, they have witnessed the struggles for integration, but believe it was a necessity.

> The long history of racial oppression in this country has made simply being born black a synonym for a position in society that can never quite touch the position or value of whiteness. It shows itself when we talk about black success, in identifying a black woman as the first something, or when we discredit the poor population of an entire city, as in the case of Hurricane Katrina's aftermath in New Orleans. Unfortunately, "it" is as American as apple pie. It is white privilege. (Givens, 2007, p. 169)

Historically, African American communities understood that the primary responsibility of educating their children rested with the home. Schools were the place to engage formalized education; however, black youth realized that the responsibility of gaining an education was theirs and this was indeed communicated by the parents.

African American parents knew and experienced the hardships of being educated and whether true or not, they believed educational opportunity and academic achievement were directly tied to one's race, ethnicity, gender, language, and class. African American parents used to believe that although schools were responsible for what was taught as they deemed appropriate, it was the home in which knowledge attainment was reinforced. This, however, has changed significantly within the black community as evidenced by the achievement divide that persists between African American youth and their white counterparts.

Crystal speaks of the lack of parental involvement:

> *I really reach out to our black parents. I want them to understand I am here for their children; however, many of them rarely come to school and will not return my phone calls. I understand many of them are trying to survive. The current economic downturn has forced many of them to work two and three jobs to keep a roof over their heads, but if they could just show some interests in what their child is doing in school. I make myself available before, during, and after school for our parents, but I rarely see the black ones, while the white ones keep knocking down my door.*

These educators hear teachers constantly shouting to black youth.

Christina describes the pain she feels when students have to endure such abuse from adults:

> *It saddens me to hear teachers shouting at students. We are the adults and we should be in control of our own emotions. Children are still developing emotionally, socially, and cognitively. We have to remember this and strive to speak to them with compassion. I hear the white*

teachers screaming and shouting all of the time. The students know which buttons to push to get that response and they will continue to do so because to them it is a part of being a kid.

Victoria speaks of how she handles this situation:

When I witness teachers shouting at kids and oftentimes it happens to be the black kids they are shouting at, I politely enter their classrooms and spend some time observing. At the conclusion of my observations, I leave a little "Note from the Principal." On the note, I write one thing I witnessed that was positive and one thing that was negative. I leave the tagline, "still shouting but not with my voice." It is a reminder to them that they have never heard me shout or scream at anyone in the building and when I use my voice to communicate, I am stern and firm but I always do so with love and compassion.

According to Gordon (2006),

Gains made in the 1960s, 1970s, and 1980s have slowed. We have not been able to eliminate or significantly reduce the academic achievement gap between African American, Latina/or, and Native American students and their counterparts who identify themselves as Asian American or European American. Not only has the gap not disappeared, rather it appears to have also increased as academic achievement and/or social-economic status (SES) rise. That is, the gap is smaller between low-achieving and low-SES Blacks and Whites than it is between high-achieving or high-SES Black and Whites. In other words, higher academic achievement and higher social class status are not associated with smaller but rather greater differences in academic achievement. African American males lag behind African American females in academic achievement. Schools that serve predominantly black student populations are more likely to be under-resourced than are schools serving predominantly white student populations. (p. 25)

The gains that were made all appear to have been lost even after integration. What has occurred to create such a phenomenon? Is it the lack of highly qualified teachers? Is it the increase in white female teachers entering the profession who are not prepared to teach effectively black urban youth? In the wake of integration and resegregation of America's schools based upon class, many teachers are struggling to keep up with the demands of the profession and the demands of an ever-changing student body. If the students who decide to resist the process of schooling have to interact with a teacher who they believe does not understand who they are and the neighborhoods in which they live, their educational experiences will be fraught with power struggles and notions of resistance. To counteract these issues, several interventions must take place. Gordon (2006) offers four key interventions:

- Reducing the relatively high levels of academic underproductivity observed in so many of our children and the schools that serve them;

- Stabilizing the social fabric of our families and communities to better protect and support the academic personal development of our children;

- Reducing inefficiencies in the underutilization of the power of schooling and supplemental education in the development of the sizable group of children of color who now achieve at modest levels or barely survive with minimum performance in many of our schools; and

- Increasing the nurturance and celebration of developed ability in the group that Du Bois called "the talented tenth" of our people on whom the black community and the nation must depend for leadership. (p. 28)

Our democratic public education has promised to provide the basis for an informed, engaged citizenry that is fully capable of their own self-governance. This promise has not been fulfilled. It has not been fulfilled because just as the implementation of our democracy was flawed so has been the implementation of court mandates, congressional legislation, and national policies on educational reforms. The flawed implementation of democracy and failed school policies are due to many factors:

- Cognitive factors: our inability to properly gather, process and weigh all the information required to make appropriate decisions;
- Personal factors: arguing for our own personal vested interests during democratic discourse while placing the common good on the back burner;
- Power factors: the majority, those with the most forceful voices, or those with the most power get their way;
- Apathy or inattention factors: people do not care enough to participate in the discourse, or they do not understand the significance of issues that are in the public discourse, or they simply are not paying attention and thus do not use the opportunity to participate in the discourse around an issue;
- Ideological factors: the intentional as well as inadvertent distortion of information by politicians, the media, and others to promote ideological agendas;
- Political factors: using a self-serving and shifting conception of democracy as a political tool to promote our personal and/or ideological interests (that is, "bringing democracy to the Iraqi people" while simultaneously repressing voice and restricting personal rights and freedoms in our own country); and

- Efficiency factors: it is impossible to adequately consider all publicly relevant issues. (Gause, Reitzug, & Villaverde, 2007, pp. 224–225)

When students are not achieving at-potential and allowed to engage in mis-opportunity, we have allowed the promise of public education to be a curse. Students, African American students in particular, continue not to excel nor succeed to the same extent as their counterparts. They are kicked out, pushed out, and dropped out without the forms of critical consciousness that allow them to question the commonsense beliefs that are near and dear to our country. Freedom will not ring for this group of young people and liberty has been replaced with bondage. In order for this to change, all educators regardless of race, ethnicity, creed, ability, or persuasion must take up the challenge as eloquently communicated by the African American educator extraordinaire Gertrude Ayer,

> It is the high duty of the Negro woman teacher to teach the Negro youth to maintain a critical attitude toward what he learns, rather than to lay emphasis on stuffing and inflating him only with the thoughts of others...Hers is the task of knowing well her race's history and of finding time to impart it in addition to all other standard facts required, and to impart it in such a way that the adolescent student will realize: 1. That, in fundamentals he is essentially the same as other humans. 2. That, being different in some ways does not mean that he is inferior. 3. That, he has a contribution to make to his group. 4. That, his group has a contribution to make to his nation, and 5. That, he has a part in his nation's work in the world. To stimulate this spirit is the most lasting and far-reaching phase of the Negro teacher's work. (McDougald, 1923, p. 770)

The democratic promise of public education has been about "leveling the playing field" so that people are not held back, disadvantaged, or discriminated against by race, class, gender, sexual preference, disability, or other markers of identity and difference. Public education must be at the forefront in fighting systems of entrenched oppression and domination. This can be achieved only through the collective spirit of our oneness, because it is through this spirit of unity that we are able to strengthen our humanity and confront the disparities that exist among us. For we struggle not as individuals but as a collective of communities. If we must shout, we must do so with one voice to express our moral outrage for the injustices we witness wherever we may be.

· 6 ·

LAW AND ORDER: POLICING THE VILLAGE

Life for me, ain't been no crystal stair.

—Langston Hughes, "Mother to Son"

Black men who stand against sexism, who choose to be feminist in their thinking and action model a healing masculinity for all black men.

—bell hooks, 2004, We Real Cool

To engage in a serious discussion of race in America, we must begin not with the problems of black people but with the flaws of American society—flaws rooted in historic inequalities and longstanding cultural stereotypes.

—Cornell West, 1993, Race Matters

Bitter

As hard as the marble without a chip or trace
No smiles to be seen only a stern face.

The smell of sulfur, dirt as black as night,
The beating of drums, the drummer pounds with might.
Red as fire smoke unseen

Your sister's envy turns you green.
Kisses of pain, anguish, and rage

The book goes unread, yet you turn the page.
Gold uncorrupted, Silver melted down

Your only reply was to beat him to the ground
Hail all heroes, great and small

Ask me how I feel
Just bitter, that's all. (C. P. Gause, 2001)

When I entered the halls of Case Junior-Senior High School, I was struck by the many forms of bitterness present there. Teachers did not want to work with other teachers. High school students did not want to share the same campus with middle school students. Members of the community were disgusted with high school students walking to local fast-food restaurants for lunch and they were angry because the cafeteria was not big enough to house them during the lunch period. Case at that time was a multiethnic learning community with students of color, white, Appalachian, and international students comprising the student body. Black parents and students were bitter because the faculty and staff of eighty were all white except for the four African Americans presented in this text. I became the fifth African American faculty member at Case. The community was changing and many of the white and Appalachian students were angry because they felt as if the black students were taking over. Case historically had been a majority white neighborhood school full of rich history, but because of the changes in the community, Case was now considered an urban school. With the designation of an urban school bestowed on it, many sociocultural issues started affecting the climate of Case. Teachers often openly stereotyped students of color and those in poverty. The students rebelled; therefore negotiating discipline issues became the main task of my day. Instead of trying to keep students in school, the faculty and staff were determined that if students could not follow their rules (many of them were archaic), they would have to be removed. Case had a disproportionate number of students attending, in-school and out-of-school detention, as well as students placed on long-term suspension or expelled for the academic year. Victoria believed in supporting her leadership team; therefore, she did not interfere in matters of discipline unless there was an appeal. To her credit, she did her best to limit suspensions and instructed the vice-principals to use suspension only as a last resort. I adhered to her policy; however, the parents and students often complained that the other vice-principal did not. The crowning moment was when I realized the police station was only a block from the school and students were always under surveillance.

Case and the Student Outlaws

According to research conducted by the Applied Research Center, a nonprofit organization that focuses on issues of social injustice, African American students along with Latinos and Native American students are suspended or expelled in numbers vastly disproportionate to those of their white peers. African American students are suspended eight times more than their white counterparts. This wielding of disciplinary power by educators is consistent with viewing students as docile bodies to be controlled as instruments. In *Discipline and Punish*, Foucault (1977) presents disciplinary power as "the specific technique of power that regards individuals as both objects and as instruments of its exercise" (p. 40). School officials and teachers view students as instruments and objects to be policed, interrogated, and assimilated into rituals of docility. Students who do not comply are removed from the learning community not only as a form of punishment, but also as a message to those who remain: it is better to be in the group than out of the group, because if you are out of the group something is wrong with you. Punishment is a fruitful site for a close-up look at routine institutional practices, individual acts, and cultural sanctions that give life and power to racism in a school setting that not only produces despair and failure among black students, but also increasingly demonizes them (Ferguson, 2000, pp. 19–20).

The images and representation of African Americans males, by the media as criminals and endangered species influences the decisions of educators, administrators, and civic community, and parent community members. I found this to be quite true at Case Junior-Senior High School. Those who were responsible for disciplining the students constantly invoked those images for identifying problems and making punishment decisions. One irony I discovered while serving as the interim vice-principal of Case was just as young black men are murdered, maimed, and imprisoned in record numbers, their styles have become disproportionately influential in shaping popular culture. Teachers were not critically deconstructing the images they saw daily about black males; therefore, their biases about student behavior were informed by these very images. I was often amused by the black male students who readily admitted they knew certain white teachers feared them. They used the fears white teacher had of them to control the classroom, resist instruction, and to perform their own rap lyrics. According to Harris (2006),

> The fear of escalating crime, even as crime rates were steadily declining, has led the public to embrace a series of "get tough," "zero tolerance" law enforcement polices—from

laws on the books like "Three Strikes" and mandatory minimum sentences to police practices on the streets like aggressive stops-and-frisks and random street sweeps. America's assault on crime over the past decade has exacted a high price, mostly paid by the African American community and frequently law-abiding citizens. Some of the harshest policing policies have been directed at youth. (p. 76)

For most young black men, power is acquired by stylizing their bodies over space and time in such a way that their bodies reflect their uniqueness and provoke fear in others. To be "bad" is good not simply because it subverts the language of the dominant white culture, but also because it imposes a unique kind of order for young black men on their own distinctive chaos and solicits an attention that makes others pull back with some trepidation. This young black male style is a form of self-identification and resistance in a hostile culture; it also is an instance of machismo identity ready for violent encounters (West, 1993). Stylizing one's body is a form of navigating the rules that are in place for establishing order. Rules are often referred to in terms of neutrality; they are impartially exercised, and the individual's feelings and personal responses are not taken for granted. For black males to not respect their feelings is a sign of disrespect. School rules are instruments of normalization. Students are evaluated, sorted, and compared to others on the basis of how they behave or misbehave, and all this is based on the things they do to violate and/or conform to school rules.

Case Junior-Senior High School was filled with students who were nonconformists to school rules. The varying youth identities, goth, hip-hop, freaks, geeks, and nerds were visible. A large percentage of the faculty and staff did everything within their power to not recognize the students' individuality. On the basis of conversations and personal observations, the faculty and staff, particularly white faculty and staff members, wanted students to conform to their own images of youth, which were rooted in the 1970s and 1980s. This became a huge challenge for the administrative team. I often felt as if faculty wanted students to be treated like outlaws.

Case administrative team comprised Victoria Page, the principal, William Kirkpatrick, and me. William and I handled all the discipline situations. Victoria intervened when her expertise was needed or when suspensions were appealed. She operated out of a social justice philosophy and believed students and their parents had the right to appeal any decision. I agreed; however, Mr. Kirkpatrick was not a team player about this decision. Many of the teachers wanted students to go to him; they often stated, "he has a sense of how to deal with students when it comes to teachers." As an outsider to the community,

I had to constantly remind them I was a former teacher and school principal and I brought a wealth of knowledge and experience to the job as well. After Mr. Kirkpatrick shared his story, I understood the basis on which the teachers made such claims; however, those claims were still biased and rooted in racial politics.

William Kirkpatrick had spent the past twenty-eight years in the classroom. He is a United States military veteran and considered to be the "military's man-man." He was "passed-over" twice for an administrative appointment and was finally granted one last year. William describes himself as a "midwestern-farm boy." The students, many of them, regardless of racial identity, felt that William was a "good-ole-boy" and a "racist." There were a few teachers who believed William had issues with individuals who did not look like him, but they rarely challenged him. He believed his decisions and judgment was sound when dealing with students. William espoused a "color-blind" philosophy; often stating, "I don't see color, I see the child." As the semester went on, William and many of the teachers adjusted to my style of interacting with students and began to adopt some of my methods. William did not stray far from his path, but he did open up and started to try new things. He was considered to be narrow-minded by some and intolerant of any difference held or shown by others.

> In a more reasonable society, in a more perfect nation, in a world beyond ugly discriminations of gender, race, and class, our citizens would live in a convivial atmosphere of community...that is why I worry a good deal about the soundness of the national mind and spirit. I worry about public voices that tout intolerance and narrow-mindedness. I worry about the politics of parsimony and isolation...I still take comfort knowing that singular acts of care and compassion take place all the time and I hope for the day when these acts become the very core of our culture. (Elam, 1995, p. A 11)

The Board of Education of Belton School District Number 74 adopted a "zero-tolerance" discipline policy. Statistically a policy of this nature has been shown to greatly disadvantage students of color, particularly African American males. Approximately 37 percent of African American males are overidentified for Special Education services, particularly in the "emotionally challenged behavior" category (District Statistics, 2000). Approximately 39 percent of African Americans, particularly males, are suspended, expelled, and/or "placed on homebound" from Case Junior-Senior High School (District Statistics, 2000). I was surprised with Case local statistics because African Americans only comprised approximately 43 percent of the student population. I realized that the culture of Case Junior-Senior High School is not about "providing a quality education for all students in a disciplined and caring environment," which is the mission of the Belton School District Number 74; it is really about custody and control. Students were considered outlaws and they had to be punished, no matter what the cost.

The faculty and staff members of Case were more like local sheriffs than educators and as the interim vice-principal I was expected to continue to suspend and hold discipline hearings for the student body. In fact, disposing of discipline cases was my primary responsibility. I was responsible for administering administrative detentions, which were commonly known as "DTs." Administrative detentions were served in the afternoon in the classroom of one of the biology teachers. It was reported on several occasions that students could not talk, sleep, make noise, or breathe heavy in detention or they would be thrown out. Detention lasted one full hour. On several occasions black male students were thrown out of the white male biology teacher's classroom with only five minutes left on the clock. I did not believe this, until I witnessed the action "firsthand." The teacher on more than one occasion referred to "those students" being involved with the police. In fact many of the teachers at Case often discussed whether certain students had been involved with the police.

The irony in all this is that the local police station was one block away from the school and the police were always on constant alert. Driving past the school many times a day was a daily ritual. The local police have on many occasions entered the school with and without being asked to do so. I have personally witnessed the police harass African American students, particularly the males. I have witnessed their harsh tone and conversation with black students and I have had several conversations with the police discussing "today's youth" and their behavior. They have arrested many of our students while on lunch break at the local fast-food restaurant allegedly for creating disturbances. When Victoria banned the students from going to the fast-food restaurants, the managers of the establishments would call and beg her to allow them to return. The students of Case were a major source of revenue for those establishments. Victoria met with each of them to discuss strategies for insuring that our students would not be arrested; however, the managers responded, "that's the police departments call, we can't control the decisions of the police."

Doug elaborates on this and his concerns about the amount of "policing" that takes place:

> The police follow these kids everywhere. When school is dismissed they follow them up different streets for blocks and they will arrest them. It's amazing. During basketball season after

practice in the evening, I have witnessed the white police officers follow the African American kids up the block. They never follow the white kids. The white teachers here have this "get you" attitude. They police the kids all of the time. It's not right and I make sure our students, especially the black ones know they are being followed.

Crystal expresses her concerns about how the students are policed and how there is a distinct difference in treatment in terms of race:

I have two students in one of my Algebra classes. The white one should have been suspended possibly even expelled for throwing a discipline referral at me, which hit me on my neck and left a bruise. I had to go to William twice and then to Victoria to get something done. The black student was suspended for "cutting too me classes." Now the black student is an A- student, the white student is a D+ student. You know this is about race. The students call Mr. Kirkpatrick a racist and if you look at some of his actions it would be hard not to agree with them.

Victoria discusses how the student code of conduct is subjective and how some teachers manipulate it to get some students into trouble.

The student code of discipline has 58 infractions. Some of them are really needed, for instance those that deal with weapons, drugs, and other illegal matters; however the issues concerning disrespect, chronic behavior that disrupts school activities, and disregard of reasonable directions or commands by school authorities including administrators and teachers, those items are quite subjective and many of our teachers have utilized them to push students out of their classrooms into ACA (Alternative Classroom Assignment), after school detention, Friday school, or home (because of suspension.) I have called for a revision; but the code of conduct was developed from district policy, so I ask members of the leadership team and teachers to utilize their best judgment when seeking discipline for our student. We have to be patient and understanding. I want teachers to also understand they take things too seriously. These are kids and sometimes you have to just allow them to do kid things, of course within reason.

Christina presents her perspective on how the students of Case are policed:

One of my students, Joshua, was arrested during the lunch period at one of the fast-food restaurants. Joshua loves to play around, however he emphatically stands behind his story that the white police officer, asked him, "what are you looking at" and Joshua told him that he was looking at "him." Joshua stated he was placed under arrest. He was made to get on the ground and placed in handcuffs in front of everyone. Joshua said the police officer kept staring at him and instead of turning away he looked back. When the officer asked the question, he gave him the answer. Joshua is a handful, we all know this, but he does tell the truth.

Case has an open lunch for those 7th and 8th grade students who are on the honor roll and all 9th–12th-grade high school students. What does this mean?

During lunch, because of the capacity of the cafeteria (115), the students are able to go to the nationally recognized "fast-food" restaurants in the community to purchase and eat their lunch. It is known as a "walking lunch period." Because of the "savage inequalities" of America's schools, this situation is very real (Kozol, 1991).

Crystal expresses concerns that many of her students cut the sixth period because it is right after lunch and many of them are late finishing their lunch and getting back to school:

> *This walking lunch is a mess. The kids are often late coming back and when they get to class, because they have just finished lunch, they want to go to the bathroom. Some of them utilize this time to drink and smoke marijuana off campus. I have been told that some of them also go home to have sex. Many of them just don't return sometimes because they are out having fun, socializing, and just don't think they need to be in class. It really is problematic. They are teenagers who have no sense of responsibility. I am trying to teach them and prepare them for state testing and college entrance examinations during sixth period. The school district needs to improve this facility by building a larger cafeteria or converting the second gymnasium into a "commons" area so kids will have a place to eat and socialize during lunch time, instead of walking up and down the streets. I wouldn't want my child to be off the campus, especially crossing that busy intersection. One day someone is going to get hurt trying to cross that street during lunch time.*

Victoria also addresses the lunch problems:

> *It has been reported that students have gone into the neighborhood bars to eat lunch, or should I say a place that sells food and alcoholic beverages, a bar and grill. The administrative team has to go "round them up" and get them to hurry back to class. Because of this the sixth period has the highest tardy and truancy rate. The police visit the local establishments to make sure the kids are "in-line." Well you know this creates even a bigger problem, because when they see two or more African American students walking together and dressed in the latest "gear" from those rap videos, the first thing they think is "some gang-related" activity is going on.*

Doug asserts that the students in the "junior" division of the school are often confined to the cafeteria and were also placed on "in house" lunch, which means even after they finish their lunch they cannot go outside, which creates a problem:

> *Junior high students need to let off some "steam" and be able to get some socialization time and exercise. When they cannot go outside even during their lunch period they become more agitated and restless. They are treated like prisoners and I understand the issue regarding space; but we have to figure out a way to let them get some fresh air after lunch. Many of them have been sitting in classes all day and they become aggressive and angry because they feel like caged animals.*

Victoria openly discusses how the district's policies concerning truancy, absenteeism, and "zero-tolerance," all contribute to an environment of surveillance:

> If students are truant to school and/or class, their parents are referred to the court system for violation of school attendance laws. We have a significant number of parents and students who have to go through the court system, because of extenuating circumstances regarding their children's attendance. The "zero-tolerance" policy adopted by the "board" also creates a significant amount of "policing." If any students are involved in any violence, including fighting, they are suspended, and charged by the school for "disorderly conduct." A police report is filed and the students are then referred to the court system for adjudication. This of course disadvantages all of our students, particularly the African American male students, because they are always under the "gaze."

Crystal discusses how the student dress code creates problems; some teachers enforce it and others do not:

> The student dress code is an issue. The young men all of them, white, black, purple, and blue, all were their pants hanging or "sagging" as they call it, and they wear these oversize shirts and jackets. Now the jackets are supposed to be in their lockers, however some teachers enforce this based upon the student and what mood they (white) themselves are in. I know it's the style for them, especially with these designers, like FUBU, Sean John, Ecko, and Enyce; however the students know that they are being treated differently. I have seen my white colleagues give Joshua, who is black, hell in the name of the dress code, and not say one thing to Adam, who's white.

Clothes are significant to you as they construct your identities. Youth often use clothes to communicate their favorite color, music group, designer label, or fashion sense. Clothes are also status symbols and represent class differences. Youth see how and what they wear speak of how much "cool factor" they possess in their peer group. Clothes are sometimes the only source of pride, dignity, and worth for young people. Yes, they are the outward status symbols of materialism and often they are markers for success in American culture; however, clothes for youth communicate who they are and what is important to them.

African American Rap on Black Males

Compensating for feelings of insecurity in a Eurocentric world has led the African American male, particularly the youth, to redefine what it means to be a man in the today's world. For most, this includes risk taking, machismo, aggressive social skills, and sexual promiscuity. The noted mannerisms include physical posture, style of clothing, dialect, walking style, greeting behaviors, and overall demeanor (Harris, 1995). Richard Majors and Janet Billson collectively refer to these attitudes and behaviors as "Cool Pose."

Doug discusses his perspective on working with black youth at Case and how the white teachers misunderstand that black male youth are about being cool. He also discusses striving to help the black male youth understand the issues of negotiating worlds—the white world and the hip-hop or black world. He speaks of the "double consciousness":

> I want our black young men to understand that it is okay to be cool. I also try to get them to understand that the world exists in many forms and they are going to have to learn how to exist in many of those forms. They like to define it as a black and white thing, which is good for where they are coming from, so I tell them they are going to have to develop the "double consciousness" of understanding,; which is they are black males living in a society whereby they are always misrepresented and under the "element of suspicion." They scream "it's not fair" and I tell them I know; however it is my job to help them learn both systems that they will be successful. I also explain to them that "acting cool" is okay; however sometimes when they are in Ms. Sweeting class, they will have to "tone it down." They immediately say that I am trying to get them to "act-white." I tell them no, I am trying to get them to use their intelligence so that they can succeed.

The black male is socialized to view every white man as a potential enemy, and every symbol of the dominant system as a potential threat. Because of this, he is reluctant to expose his innermost feelings. (Playing it cool becomes the mask of choice. Cool Pose is a well-developed and creative art; it also exacts a stiff price in repressed feelings and suppressed energy.)

Victoria describes how she spends time discussing with many students, particularly the African American males, how their "coolness" may be perceived as a "threatening demeanor." She further describes how many of the African American males like to evoke fear in the white teachers, but they fail to realize that the white teachers have the power of the system on their side:

> I have spoken to Rashawn, Ahmed, Ahmad, J.D. and Joshua, about how these teachers perceive their "coolness" as aggressive behavior towards them and their demeanor as "threatening." I also explained to Joshua that was the "real" reason he was arrested during lunch the previous week. I also tried to get them to understand with the shooting of the unarmed African American male by the white police officer which took place a couple of months ago and with Metropolitan experiencing all of the rioting. Who did the "white establishment" hold responsible? The black males. They confessed to me that they like making them (white teachers) feel afraid of them, especially after that situation. I told them that the teachers still have the power of the system over them and that they must learn to negotiate how to exist at Case bringing very little negative attention to them.

National telecasts of African American males being apprehended by law enforcement locally and regionally are a daily ritual. Contemporary images of black masculinity continue to challenge hegemonic constructions of whiteness even as they rewrite and reproduce forms of patriarchal authority, enveloping some of its most disturbing aspects in black vernacular style and expressive performance. This was quite evident during the race riots at the Metropolitan caused by the unarmed shooting of a black "teen" by a white police officer.

Crystal interjects with her thoughts about how African Americans, males in particular, are policed because of the culture of hip-hop:

> These young men do not understand that the culture of hip-hop is one in which the "white establishment" does not like, except for how it has made the big white executives a lot of money. Middle-class white folks, still have a strong distaste for anything that is different and they see hip-hop and rap music and those who partake of it as criminals. Gangster rap is a prime example. These teachers (white) base their perceptions of our students on the images they see and because we live in a mediated culture and society, those images are everywhere.

Victoria, Doug, Crystal, and Christina believe the political disturbances locally and globally along with the culture wars within our own nation require a new reading and analysis of the black male image. They also believe it will take new instructional strategies and practices to reach the black male presently in America's schools because they are competing against the forces of black heterosexual masculinity perpetuated by popular culture. They realize the images of superathletes, gangbangers, and rap superstars are more powerful and alluring than those found in schools.

Christina presents this perspective of how she believes her white colleagues and parents base their assumptions of who she is as an African American on what they see on television and the media:

> I have parents who judge my knowledge of education and the decisions I make concerning their child on what they see from the media. I believe anytime that I have to assign their student a detention or any type of discipline infraction they want to challenge it, and not because of the situation, but because of my "black authority." I have had parents to try to get decisions overturned because of my "racial identity." If the white parents would just engage in a coherent dialogue they would realize I am not like what they see on television.

Victoria also continues along the same vein and talks of her authority being challenged not only because she is an African American but also because she is a woman. She says that gender has played a role as well:

> I have made decisions and parents threaten me with Mr. Grainger the superintendent, which is fine. I stand my own ground. However I have also noticed how some parents will challenge

certain teachers and leave others alone. I have seen black parents challenge white and black teachers. But the white parents never challenge the white teachers, but they always challenge the black ones. I believe our parent community is more in-tuned to their rights as taxpayers, so they believe they can come in and influence the school.

Based on the works of Foster (1990), the following assertion can be applied to Case Junior-Senior High School:

> The behavior of African American boys in school is perceived by adults at Rosa Parks School through the filter of overlapping representations of three socially invented categories of "difference": age, gender, and race. These are grounded in the common-sense, taken-for-granted notions that existing social divisions reflect biological and natural dispositional differences among humans: so children are especially different from adults, males from females, blacks from whites. At the intersection of this complex of subject positions are African American boys who are doubly displaced: as black children, they are not seen as childlike but as adults; as black males, they are denied the masculine dispensation constituting white males as being "naturally naughty" and are discerned as willfully bad. (p. 80)

Black heterosexual masculinity is used in policy debates, in television news, and popular film representations to link the signs of patriotism, whiteness, family, nation, and individual responsibility. Discursively located outside of the "normative conceptions," mainstream moral and class structure, media representations of poor black males serve as the symbolic basis for fueling and sustaining panic about crime, the nuclear family, and middle-class security, while politicians displace attention from the economy, racism, sexism, and homophobia. The result is that black youth have limited opportunities to construct positive self-identities. Contemporary expressions of black masculinity work symbolically in a number of directions at once; they challenge and disturb racial and class constructions of blackness; they also rewrite and reinscribe the patriarchal and heterosexual basis of masculine privilege and domination derived from gender and sexuality.

This figure of black masculinity consistently appears in the popular imagination as the logical and legitimate object of surveillance and policing, containment, and punishment. Discursively this black male body brings together the dominant institutions of (white) masculine power and authority, criminal justice system, the police, and the news media to protect (white) Americans from harm. Working in this heavily surveyed and heavily illuminated public arena, the figure of the menacing black male criminal body is also the object of adolescent intrigue, fascination, and adulation. Rap artists have used cinema and music video to appropriate this surveyed and policed space for different ends, namely, to construct or reconstruct the image of black masculinity into one of hyperblackness based on fear and dread. This is the mechanism for selling their music. The thug image is about consumerism. Christina presents her perspective on trying to get students, particularly African American students to really look at rap videos as forms of entertainment that degrade women:

> I tell my students, especially when they want to discuss Drama, that "Rap" videos maybe the new "urban plays" of today, but they are limited in terms of artistic value. I get them to see that they portray women negatively only as possessions. Black women are objectified and utilized as tools for sexual pleasure in some of these videos. Many of the videos are violent in nature and never show the intellectual abilities of our people. Violence produces more violence and those videos don't represent all African Americans.

Crystal continues and says that she believes those videos affect youth and the public. She believes that their attitudes and their identity are constructed on the basis of rap videos:

> The content that is present in the media, television, and Internet influences these students. The topic of conversations majority of the time is no hip-hop culture, the best lyrics, the "bling bling" The best ride, the best gangster videos, and many of these kids worship those rap stars, and now since many of your basketball stars are trying to be rap artists, it's taken this entertainment issue to a whole new level.

Victoria discusses the overall perception of the school and the community:

> Parents and teachers, particularly white parents and teachers, see the kids dressed like he images on the videos and they automatically assume that it's about violence and gangs. Mr. Grainger and a board member saw some students wearing bandanas, and of course that is against the dress code and student code of conduct, but they called me to discuss the level of "gang" activity that is present at Case. It is an automatic assumption that whatever a student wears to school is a part of the hip-hop culture that it has to be connected to violence or some form of criminality.

Doug discusses his perspective on the assumptions that individuals make about rap and its evolution:

> Rap started out as party music and it has evolved to include gangster rap, hip-hop, pop, and other forms. Rappers have to sell records and whatever the consumer continues to purchase will sell, however the only form of rap music that has been largely contested is gangster rap. The majority of the students have moved beyond gangster rap, they are more into the rap that deals with having "props," material possessions, or material wealth, which is what made

America. "It's about getting mine." The students also remind me of this, by saying, "Bill Gates, got his, I want mine." The students also believe that rap was not a problem until black youth were becoming powerful.

By drawing on deeply felt moral panic about crime, violence, gangs, and drugs, rappers have attempted, often successfully, to turn dominant representations of black male bodies into a contested cultural field. Black rap artists rework and rewrite the historic tropes of black heterosexual, masculine (hyper) sexuality, insensitivity, detachment, and cold-bloodedness into new tropes of fascination and fear for the dominant culture.

The cultural effects of these images are as complex as they are troubling. The complex cluster of self-representations, embodied in images of the black heterosexual body as hip-hop artist, athlete, and movie star reify negative connotations of black masculinity. Until black entertainers challenge racist depictions of black masculinity as incompetent, oversexed, and uncivil—ultimately a threat to middle-class notions of white womanhood, family, and the nation—black males will continue to be their own oppressors. Black male youth will continue to define their manhood on the basis of deeply held traditional notions of heterosexuality, authenticity, and sexism.

The images of black manhood as threat and dread not only work to reify dominant white representations of black manhood, but they also stand in a conflicted relationship with definitions and images of masculinity within black culture. This is found most notably in constructions of black masculinity produced by the middle-class wing of the civil rights movement and those produced by black gay men. My journey at Case Junior-Senior High School was one I shall never forget. It provided me the opportunity to work with post–civil rights African American educators who were committed to transforming their school community and the lives of the students they touch. I learned about life, liberty, and justice in the context of policing and interrogation.

· 7 ·

COLLABORATIVE ACTIVISM: KEYS TO TRANSFORMING LEARNING COMMUNITIES

> If...one managed to change the curriculum in all schools so that [African Americans] learned more about themselves and their real contributions to this culture, you would be liberating not only [African Americans], you'd be liberating white people who know nothing about their own history.
> —James Baldwin, 1963, A Talk to Teachers

> The courage to teach is the courage to keep one's heart open in those very moments when the heart is asked to hold more than it is able so that teacher and students and subject can be woven into the fabric of community that learning and living require.
> —Parker Palmer, 1998, The Courage to Teach

The new millennium arrived with great economic prosperity; however, currently the United States is facing a weaker economy, a depressed housing market, a costly Iraq war, and all the old problems of the late 20th century— power, race, identity, violence, and ethics. Current challenges for educators are: (1) the increase number of charter schools; (2) voucher programs; (3) increases in immigrant populations; (4) for-profit educational organizations; (5) inadequate funding for No Child Left Behind; (6) inequities regarding accountability, and; (7) and the resegregation of public schools along class/racial lines. These challenges have broad implications for higher education. According to Hopkins

(1997), education is considered to be the most accessible means for achieving social, political, economic, and cultural liberation in the United States. This traditionalist view accepts the idea that public schools are vehicles of democracy and social and individual mobility. Educators and laypersons alike believe that the nature of public schools is the major mechanism for development of a democratic and egalitarian society (Hopkins, 1997).

Gutmann and Thompson (1996) posit:

> In any effort to make democracy more deliberative, the single most important institution outside government is the educational system. To prepare their students for citizenship, schools must go beyond teaching literacy and numeracy, though both are of course prerequisites for deliberating about public problems. Schools should aim to develop their students' capacities to understand different perspectives, communicate their understandings to other people, and engage in the give-and-take of moral argument with a view to making mutually acceptable decisions. These goals, which entail cultivating moral character and intellectual skills at the same time, are likely to require some significant changes in traditional civic education, which has neglected teaching this kind of moral reasoning about politics. (p. 359)

Democratic education involves educators empowering students to engage in free and open discourse, and offering consistent opportunities for students to engage in inquiry, reflection, critique, and ultimately, social transformation (Knight and Pearl, 2000; hooks, 2003; Nagda, Gurin, & Lopez, 2003). This must be done to counteract the despair that is clearly visible locally and globally.

Our lives today are filled with the availability of nonstop global media at the click of the mouse. We are able to garner attention to our cause and even gain support for it rather quickly through the use of the Internet. Presidential campaigns are raising more money through the World Wide Web than through traditional means. We can view the supporters of individual campaigns through videos made for airing through social networking sites. This is taking place in virtual reality; but what about in our current/physical reality? The days of marching on Washington or any other city en masse are over. The convenience of the Internet allows us to e-mail our petitions for virtual signatures to be digitally delivered to multiple entities at the same time. Our activism has moved from being collaborative and present to individualistic and absent. I do realize the Internet is filled with instances of large group collaboration; in fact it has redefined it. Yes, the media are filled with situations and circumstances that are detrimental to the human condition, such as war, famine, disease, and greed; however, we cannot deny the fact that now instead of waiting for days for responses to a cause, we can receive them instantaneously. My concern is when our activism was current and present, we came face-to-face with the reality of our destructive behaviors. Now that we see them so often in real-time, we come to expect and accept them as everyday experiences. I believe this is why we no longer focus on providing an equitable education through which all students can gain success and academic achievement. I believe our calls for accountability are devoid of any true sense of democracy, social justice, and moral responsibility. I believe youth today realize the promises of their parents and adults are empty of meaning and commitment. Today's youth are experiencing despair, rage, pain, and frustration. Our youth are able to witness the impact of our decisions on our local and global communities in an instant. The impact of not being good global citizens, the use of cheap labor for greed and profit, and the ability to invade sovereign nations because of faulty intelligence, all these force them to call into question the integrity of their adult role models. If the intelligence was faulty, why didn't someone do their homework? If I were a youth of today, that would be my first question posed to the Bush administration about the decision to invade Iraq.

Education is often touted as being the essence of America's success. The ability to learn and achieve were once considered synonymous with the American dream. This no longer holds true in our land of the free and home of the brave. It is now about corporate profits, consumerism, and economic domination. Do we want to continue on this self-destructive path? Education was once presented as "the great equalizer"; however, the ability to make large sums of money at an alarming rate and at the expense of others seems to dominate now. It has become more and more about "The Benjamin's" and less and less about education. Let's look at the world of entertainment as an example.

The world of entertainment in its many facets has grown into a multitrillion-dollar business while education has taken a "back seat." Many cities in the United States are striving to build new stadiums for football, basketball, and baseball instead of building new infrastructure and school facilities. This perspective has created a generation of students who believe the desires of the individual are more important than group success. Because of this, there has been an increase in the "underworld" economy. More students are engaging in selling drugs, prostitution, and illegal gambling now than at any other time in our history. Students are becoming substance abusers at alarming rates. Recreational drug use and underage drinking are more prevalent in high schools today than textbooks. The War on Drugs has been replaced with the War on Terrorism, which is indeed a political act, because America was losing the War on Drugs anyway. Students are smart and they are aware because they are socially and technologically connected.

While the American public educational system continues to battle budget-cuts, high-stake testing, accountability, and capitalism, students are committing acts of violence in increasing numbers, recording them, and selling them on home constructed DVDs for profit and/or placing them on the Internet for everyone to see. They are "hooking up" for sex and recording their experiences and selling them for profit on the Internet as well as passing them through their cell phones to gain a larger audience. While teachers, parents, and administrators spend time arguing over "school-choice," "vouchers," and "charter schools," today's students are holding classes on identity theft, drug trafficking, and "pimping" the system. Is this what we want for our youth? All this is occurring while the present sociopolitical environment continues to navigate the "waves" of corporate scandals, terrorism, racial inequalities, and poverty and through all this we have forgotten that the advancement of our democracy is dependent on the education of its citizenry.

Purpose of Schooling

The national economic downturn, the last wave of horrific budget-cuts, and the present political climate are adding to the hurdles for educators, particularly administrators, who must successfully educate students with less than adequate resources. These resources are not just monetary but human as well. The current sociocultural political climate in the United States, the renewing of the Patriot Act, disaster relief or the lack thereof, terrorism and homeland security, the demonization of those in poverty, and the privatization of a free public education force me to ask the following central question: What is the promise and purpose of a democratic education? Higher education and K-12 public schooling both have changed significantly in the past ten years. The advancement of the democratic promise of public education continues to be challenged by political and economic forces that constrain the opportunities for America's citizenry to enhance the value of their lives by accessing public colleges and universities and by benefiting from a "free" public education. According to Carlson and Gause (2007), "In its most radical terms this promise has been that public education can provide the basis for an informed, engaged citizenry, fully capable of their own self-governance, and armed with forms of critical consciousness that allow them to question the commonsense beliefs embedded in political speech and popular culture texts" (ix).

Given the promise of public education, this chapter implicitly and explicitly explores the following questions:

- What are the pedagogical challenges of cocreating democratic spaces with practitioners to provide for seamless learning through the K-12 educational experience?
- How do faculty members of color who are committed to social justice confront student resistance in their higher education classrooms from K-12 practitioners?

I believe in transformative leadership, a leadership that speaks of the moral and spiritual dimensions of decision making founded on the principles of social justice. Education is about freedom and democracy for the betterment of the global society. As a creative educational leader who embodies education as a praxis of freedom (hooks, 1994), my perspective on democracy is evidenced in my practice. I strive to cocreate learning environments in which all member-voices are given the opportunity to be heard, shared, and awakened. Consensus building is essential in this process. The dialogic encounter is central to (de) constructing and (re) constructing spaces for knowledge acquisition and development. Gause in Gause, Reitzug and Villaverde (2007) asserts,

> Because the personal is political and because I view my role as a teacher/activist within a framework that my perspective of democracy cannot be de-linked from what I do as a teacher/activist in the academic space; I envision democracy as the interconnections that lie within the quest of knowledge; the faith that our humanity exercises as we navigate the manifestations of our destinies. (p. 221)

As educators we must engage in collaborative activism: a coming together and unity of our pedagogy to bring love and compassion to our communities. For the citizens of the United States to continue to engage in "life, liberty, and the pursuit of happiness," democracy must exist in institutions that encourage us to transform our environment, communities, neighborhoods, and schools into arenas where dialogue, discourse, and dissent are not silenced but celebrated. The aforementioned should be the foci of K-12 public and private education in the United States.

Students who enter graduate programs seeking answers to reform schools should first critically reflect upon the personal and professional practice as citizens of this democracy. If they have not done so, it becomes difficult to engage in a discourse that moves beyond school reformation. If the technical aspects of schooling are their greatest concern, they must be able to navigate and gain skills juxtaposed with gaining experiences in transformative leadership. I do understand the importance of gaining technical skills to operate schools, given the pressure to meet so many political mandates; however, this should not supersede the purpose of schooling: to transform our humanity. These educators enroll in our program, hoping someone will help them make sense of dynamic school cultures. Educators, who come to the academy, are searching for answers. Some are looking for the "quick-fixes," while others understand transforming schools into vibrant, dynamic, and engaging learning communities in which all students experience academic achievement and success requires time. Yet all of them struggle with how to implement local, state, and federal legislation, seek efficient and effective ways to provide optimal learning experiences for all members of the learning community, and strive to make sense of the dynamic cultures in which they work professionally. During this era of market competition, globalization, and educational accountability, the challenge of the academy is transforming those aspiring educational leaders who are concerned more with "the bottom line" into critically conscious democratic leaders who seek to develop free-thinking members of our society. Given the call for "principal executives," democratic education and freedom have been reduced to the ability to achieve academic standards and acquire material goods, wealth, and power without critiquing the consequences of inequity, greed, and inequality.

Moving Adult Learners beyond Postsecondary Education

According to Rusch (2004), "Women and men from diverse backgrounds and communities arrive at the doors of the academy, eager to learn how to lead the nation's schools to a better place these educators enroll in leadership programs, hoping someone will help them make sense of dynamic school cultures" (p. 17).

As schools are hegemonic reproductions of the larger society, engaging graduate students in discourse of power, knowledge, and pedagogy creates "tension" I find myself encouraging students to understand the culture of school, particularly as it engages in an oppressive system of sorting and selecting students. This presents a barrier to resolving many of its problems. However, because of the linear and hierarchical decision-making structures that are inherent in the tight coupling systems of K-12 schooling, students find courses in which social justice, liberatory practices, and multimodal learning devoid of meaning to their practice. I move beyond this and strive to create classroom environments that displace the otherness of humanity by honoring the differences that students bring to the learning community. I reconstruct the classroom into a hub of inquiry, a safe haven to critique the role of education in our society. I want students to feel they belong in our classroom environment while wrestling with the tough questions we must engage on our democracy. In coconstructing the learning environment I want students to feel the passion and pain that coexist while paving the road as we walk along an undone path. The challenges of today's educational leaders are indeed numerous and aspiring educational administrators believe that to meet those challenges they must operate out of a technical/rational model of leadership ignoring issues of equity and social justice. Shields (2004) asserts, "educational leaders are expected to develop learning communities, build the professional capacity of teachers, take advice from parents, engage in collaborative and consultative decision making, resolve conflicts, engage in effective instructional leadership, and attend respectfully, immediately, and appropriately to the needs and requests of families with diverse cultural, ethnic, and socioeconomic backgrounds" (p. 109).

The fact remains that mainstream America is "ignorant" about education that is culturally relevant and the impact of that education on today's classrooms. To address the "ignorance" of mainstream America, we must answer the following questions:

1. What must school districts do to respond to this pervasive culture (any culture that is not the dominant one)?
2. What is the role of leadership? How must it change and/or adapt?
3. What is the role of teacher preparation and educational leadership programs in universities in this process?

Schools will always be sites where the politics of culture are always present. From the struggle of integration, bilingual education, and prayer in schools to the present ones of SMOD (Standard Mode of Dress), the use of iPods, and high-stake testing, cultural politics will remain front and center of schooling. Why? Central to the politics of culture is the struggle of meaning and identity. Schools are filled with groups who engage in conflict surrounding the identity of the school community and the meanings constructed from this identity. School climate is often informed by this identity. Schools are often known by their identities, that is, a certain school is known for its athletic program or another school is known for its band and music program. It is inherent in how we make meaning out of the educational process. One model that speaks of negotiating the competing and conflicting behaviors we engage in fostering school identity is the Cultural Proficiency Model.

The Cultural Proficiency Model (Lindsey, Nuri-Robbins, & Terrell, 1998) provides individuals and institutions with a framework for systemic change in reflecting on an individual's values and behaviors, along with analyzing the policies and practices of an institution. It is pertinent that teachers, faculty, education programs, and institutions be more skilled and self-reflective in recognizing their own behavior, using the essential elements of cultural proficiency along with the range of the cultural proficiency continuum. This model provides teacher education programs and education administration programs with a forum to deconstruct the present notions of power and include in the present teacher education and educational leadership preparation discourses culturally relevant "new" ways of knowing; by doing so, educators, educational administrators, teachers, and policymakers will begin to address the politics of culture in schools. The need for institutions of higher education to produce culturally proficient teachers, leaders, and educators cannot be overstressed. "Cultural proficiency is the policies and practices of an organization or the values and behaviors of an individual that enable the agency or person to interact effectively in a culturally diverse environment. Cultural proficiency is reflected in the way an organization treats it employees, its client, and its community" (Lindsey, Nuri-Robbins, & Terrell, 1998, p. 21). They continue by asserting the following:

> Culturally proficient educators recognize that culture means far more than recognizing racial and ethnic differences. It suggests that we must always be willing to be in a state of learning in order to demonstrate an understanding of various cultures. We need to be able to respond effectively to issues of culture and diversity in order to facilitate student learning. This approach can lead to positive community relations, foster effective leadership and enrich the teacher's ability to learn and teach. The authors contend that a culturally proficient school "promotes inclusiveness and institutionalizes processes for learning about differences and responding appropriately to those differences." (p. 25)

Moving students from the language of reformation to transformation is often difficult and viewed as counterproductive; however if schools are to be sites of democracy, this is the path of liberation. I encourage students to view themselves not as mere custodians of buildings of learning, but as proactive transformational leaders. This involves understanding the school culture and transforming custodial organizations into creative learning communities. This change requires transformational leadership that is creative, courageous, and visionary to meet the needs of today's youth who are experiencing economic, social, and political challenges in our society.

Conclusion: The Cause of Education

Teaching is practice that requires tenacity, integrity, and courage to change the status quo. Our freedom depends on the development of enticing and exciting democratic learning communities in which the pursuit of knowledge is the primary objective and students are given the tools to critically examine the world they inhabit. Because American democracy is under a reconstruction situated within globalization, evangelical fundamentalism, free market enterprise, and sociocultural politics, the educational leader of today must be able to negotiate and navigate the often competing and conflicting forces of our democracy and facilitate the development of a learning community that fosters collaboration and activism within its environment.

Teaching, learning, and leading democratically require activism that is purposive, pragmatic, and transforming. The purpose of higher education and K-12 public education is to provide opportunities and spaces for the global citizenry to engage in democratic practices for the public good. Democracy is an enacted daily practice through which people interact and relate through personal, social, and professional routines with a primary focus on continuing the betterment of our humanity. "Democracy is not just a form of social life among other workable forms of social life; it is the precondition for the full application of intelligence to the solution of social problems" (Putnam, 1991, p. 217). This is the cause of education. To do this, higher education must prepare critical transformative leaders who are willing and able to draw upon culturally relevant, critical, and counternormative pedagogies. I do this by infusing cultural studies in the leadership discourse of our educational leadership program (Gause, 2005c).

Critical change occurs with significant self-sacrifice, potential alienation, rejection, and costly consequences. As critical transformative educators, we must do justice to the larger social/public responsibility of our positions and roles, particularly in higher education. In (re) crafting the education of critical transformative leaders, we must demystify change, courage, and risk as we (re) imagine the language and fluency of multiple discourses in the rediscovery of democracy and social justice. This occurs in the development of the democratic classroom, which should be the hallmark of higher education. I practice this by having students reflect upon one of hooks' (1994) most powerful statements about vulnerability and empowerment: "any classroom that employs a holistic model of learning will also be a place where teachers grow, and are empowered by the process. That empowerment cannot happen if we refuse to be vulnerable while encouraging students to take risks" (p. 21). This very act affronts the pedagogical challenges of seamless learning from K-12. Critical transformative educational leaders who develop through the seamless K-12 educational system in the United States will facilitate the development of inviting, engaging, and dynamic learning communities that (1) transform the human condition, (2) till fallow ground, (3) interrogate and rupture the status quo, (4) question multiple political spaces critically, and (5) seek multiple epistemologies to re-create constructs that better serve our humanity. To further our thinking about the challenges of seamless learning from K-12, I call on all higher education faculties who actively serve in teacher education and/or educational leadership preparation programs around the country to (re) think the following by Gause (2005b).

> We are educating in a time of expanding globalization whose impact we witness via 24-hour digitally mediated discourse. How are schools and educational leaders keeping up with this global transformation? What type of impact does this transformation of schools from sites of democracy to "bedfellows" of consumerism have upon the school and much larger global community? How are the "souls" of schools affected? In the journey of school reform are educational leaders acknowledging that the "process of schooling" is filled with "cultural politics"? How are educational leadership programs preparing future school leaders? Are educational leadership preparation programs equipping schools' leaders for the "journey of the self" or for the "journey of the soul"? (p. 242)

As a former teacher, K-12 school administrator, principal, and current faculty member in an educational leadership preparation program in the southeastern part of the United States, I work to cocreate and decolonize democratic learning communities as a form of political activism. As a critical transformative educational leader, I inspire and transform others to become more conscious of the human condition. Parker Palmer in his work, *The Courage to Teach: Exploring the Inner Landscape of a Teacher's Life*, speaks of the importance of connectedness. He offers this: "If we want to develop and deepen the capacity for connectedness at the heart of good teaching, we must understand—and resist—the perverse but powerful draw of a 'disconnected' life. How and why does academic culture discourage us from living connected life? How, and why, does it encourage us to distance ourselves from our students and our subjects, to teach and learn at some remove from our own hearts?" (p. 35). I seek to remain connected situating my teaching and practice toward social vision and change, not simply, or only, by organizational goals. My teaching is a form of protest. In conclusion, I understand that it is my duty and responsibility to encourage other human beings, particularly those who are involved in the educational process, to transform our environment, institutions, communities, neighborhoods, and schools into arenas where those with whom we come into contact will become agents of democracy and social justice. Together we must face the struggle of educating our citizenry with nobility and commitment. For to be together in the struggle is to be one.

Educators who are passionate and committed to social justice and democracy should be angered by the current state of education in the United States and seek to deconstruct the practices, policies, and procedures that exist in their specific district and school community. They must engage in collaborative activism. "Collaborative activism is a democratic education approach that unites educators and learners in raising consciousness and rupturing the status quo in order to socially deconstruct, politically transform, and share a sense of hope. Collaborative activism is the essence of transformative leadership" (Cooper & Gause, 2007, pp. 209–210). I believe this is the primary responsibility of all members of a learning community: It is an essential part of the process of advancing knowledge for the purpose of transforming the human spirit and human condition.

Educational leaders are "agents of change." Every member of a learning community is an educational leader. This includes, but is not limited to the paraprofessional, cafeteria staff, custodial staff, bus driver, teacher, volunteer, clerical support, and administrative team. It is the duty and responsibility of every member of the learning community to encourage other human beings, particularly those who are members of that community in transformation. The proper criterion for deliberative democracy is indeed "equality as effective social freedom, understood as equal capability for public functioning" (Bohman, 1997, p. 322). How should schools prepare for conditions in which this criterion could be met? Deliberative conceptions of democracy must have rigorous and relevant requirements of political equality. They must not favor any individual based on their class, nor seek to reproduce cultural hegemony. I conclude this chapter by sharing what I consider keys to successful collaborative activism. Many of these strategies, techniques, and thoughts come from my observations as a teacher, school principal, and student of learning. I have used them in various situations and contexts and often reflect upon them to move my thinking forward in new directions. Some of them are written as maxims and others as text with subtext. I hope they serve you well.

Keys to Successful Collaborative Activism

Keys for School Administrators

Creating successful learning communities will require **school administrators** to do the following:

Build trust with all members of your learning community regardless of position or privilege.

First and foremost a successful school administrator along with the members of the learning community must develop a vision of learning that promotes success.
This process takes into account standards-driven curricula, federal legislation, and/or policies that speak of educational standards. The very core of this vision is based on foundational and cultural leadership principles that have as their premise the following: All members of the learning community regardless of backgrounds are provided opportunities for academic success.

Build open and trusting relationships with your students, faculty, staff, and parent community. This is the key to developing a successful school.
Sustainable change, in a learning community, occurs when trusting relationships have been developed. People are willing to try new and innovating ideas when support from colleagues and supervisors is evident.

Transform ordinary schools into vibrant learning communities that are creative, equitable, and "just."
Creative learning communities ignore rules; they seek to develop procedures for encouraging desirable behavior versus establishing levels of discipline and punishment. These communities also look for innovations in providing optimal learning experiences for their stakeholders. Creative learning communities remain on the cutting edge by establishing new missions, thriving on unpredictability, and broadening their scope for new horizons. They avoid the mechanization, simplification, and predictability found in custodial organizations.

Seek multiple methods and techniques to promote a school culture that is positive and inviting.
Culture includes both past and present perceptions; and its perceived reality is reflected in its symbols, rituals, and purpose. The school's culture is a representation of what its members collectively develop as their vision; it is their self-concept. The school's culture reflects what the stakeholders value and what they express to others as being "important around here." For school reform to occur, educators must realize that the culture of the school and the way the school operates must be transformed inside and out, not only physically but also mentally.

Affirm, encourage, and support all members of the learning community.
Teachers are the troops. They must be well taken care of for the vision and mission of a successful learning community to be realized. It is the job, duty, and responsibility of the school administrator to provide all the necessary resources to insure effective instruction. Without adequate instructional tools, support, and preparation, teachers will not be effective in delivering a top-notch curriculum. The little things do matter.

Schools that are successful are led by transformative leaders.
Transformative leaders continually seek out opportunities for improvement. These individuals look for solutions to problems and encourage the free exchange of ideas. No one has all the answers. Problems are part fact and part perspective. When individuals come together to discuss issues, it opens the space for a "dialogic encounter." Within the discussion people's perceptions often change and/or become redefined.

Being an exceptional educational leader requires functioning as an effective school motivator, as well as an effective school administrator. This is accomplished by striving to "do things right" and by "doing the right thing."
Organizations are socially constructed realties that exist in the minds of their collective members as well as in the concrete sets of rules and regulations that those members develop. According to those rules and roles, educators are, indeed, accountable for the dissemination of knowledge. They are also accountable for the advancement of the human spirit! It is important to make organizations effective; it is important, as well, to foster humane social conditions. Remember: we need leaders who will respond to knowledge in ways that will benefit not only the organization and its members, but the social order as well.

Keys for Teachers

Creating successful learning communities will require **teachers** to do the following:

Develop sustainable trusting relationships with your students.

Teach from the heart with your subject and student at the very core of your being.

Provide opportunities for students to share their talents with you and encourage them to do so with others.

Job satisfaction is based upon what you give and not what you get; pour your heart and soul into your students so they will become agents of change and democracy.

The new millennium has arrived and schools are still faced with issues of power, race, identity, violence, and ethics, and because of this, the meaning and purpose of schooling are being redefined. Do you teach for freedom and democracy or to develop a citizenry that will maintain the "status quo?"

Spend more time looking for solutions than discussing the problems.

Conduct weekly conferences with your students and make a point to address their concerns before you discuss yours.

Listen to your students without interruption. Allow students to present all their concerns without value-judging them.

Making a difference in the lives of young people requires every fiber in the fabric of your "being."

Teaching in the 21st century is hard work. The competing forces of popular culture and individualism oftentimes present great challenges. To overcome those challenges you must establish genuine lines of communication with your students. Establish rapport, relationships, and realness. This will give you more credibility than knowing your discipline.

Be the #1 advocate for your students and they in turn will become your #1 supporter.

Even if the relationship between you and your students enters a critical stage, still seek to create a space with the learning community to allow the democratic process to take place. In the process do not give up on them and they will not give up on you.

Teaching is an investment in the future.
We live in a culture that dictates you should witness immediate returns on your investment. Forget about the immediate return. You only see the growth in your investment as it matures. Apply this principle to the students whom you serve. They come to you at one level of maturity and as you invest in them, they grow. The more you invest, the bigger your return.

Students believe the knowledge they have is of greater value.
Allow students to engage in the democratic process by giving them authority, bolstering their own position, and discounting your knowledge and wisdom. Teach them how to do this with dignity and respect. The ability to communicate and articulate their position in a manner that is conducive to the learning environment will foster an understanding of peace and justice.

Give of yourself, time, knowledge, and skills to serve humanity.
Remember when you decided to become a member of the teaching profession. By making that decision you decided to give of yourself in all aspects of your life to serve humanity. Yes, what a great responsibility and challenge! Are you still up for the task?

Realize you are teaching the "echo-boomers" and develop strategies to educate them on the importance of earning their way through life.
An echo is given a free space to roam without parameters, guidance, or structure. It continues on its journey until it strikes an object or barrier; then it returns to its point of origination. This generation is the "echo" generation. They have been given everything and when they hit a barrier, they return for more things. Instead of things, teach them the ability to think "critically."

Use your students' daily life experiences to make connections to the lessons you are teaching.

Listen to popular music at least once a week to share a common experience with your students outside of the classroom.
Popular music has always had an impact upon the lives of young people. Throughout history, parents and teachers alike have striven to teach young people to arm and protect themselves from the ideological power of popular music. Use your listening experience to establish a "point of entry" for conversations with your students.

Seize every opportunity to create a "space for change. You are the authority!" Remember:

Change is a process.
Change is accomplished by individuals.
Change is a highly personalized process.
Change involves developmental growth.
Change is socially constructed and context specific.

Believe in the work that you do and know that you make a difference in the lives of young people daily.
As educators it is your responsibility and duty to liberate, educate, and motivate individuals toward social transformation. Without you, the ideas of democracy and social justice are just that—ideas.

Say what you mean and mean what you say.
Language, verbal and nonverbal, is the method in which humans develop understanding. The messages we send should be clear and concise. All educational jargon should be eliminated when we speak to members of our community.

A mean struggle yields mean results; however, a great struggle yields great results.
The struggle in delivering successful academic programs involves negotiating two sets of goals. First, students and their development should be the primary focus of schools. Second, the schooling process should be designed to deliver instruction and knowledge to prepare a citizenry who will perpetuate notions of democracy. Together we must face the struggle of educating our citizenry with nobility and commitment. For together in the struggle we are one.

Keys for Parents

Creating successful communities will require the **parents** to do the following:

Believe in your educational system.

Support your educational system with as many resources as you can.

Support your children by nurturing the gifts and talents they possess.

Listen to every word your child speaks; by doing so you will come to understand how they view the world in which they live.

Set a regular scheduled time to engage in a dialogue with your children daily.

Do not give your children everything.
This creates dependence, which is the precursor to victimization. Teach your child to be independent in mind and deed. Also model the importance of understanding the value of money, worth, and ability. Teach them the value of money by showing them how to earn it. When you give a child everything, it stifles their ability to understand how to earn what they want. Giving children everything also colludes their understanding of how to place value on the work in which they do.

Regardless of how you look on the outside, the inside really does matter.
Parents often do not like to come to school events because they worry about how they look, especially those parents who are considered to be "working class" and/or in poverty. We are taught that the importance of communicating, "who you are" can be surmised from how you walk, the integrity of your reputation, the smile on your face, and the clothes which you wear; however, many corporate scandals have revealed that if you look like a million dollars you probably stole it from the stockholders. Parents do not allow how you perceive the way you look keeps you from taking an active role in your child's school. Show up and get involved!

Intelligence along with wisdom will insure the success of your children.

Children will remember your indifference and your silence.
It is important to be attentive to youth at all times. Everything they experience is important to them. By showing indifference, youth will come to believe that they are not important to you. Silence is only golden when someone else is speaking.

Attend all PTA meetings, "Open-houses," and schedule conferences.

Read to your child at least thirty minutes a day.

Monitor the amount of time your child spends in front of the television and playing video games.

Provide a significant number of books for your children.

Visit your local public library every two weeks.
Encourage your child to help prepare a meal to evaluate and teach them "standard units of measurement."

Attend your local school board meetings.

Volunteer a portion of your time every six weeks in a teacher's classroom.

Become a member of the School Improvement Team.

Become a member of the Monday Moms volunteer organization at your child's school. If one does not exist, create one.

Become a member of the Friday Fathers volunteer organization at your child's school. If one does not exist, create one.

Spend time in the Commons Area to observe the activity of the school. By doing so, you will develop an appreciation for the work educators do on behalf of society.

Keys for Students

Creating successful learning experiences will require **students** to do the following:

Enjoy learning and seek to complete every assignment by giving it your best shot.

Do not post anything you would not want your grandparents to see on the Internet.

Be prepared to achieve the impossible regardless of conditions and/or circumstances.

Integrity is your moral compass.
If you are going to be a part of the crowd, be the leader and lead with integrity. Earn your way through school by doing your best with all the power that lies within you. Complete all assignments on time and with integrity. Do not settle for mediocrity and understand that your participation in the educational process is not a sport or extracurricular activity, it is your job!

You exist in body, mind and spirit; therefore, cultivate and nurture every aspect of your being.

Envision where you want to go and what you want to achieve in life and then focus all your energy toward the outcomes.

Honesty, integrity, truth, justice, and respect coupled with hard work, dedication, compassion, and love will determine your success, not the amount of money you earn.

Nothing in life is fair; however, you have the power to make it "just."

A change in your behavior is the only thing that will change your outcome.

Commitment to your dreams and goals will get you closer to achieving them than your talent alone.

Transform your community by engaging in volunteerism and community service.

Let go of old hurt, pain, and regret; they only serve as stumbling blocks toward achieving your destiny.
Forgive those who wrong you and ask forgiveness from those you have wronged. Life is a precious gift and the loss of life can be traumatic. It is better to live in peace and harmony than in regret.

Conflict is a natural occurring phenomenon, how you deal with conflict will be the anomaly.

Listen before speaking, and then decide if what you have to say is important enough to share with everyone.

Treat your siblings with love and respect, because one day they may be your employer.

Limit the amount of time you spend in the virtual world on social networking sites.
Spend less time in the virtual world and more time in physical contact with people. The spirit of our humanity is only synergistic when human beings are in physical contact with one another.

Volunteer your time and a portion of your earnings once a month to a charity that aids the needy.

You are closer to greatness than you think.

Your knowledge, skills, and dispositions (attitudes) serve as the foundation for your academic success.

Perseverance is the key to overcoming life's challenges.

Honor your parents, your teachers, your friends, your neighbors, and yourself.

Just because you can does not mean you always should.
Opportunities will always come your way; however, it is important to choose wisely and carefully those in which you will engage.

Acknowledge your God-given gifts, talents, and knowledge by using them for good and not evil.

Determine to be the best and the brightest in all aspects of your life and share that belief with everyone.

Challenge yourself by loving who you are and those that are around you.

Failure is not an option and does not exist when you exercise your beliefs.

Develop and maintain a positive attitude.

Dress for success.

Eat nutritious meals and receive an adequate amount of rest.

The talents, gifts, and knowledge placed within you by the "Divine Creator" should be used for the good of the community and not selfish gain.

Achieving the impossible regardless of conditions and/or circumstances is the manifestation of great determination.

Serving those in your community is indeed noble. Serving humanity is indeed greatness.

Give back to your community by mentoring.

· 8 ·

THE COURAGE TO LEAD: NAVIGATING IDENTITY

Today: I Opened My Eyes

I opened my eyes, today
And saw the light of the Divine Creator
Beaming ever so brightly in the corridors
Of my heart for life, liberty and
You

Today, I saw opportunities for love
And the challenges of conquering my fear
A fear always present but yet never acknowledged
Until today when the eyes that I opened
Revealed a look within my soul

I conquered
What I saw
My insecurities
The need to be heard
Blaming, complaining
No attitude of gratitude
But yet
I conquered
Only with the Vision of
Your patience, love
And fiery commitment to move forward

A vision of change and completeness
Multi-colored radiating so divinely
From you to me
Because you care and that is why
Today, I stepped out of myself
Into a new existence
One of understanding, not me but you

I opened my eyes, today
I sought not to be understood
But to hear
No defenses, just
Compassion, healing and a little more love
You care about me as I you

Today, I opened my eyes
Moving beyond the trauma of tragedy
Towards our road of triumph
Knowing that I now see
Not just you
Not just me
But we
A togetherness that
Withstands the tests of mountains
A unity that weathers the storms of yesterday
By bringing the sunshine of tomorrow

I opened my eyes, today
And listened to the beat of a new
Rhythm that smiles the way you do
Drums of pain and rage are replaced
By
Symphonies of melodic love
Cymbals of peace are struck
Not
With the sticks of discord but of your voice
A voice that sings sweet harmonies of life

Today, I opened my eyes
And I witnessed a new birth
A
Genesis
The creation of all that is good
Our lives becoming fine tuned
For the journey we share

Today, I opened my eyes
And I realized
That I needed you...
To see Me! (©Charles P. Gause)

Minras Gause, my great-grandfather was born into slavery in 1832 in Marion County, South Carolina. My grandfather, Charlie Gause, was born after the Civil War and the ratification of the Thirteenth Amendment of the United States Constitution that abolished slavery. He was a sharecropper in Marion County, South Carolina all his life. My father Walter T. Gause, Sr. was born after the Great Depression but before World War II. He and his brothers were part of the Great Migration to the North. He was a member of the 716 Military Police Battalion of the United States Army and later became a member of the NYPD (New York City Police Department). While a member of the 716 MPs, one of his tours of duties was to protect James Meredith, the first African American to integrate the University of Mississippi, *Ole Miss*. He later served as a member of the NYPD and was on duty on April 4, 1968 the day Dr. Martin Luther King was assassinated in Memphis. He talked about these events after I asked him what his thoughts were about integration and the state of black America. I have often asked him these questions; however, this was the first time I had ever heard the stories about his time in the army and his time while serving on the New York police force.

> WTG: *Young people today don't realize how blessed they are and what my parents, their grandparents and great-grandparents had to go through. My father, your grandfather was a sharecropper. They worked and toiled land that didn't belong to them just to keep food on the table. Dad had an 8th grade education, that's as far as you could go in school back then, especially if you were black. You stayed home and worked the farm. Your great-grandfather was born into slavery and lived to be a 98 year-old; but he didn't become free until he was in his 70s. Every group of people that come to America has been able to make it. They develop businesses, establish networks and educate their children. Our people, black people still can't seem to get it together. While at Ole Miss protecting James Meredith, the army was integrated at that time, but the towns were segregated. I think about how I slept on the ground in pup tents to fight for integration and now you got kids who call each other the N-word, with pants hanging off their behinds, and who refuse to go to school and get a good education. These kids can go to school for free and gain all types of skills and will not go. The night Dr. King died, bullets ranged out all through Brooklyn. I had to walk my beat anyway to make sure people were safe. I could have been killed; sometimes death is the ultimate sacrifice when you want freedom. We as a people are better off due to integration; but young people today are squandering the opportunities we worked so hard to have in this country.* (Personal Interview, May 2007)

My siblings, cousins, and I are the first generation recognized as beneficiaries of the post–civil rights revolution. We received great opportunities from the Voting Rights Act, the Fair Housing Act, and the policies of affirmative action. Our parents and foreparents marched through the streets of many cities seeking equality. They protested the Jim Crow laws of the South and demanded better educational, social, and political opportunities. They risked beatings, dogs, and water hoses just to have the same advantages and rights that were given to whites; they even risked death in their struggle to have a better way of life. What have we done with these gifts our ancestors granted us through their legacy of hard work and determination? I ask this rhetorical question to provoke thought about how far we have come, but yet how far we still must go. It saddens me to read the statistics on black males in our society. I understand the issues many of them must face. I wasn't born with a silver spoon in my mouth and I know the inequities that exist in our system of education. I am the product of a public school education. I am also a former public school educator and administrator. The difficulty of receiving a quality public school education in the 21st century is far greater than it was in the 20th century. It requires great ability in negotiating the power and politics inherent in our school systems; however, I am not anti–public schools. I believe they are the greatest institutions in America, if they are led by exceptional leaders and filled with great teachers. It is in public schools we develop the skills, dispositions, and knowledge to be good neighbors and to understand how to embrace and affirm cultural and political differences. They are a necessity in transmitting the important ideas of our democracy.

Recently I read an e-mail from a student with a picture attached that revealed the text, "I Hate Niggers." The text was in white lettering on a major street, eight blocks from my office at the University of North Carolina-Greensboro. I was appalled, disturbed, and outraged. My student later told me that when he called the city to come and clean it up, they had a problem not with the text, but with the fact that a citizen had contacted them and asked for the street graffiti to be removed. How could this happen in a city filled with a legacy of civil rights? I asked the question, but I already knew the answer. It is one that is not difficult by any means. When we focus only on our individualism and how we construct our own identities devoid of any connection to our humanity or culture, we are capable of unleashing venomous hate on the world.

I wondered if the individuals who painted that particular text on the street attended a school that was integrated and in which multiculturalism was celebrated and difference was affirmed. If they had attended such a school would they have left such an indelible mark of hate on the streets of Greensboro? Like all cities there are problems here too; however, I cannot accept that the city known for the Woolworth civil rights sit-ins continues to be complicit in perpetuating oppressive practices. I say this after watching many city-council meetings on television and realize the legacies of race are still major issues, and politics around race and centered on race is ever present. Whenever I was frustrated, I remind myself that as an educator it is my moral responsibility to assist individuals who strive to connect human beings to their identity. As global citizens we must understand the larger global context of our citizenry informs who we are in within our community, for in this connection to humanity and global citizenry our identities will be constructed.

I wrote *Integration Matters: Navigating Identity, Culture and Resistance* as the effusion of the total sum of symbols, texts, and signifiers of the sojourn my ancestors began so very long ago. I wrote this work as a testament to honor those who have gone before on the path of educational liberation toward a democracy of freedom and justice and also for those who remain in the struggle.

I consider my father, mother who is deceased, siblings, friends, ancestors, and relatives as revolutionaries. I consider the African American educators and "street" educators in this text as individuals who engage in revolutionary leadership. I do so because their stories of faith, courage, and hope in times of adversity have changed my life and the lives of others. My friend and colleague Glenn Hudak speaks of this very idea.

> Revolutionary leadership emerges from the group, as embodied, as authentic, and where its stance is one of returning the community its memory of itself—as a mode of disclosure—as that space where the community can affirm and confront, within tolerable limits, the limit-situations of its existence. (Hudak, 2007, p. 355)

I have been a member of many groups throughout my life and in many of them I emerged as the leader, but not by choice. I realize I am passionate about my commitment to my beliefs, values, and ideologies. I am also committed to the process of inquiry and discovery and have been privileged to have those perspectives recognized by others. I accept the fact that I am a leader, a transformative one at that; many burdens come with this responsibility and I don't take my call and passion for this work lightly. It takes courage to lead, but greater courage to lead with passion, heart, conviction, and with a commitment to social justice. My mother who died on October 17, 1980 at the age of thirty-six often spoke these words to me, "baby you will often be misunderstood, but keep true to your conviction because good guys don't always finish last. You can be anything you want to be even when all of the odds are against you and at times they will be, just remember you are a precious gift." I was fourteen-years old when she died and was in the 9th grade. My sister was eleven years old and my brother was fifteen. My father then became a widower with three children to take care of and no direction. For all things I am grateful. She was right, adversities did come. I learned how to navigate the many adversities I experienced along my journey while remaining true to my purpose. I offer you a glimpse of my service as a transformative educational leader who is committed to social justice.

> As I sit here upon the dawn of a new day, my mind travels across an uncontested terrain of impossibilities. I, feel so alone. Presently serving humankind to transform the very thought of how we educate and for whom, continues to create not only an uneasiness, but a chasm of tension within the very fabric of my being. I often wonder sometimes how the ancestors that have gone before managed to overcome adversity even with the wind at their backs. I now have my answer. The epiphany to the multiple identities that layer the fabric of my being is often for others very confusing, however for me, it is indeed who I am. I guess being a Same Affection Loving, African American Educator who holds a Doctor of Philosophy along with four other degrees probably would disrupt the hegemonic paradigms to which our society subscribes, however; to borrow a line from the phenomenal work, "Mother to Son" by Langston Hughes, "life for me...ain't been no crystal." I am constantly reminded of my purpose and I am thankful for these opportunities; however how much more can a brother take, especially in this fragmented city? Spending a significant amount of my life in the South and now returning to the South to assist in school reform haunts me. I feel as if, I am (re) closeting myself. I have discovered a level of hypocrisy beyond belief. Based upon personal observations and interactions; there are very few black men who live openly in the Triad area of North Carolina. What did I expect, in the home state of the dead Senator Jesse Helms; I guess I held "pedagogy of hope," a hope that speaks of the notion that presently in 2004 the high level of overt and covert racism, classism, and sexism. Covert could not exist anywhere in America. Boy, I am certainly wrong. What must a man do to achieve his dream in American society? What must a black man contend with as he strives to make his dreams a reality in America? The same affection loving black male must go beyond his white straight counterpart, his black straight counterpart, and his white gay counterpart. I assume the black same affection loving male is the antithesis to and the presupposed binary opposition of the heterosexist black male, but is this accurate? Does the socially constructed marker of race serve as the primary identifier for the black male in our society? How will I navigate my identities and black masculinity while still remaining true to the call of social justice? Should I just keep silent and wait until tenure? (Personal Journal Entry-Fall 2004)

Black Identity and Masculinity: Politics of the Academy

Students who enter the learning space I facilitate come seeking answers to how to educate culturally and linguistically diverse populations; however, most of them have a hard time receiving the messenger as well as the message. Having spent many years living in various cities in the United States and having visited many abroad, living and working in the South is a very unique and different experience from any other. I have served as a principal in very rural South Carolina and I now teach at the college level in the third largest city in North Carolina, Greensboro. To be a teacher in the academy is a position of privilege and one that I enjoy immensely; however, it does come with its own set of challenges. I am the only African American male faculty member in my department and for the past three years I have been the only African American male faculty member in the entire school of education. So when I think of democratic education and the purpose of public schools and my own academic identity situated within that context, I carry the weight of race and gender on my back. Understanding the environment which I inhabit, I also realize my black male identity is formed out of those who were enslaved by individuals who framed this country's democratic experiment and institutions of higher learning (Gause, 2005a).

> The paradox of teaching for social justice in higher education—which comprises revered institutions grounded in patriarchal, Anglocentric norms—challenges any faculty member striving to use critical, liberatory pedagogies. Faculty members of color doing this work, however, must confront a second paradox: that of being disproportionately oppressed, devalued, and scrutinized by the same structures, institutions, and social norms that we work within, critique, resist, and encourage others to defy. (Cooper and Gause, 2007, p. 201)

Many of the critical perspectives I as an African American male academician hold on the intersections of race, class, and gender affront the white southern Christian values my students hold near and dear. The expectation is for me to operate out of false civility and behave as if these values should not be critiqued and/or interrogated, but honored and celebrated regardless of how they assault the plurality of values students bring into public schools daily. When this is coupled with my being a faculty of member of color, regardless of credentials, ideological orientation, and instructional style, my students at times implicitly and explicitly challenge my professorial authority, scholarship, intellect, and political agenda (Antonio, 2003; Baez, 2003; Bonner, 2004; Hamilton, 2002; Lawrence, 1995; Tate, 1994; Thomas, 2001). After speaking truth to power in many of our dialogic encounters I have often heard students call me "the angry black man" or "Dr. Thug." I find it interesting how they construct my passion for the subject and fiery delivery style as a place of subjugation. Given the atrocities occurring in public education in our nation today, we should all be angered to action and to express moral outrage. Shields (2004) suggests,

> Educators, policymakers, and indeed, the general public are increasingly aware that despite numerous well-intentioned restructuring, reform, and curricular efforts, many children who are in some way different from the previously dominant and traditionally most successful White, middle-class children are not achieving school success. (p. 111)

To transform schools we must hold our students accountable. We do this by shifting them from a traditionalist view of education and democracy to one that is radical and transformative. We can do this by promoting environments that require students to engage in independent thinking, by motivating them to take ownership of their learning process, and by providing opportunities for rigorous intellectual study and committed activism that moves beyond arriving at the "right" answers. This requires critical change in teaching PreK-12 and the courage to lead.

> In forging a democratic discourse on progress in American education, the most immediate and pragmatic response among progressive educational leaders may well be a politics of individual and collective resistance to the "machines "of urban schooling, including "high stakes" testing. As I have long argued, teachers represent a potentially powerful counterhegemonic power bloc in democratic educational renewal and there is much good, progressive work to be done in teachers' unions and professional organizations. At some point, however, progressives also must move beyond critique and resistance toward the forging of a countermovement for progress in America, linked to a new commonsense discourse on the renewal of public education and public life." (Carlson, 1998; 2007, p. 23)

I consider myself a charismatic activist educator with radical consciousness who strives to make a difference in people's lives; however, being the only African American male in the professoriate in the school of education at the University of North Carolina-Greensboro, who at the time of this writing is waiting be tenured, I constantly struggle with not allowing neither myself nor the multiple identities I navigate to become co-opted. bell hooks in *We Real Cool: Black Men and Masculinity* asserts, "Individual charismatic black male leaders with radical consciousness often become as enamored of their unique status as the black man who is different that they fail to share the good news with other black men. Or they allow themselves to be co-opted—seduced by the promise of greater monetary rewards and access to mainstream power that are the payoffs for pushing a less radical message" (p. xvii). To remain true to yourself resisting this kind of co-optation at times can be difficult, particularly if you are the only one doing it. I believe it is virtually impossible to integrate our schools, churches, civic groups, businesses, leadership ranks of our society, and professions until students from underrepresented groups become high achievers. The African American educators in this text espoused those beliefs and spoke of the failure of various communities to encourage our young people to become high achievers. Teachers must set high expectations and empower our young people to develop the resources to engage in inquiry that is critical and dynamic.

Courageous Leadership

This book is my attempt to exemplify courageous leadership. I was advised to wait and write a book of this nature after tenure while I was in graduate school. The individuals to whom I floated the idea felt it might be too controversial for the academy. But after the publication of the edited volume, *Keeping the Promise: Essays on Leadership, Democracy and Education* with Dr. Dennis Carlson, my friend and colleague at Miami University, I knew this work had to be published because of the many stories and life histories it represents. I often debated with myself wondering whether I was doing the right thing. My father, a wise a great man, told me to do what I felt was right and write the book. He exemplifies courageous leadership and I knew that once he spoke, all things fell in order. I revisited many of my writings over the years to gain some inspiration and I included two of the pieces that inspired me to be courageous to bring this work to fruition.

The poem that appears at the beginning of this chapter I delivered at the School of Education's Equity and Diversity Conference held early spring of 2008. The journal entry was written after a very challenging experience at the university. The purpose for writing both pieces was to push my thinking around the intersection of the multiple identities that I enact juxtaposed with the difficulty of remaining silent during moments of personal injustice. I use the term enact, because I believe we perform our identities given the situations and circumstances that occur in our daily lives. I wrote the poem as a way to feel liberated from my own oppressive practices. I was struggling with writing a journal article about sexual identities and educational leadership and realized how I was subconsciously avoiding using any of the GLBTIQQ (Gay, Lesbian, Bisexual, Transgendered, Intersexual, Queer, and Questioning) language in the article. As I interrogated my own position as the author of the text, I closeted myself from how I viewed myself as a *same-affection loving* black man in the academy. I use the term *same-affection loving* to speak of the spiritual attractions I have for individuals devoid of the performance of a sex act. My attraction to someone begins with a spiritual connection. It is through the affection of soul connection that speaks of my desire for another human being and because this is soul-practice; the body inhabited has little meaning in establishing a relationship. Their physical appearance, cognitive abilities, and social/cultural capital are not the first things I experience when they are introduced to me. Through the spiritual realm of our existence my desires are awakened and my senses are aroused for the individual. The current terms for expressing alternative gendered identities is too limiting to describe how I construct my own sexual identity. I am first attracted to an individual spiritually and then intellectually; therefore, the person can be housed in a biologically male or female body. I offer you this personal definition because it is mine and also to problematize how we recognize gender and sexual identities in this society. I will pick up the notion of *same-affection loving* in a future piece of scholarship. I realize the reason I was closeting myself in my own scholarship was my fear. Parker Palmer in his work, *The Courage to Teach: Exploring the Inner Landscape of a Teacher's Life*, explores this notion of fear. He asserts:

> Fear is what distances us from our colleagues, our students, our subjects, ourselves. Fear shuts down those "experiments with truth" that allow us to weave a wider web of connectedness—and thus shuts down our capacity to teach as well." (p. 36)

I was fearful of professing to be who I saw myself to be because being the "other" in our society is a badge of hatred and shame. Living an alternative gendered identity in America when one can clearly see that I am an African American male is difficult at best in the academy, and quite problematic at worst in everyday African American communities. How could I speak truth to power as an African American male who is partnered with another African American male when homophobia still continues to be the norm in black communities and institutions particularly those in the South? For a *same-affection loving* black man like me teaching aspiring educational leaders, to engage in transformational leadership at a major southern university as a pretenured faculty member is unimaginable. It takes courage to lead and navigate the multiple identities I perform, given the cultural resistance inherent in southern communities. So the poem is a journey of self- reflection.

"Today: I Opened My Eyes" is a reflection on how I see the world viewing me. From the perspective of the academy, I am a relatively young tenure-track faculty member of color who holds doctoral and other advance degrees from tier-one research institutions. I was mentored by highly distinguished educational scholars who were from diverse ethnic and gendered identities. I have various experiences leading public, private and nonprofit organizations. I teach, research, and evaluate K-12 schools situated in a range of political, geographical, and cultural contexts. The additional elements of my identities are African American, male, *same-affection loving*, Christian, northerner, southerner, mid-westerner, and my praxis is rooted in collaborative activism, social justice, political struggle, and resistance. Parker Palmer in his work, *The Courage to Teach: Exploring the Inner Landscape of a Teacher's Life*, explores this notion of courage. He asserts, "The courage to teach is the courage to keep one's heart open in those very moments when the heart is asked to hold more than it is able so that teacher and students and subject can be woven into the fabric of community that learning, and living, require" (p. 11).

The codifying of the experiences of African American educators is very limited in first-person narrative form. Their "stories" and their "voices" are virtually silent in educational discourses. African American educators of course are not nonexistent; however, the accounts of their lives, contributions, and experiences in educating youth are quite limited. "Research on teachers; though extensive, has generally failed to include the experiences of African American teachers" (Foster, 1990, p. 123). The stories of people's lives are communicated through the use of narratives. Personal narratives of the *Brown* ruling and its impact on African American educators are very limited in academic discourse. In 1954, only .001 percent of black students attended majority white schools. As a result of the decision the number of African Americans attending majority white schools increased significantly. From the late 1960s through 1988, almost 43.5 percent of southern black students attended majority white schools; however, this was at the expense of black educators. Chesley and Lyons (2004) posit one of the first negative impacts for African Americans stemming from desegregation was the dismissal and demotion of black principals and teachers. I add many all-black high schools were also casualties in the integration experiment. Booker T. Washington High School in Columbia, South Carolina, my mother's alma mater is one notable example. Personal stories and their role in identity construction are important in to the educational discourse. "[P]ersonal stories are not nearly a way of telling someone (or oneself) about one's life; they are a means by which identities may be fashioned" (p. 1). Bruner (1990) argues that narratives are the natural mode in which human beings make sense of lives in time. "People do not deal with the world event by event or with text sentence by sentence. They frame events and sentences in larger structures" (Bruner, 1990, p. 64, as cited in Polkinghorne, 1997, p. 12).

Hearing the voices of the "other" three African American women and one African American man telling their "stories" of daily encounters with students, parents, other teachers, and negotiating their own lives began to resonate within my own self. My critical reflection made me even more critical of my role as the researcher, as an educator, as an African American male, and all the other multiple identities that construct "me." I realized the struggle of which we were all a part began on the "backs of our ancestors." Knowing this created in me a desire to rise up against injustice wherever it may be and this became my purpose in life. The educators and their experiences found in this text are courageous for telling their stories. The African American educators and the "street educators" wanted their stories to be told and I happened to be the conduit so this text had to be written. Because of the nature of this work and how academic texts are viewed by general audiences and how texts for general readership are viewed by academics, I have to code-switch. The following text is designed to be written as a journal article; however, I think no academic journal would publish this; therefore, I include it here as a representation of how I negotiate my identities as I navigate the sociocultural politics of my profession even in the academy. In a sense for me it is a form of protest and resistance, because scholarship, especially research in educational leadership, is often evaluated and assessed through white heteronormative dimensions.

CP! Academically Speaking—The Lost Journal Article

A discourse on the intersections of black masculinity, queerness, and educational leadership is quite limited in academic scholarship. This project moves beyond the questioning of masculinities to advance one that interrogates the bestial, hypersexualized, and endangered imagery of African American males within the public sphere. I further use this chapter as a platform for interrogating my role as a school administrator in the late 1990s juxtaposed with my current position as educational leadership faculty in a major university in the southeastern part of the United States who seeks to coconstruct democratic learning communities with current practitioners.

When RuPaul arrived on the music scene in 1993 as an African American "brotha" turned drag queen with the single hit *Supermodel*, the American mainstream music scene was blindsided. The song lauded the beauty of the international models of the fashion industry and how they worked the runway bringing the designer clothes on their bodies to life. The tagline of the song, "you better work" was gay slang for, "do your stuff and do it well." *Supermodel* peaked at #45 on the Billboard Hot 100, which was regarded as an unlikely accomplishment for the drag entertainer. It found the most success on the U.S. Billboard Hot Dance Music/Club Play where it peaked at #2.

How could a 6'3" pecan tan 200lb. black male put on a blond wig, sequin gown, and makeup capture the American music scene? Boy George, Culture Club's androgynous front man did it in the early 1980s but he was white and could sing by some standards. His androgynous costumes spoke of the fusion of the 80s punk scene with queer exploration. No other African American male except Sylvester, a transgendered songstress of the 1970s and 1980s made an attempt to display his sexuality in the public sphere by using mediated imagery. Sylvester was a big disco star with several hits but did not achieve the level of success RuPaul experienced. With MTV being viewed across the entire country, RuPaul was able to move gay camp female impersonation from the stages of gay clubs in cities across the United States into mainstream popular culture. RuPaul hosted MTV's Spring Break, made various appearances at many of the entertainment industry's award shows, and played at major concert venues throughout the country. RuPaul became so popular that he even had his own talk show sponsored by MTV.

RuPaul was most popular with young white kids from the suburbs (Magubane, 2002). This was not to say that he did not have any African American fans; however, his following consisted of white club kids, just like hip-hop is purchased and consumed more by young white males than any other demographic in the United States. I experienced the RuPaul craze of the 1990s and was reminded of my dance club experiences when one of my lifelong friends saw a copy of *Keeping the Promise: Essays on Leadership, Democracy and Education* (Carlson & Gause, 2007) and decided to call me up. We talked about life and work, and he wanted to know whether I was still single. I told him, "of course, because the right person has yet to come along and win my heart." He said, "C. P., I saw the book, honey they aren't ready for you, you better work!" I laughed for a moment and then I began to realize some of the difficulties I experienced as a *same-affection loving* tenure-track faculty member of color in a majority-minority research intensive university located in the southeastern part of the United States. Before ending our call, we vowed to remain in touch and to continue on our paths of liberation. Given the media representations of

African American and Latino males in this country, I could only think about the line Oprah Winfrey delivered as Sophia in the movie the *Color Purple*, "all my life I had to fight."

Fighting the Fight

This work, unlike the work of the sex-role reformers in the 1970s, is not a push for androgyny in schools or our communities, although I do see a need for change. However, the sex-role reformers of the 1970s "underestimated the complexity of masculinities and femininities, [and] put too much emphasis on attitudes and not enough on material inequalities and issues of power" (Connell, 1992, p. 205). This work strives to "trouble" the inherent power of the construction of race, gender, and sexuality, particularly as enacted and performed in schools (Butler, 1990; Foucault, 1979). I think my experience with public schools and how it silences anything outside of the dominant culture provide me the space to speak of these issues as a scholar, practitioner, and student. As I journeyed through K-12 education, first as a student, then as a professional, I thought often of my race and position as a black male, particularly as a black male educator who negotiated multiple public spheres. It was not until I began my doctoral studies that I began to interrogate my sexuality and the ways in which I viewed gender. I did give some thought to sexual orientation and the ways in which it was constructed by dominating discourses, but I did not fit those little boxes. My phrase, *same-affection loving* was how I described myself, a form of spiritual lovingness where sexual performance was decentered. It was my way of *queering*. To others this was a form of passing, sexual passing, which shares the same connotation of racial passing. If I am light enough, no one can see my blackness and therefore, I am white. If I am *queer* enough no one can see my gayness, which in the African American community is a sign of weakness; therefore, I am perceived to be straight. According to Heasley (2005),

> The hegemonic heteromasculine is represented culturally in the icons of religion, sports, historical figures, economic and political leaders, and the entertainment industry; however, in these arenas, males are presumed to be straight and hold stereotypically masculine beliefs, attitudes, and values unless and until they present themselves as other. (p. 310)

Within the black church, considered by some to be the most homophobic institution of the black public sphere, gayness and queerness are often perceived in stereotypical forms—the flamboyant preacher, the faggot choir director, and the sissified musician. Many members of the black church community have come to embrace the talents of the homosexual in our churches but we refuse to acknowledge their life partners, their openness about how they sexually identify as well as their leadership capabilities. I doubt we will ever witness openly queer pastors, bishops, or national leaders of any traditional mainstream black religious denominations or spiritual organizations. This speaks of the prejudices and homophobia in the black community. We are committed to sexist thinking, but we scream racism when other groups remain committed to racist thinking. According to hooks (2004), "Allegiance to sexist thinking about the nature of leadership creates a blind spot that effectively prevents masses of black people from making use of theories and practices of liberation when they are offered by women" (xvi). I concur with hooks; however, I would argue the allegiance to sexist thinking becomes greater when such theories and practices of liberation are offered by nonheterosexist black males. Lemelle and Battle (2004) assert,

> Stigma associated with homophobia and homosexuality helps us to understand that in everyday and face-to-face interactions, black masculinity is unique in the management of identity. For one thing, black masculinity is a stigmatized status (Lemelle 1995). This means that gay black males' identities are spoiled on tripartite dimensions: as black males, as gay black males and as mortified gay black males who have internalized civil and health experiences of discrimination. (p. 48)

I experience this "oneness" in terms of my position at the university. Although colleagues in my department and the School of Education have been extremely supportive, I am speaking of the challenges of being "the only one." According to Stanley (2007), African Americans, American Indians, Asian Americans, and Latinas/Latinos, in particular, constitute between 20 percent and 25 percent of the U.S. population. However, they represent 13.4 percent of the faculty at degree-granting institutions of higher education (Internal Citation omitted, p. 1). I am the first and only African American male faculty member in the history of my department and currently I am the only African American male faculty member in the School of Education. I am very open and pragmatic about gender identity, equity, and full representation of those who are considered "the other." There are white male faculty members who are indeed allies and who demonstrate queer masculinity. Heasley (2005) defines queer masculinity. He posits:

> Many straight men experience and demonstrate "queer masculinity," ways of being masculine outside hetero-normative constructions of masculinity that disrupt, or have the potential to disrupt, traditional images of the hegemonic heterosexual masculine. (p. 310)

I am thankful to those men and women who challenge what it means to be a scholar and colleague in my department and within the School of Education at the University of North Carolina at Greensboro; however, few and far between they are, I forever remain hopeful.

Stop! The Love You Save Maybe Your Own

As a former school teacher, principal, and administrator I was not open about my sexual identity for fear of repercussions. I taught in the South during the mid 1990s and being *same-affection loving* was for white boys. The sociocultural and political dynamics of sexual orientation was one of liberation and the good life. Circuit parties, Fire Island, and P-Town were subversive and the media represented them as such. I became a school administrator during the mid-to-late 1990s and was able to witness how gay culture was being commodified by the mass media and industry. However, I was not represented in the *Advocate* or *Out* magazines. The media communicated to me that I was threatening, aggressive, and intimidating (Gause, 2005a). I did not see anyone on the fashion runway in America that I could identify with, but I did hear many students, black and white, explore the use of the words "gay" and "fag" in the classroom, on the playground, and in the cafeteria. I was horrified by the open expression and use of these terms by kids, and did not know the sociocultural and political meanings of these terms. This was not appropriate and it could not be tolerated. This language was not acceptable.

The faculty and staff of our K-8 school, under my direction began a character program that communicated democratic and community values to our students. I did not tolerate bullying of any kind; however, I never had conversations with those students who were questioning their identities. I did bring in a community liaison that had a program that spoke of puberty and abstinence; but I stayed away from those issues. I had to, for fear of being perceived as "one of them." It would have been death to a career that I worked so hard to achieve and to me who I was and what I did in the privacy of my home were my own business.

As a professor in higher education whose pedagogical framework is rooted in equity, social justice, and antioppressive education (Carlson & Gause, 2007), I have often used the aforementioned scenario with my students to discuss the intersections of race, class, gender, and power. I was not pragmatic or genuine while I was a teacher and administrator in sharing my narrative as a black queer male. The interesting point of it all is there were teachers and students who knew that I was queer. The reality was that I did not ever want to be in a situation in which I would have to "out" myself. I also knew that I was an outsider for that community (I lived seventy miles away) and did not want my sexuality viewed as a deficit in my leadership abilities especially if I made a decision that was not popular.

Transforming the Lives of Black Males

As I come to a close, I would like to offer some insights. Not all black men in America are committed to a life of criminality. Many of us are committed to our professions, families, and our communities. I believe for every negative image of us spewed across the television and the Internet, there are many more positive images of who we are and the lives we live. The challenges of our communities are rooted in our own self-image. Everything we see about our images in popular culture is digitally enhanced and (re) packaged bodies designed for consumption. The economic gain does not benefit our communities or our self-worth. We must also not be complicit in this production. The responsibility is ours and ours alone. We must be vigilant in the quest to transform our own lives if we want our lineage to continue. As a black male or individual who is connected to a black male through school, community, church, or other organizations and institutions, I implore you to engage in the following seven principles of transformation:

- Speak truth to power.
- Engage in intellectual enterprise.
- Engage in a work ethic based on integrity.
- Be committed to your own self-development.
- Delay immediate gratification and invest in lifelong learning.
- Engage in spiritual practice and a renewing of your faith daily.
- Develop a mission and vision for your life and be committed to bringing them to fruition.

There are many strategies across multiple disciplines that speak of working with black males. I like to add the following twenty to those that already exist. This list is based on the philosophical, spiritual, and educational dimensions of my journey as a black male from youth to adult and from student to educator. I purposely did not situate them in the context of specific organizations, institutions, or educational arenas. I wanted them to be as broad as possible, but not devoid of meaning so that individuals could use them to develop specific goals and objectives for their own communities. These strategies are designed to be dimensions for policy development, for realigning curricula, and for developing programmatic offerings within K-12 educational institutions. They can be used to inform task force initiatives as well as initiatives to broaden the conversation abut meeting the needs of all students, particularly black males.

Twenty Strategies for Working with Black Males

1. Embrace the multiple identities they perform.
2. Respect their feelings, thoughts and ideologies.
3. Do not be dismissive about who they believe themselves to be.
4. Maintain high expectations and often express them consistently.
5. Provide ongoing timelines for tasks to be completed, particularly in relation to classroom instruction.
6. Deconstruct your biases and be open and honest about your own perspective.
7. Be equitable in your decisions about consequences and enforcing policies.
8. Seek to be "just," not fair.
9. Build authentic relationships and maintain open communication.
10. Listen to their voices to discover what they are saying and most importantly what they are not saying.
11. Do not judge their life, community, relationships, or identity.
12. If you do not know the answer to the question, be honest in communicating this and seek their input.
13. Function in the role of student to gain an intimate understanding of the struggles in which black males engage.
14. Value their lived experiences.
15. Allow your engagement to be fluid and do not force your values, beliefs, and ideologies upon them.
16. Make sure your actions are in line with your statements by being a living epistle and role model.
17. View black males not as monolithic beings but as individuals who bring multiple perspectives to the worlds they inhabit.

18. Mentor black males beyond the occasional lunches and social outings to engage them intellectually, socially, spiritually, and emotionally.
19. Provide them multiple environments to interface with so that they can broaden their own worldview.
20. Build unguarded bridges across the multiple landscapes we inhabit so that black males will feel open to crossing those bridges without fear and retribution.

AFTERWORD

In *Integration Matters: Navigating Identity, Culture and Resistance* the maturation of a black man in America reveals harsh realities to those who observe the changes and to the man negotiating his painful growth. One of the greatest lies expressed to a young black male in the halls of education is "Dreams are free…" The spirit of the statement is not without applause, yet the irresponsibility of it should and must be condemned. How do you encourage the mind and body to engage in contexts that place one in jeopardy without regard to the social practice of race, sexuality, appearance, and orders of behavior? Seemingly responsible, well-intended educational leaders fail to realize the complexity of the hopeful statement, making it difficult to argue such a positive statement. But young black males who take educational authorities on their word find themselves in a web of contradictions with no map or resource of resolution. The loaded historical pretext of "free" is conditional on all accounts. In the failure to experience the free(ness) of a dream, left is only a dim ringing of the hopeful ideal soon fading into an abstract distance. With the fading of one idea in the face of contradiction another is born. This one not so pleasant, lacking hope and possibility fosters fatalism, hostility, and sometimes violence to himself and/or others.

There is clearly nothing wrong with hope and aspiration. It is necessary, however it can be dangerous if not placed within a context of living openly as Gause reiterates. But, the pain of the rupture of experience is compounded when the simplicity of idea intersects the complexity of a lived practice that is anything but open. The institutional (and traditional) recourse of the educational leader is only to punish the anger and hostility that projects outward from the ruptured dream because the external social pressure of discrimination and racial profiling is greater than the resiliency of the dream. It is dangerous to let dreams fade and even more so to not let them exist.

The black male as an "endangered identity" must be given the critical resources to own his dream. Why single him out? What places him in such a jeopardizing situation? We all have witnessed the media reports of young black males that are high school drop-outs, unemployed, incarcerated, in gangs, and accused of committing or are victims of violent black on black crimes. The correctional centers are filled with the defaulted dreams of our black male youth. Young men looking for points of social and professional access find themselves in contrast with the conditions of tradition and practice.

The hustle is the rejection of tradition and becomes an individual search for opportunity by any means necessary. The goal of the hustle is the attempt to reach the next wrung on the status ladder. It is this hustle that places our black males on the endangered list. Young black men, often times absorbing the role of father in the family, set out to do whatever it takes in order to make a better life for himself and his family. Faced with the reality of a shrinking American job-market and diminishing federal aid and training programs the quest for education and prosperity are in direct relation to a social education that reduces intolerance, ignorance, and racial fear. The contradictions of the American dream and American reality illustrate the preconceptions and social restrictions that he is certain to crash into on the path to affluence and social independence. Clearly, when society observes the willingness of a young black male to do whatever, wherever, whenever in order to get what others appear to have perpetuates deep racial fear and intolerance. The institutional continuation of ignorance is formed from a lack of understanding the complexity in experience and opportunities preceding the willingness to do whatever it takes. The conformation of white fear and black male disillusionment is threaded throughout popular culture. We read, watch, live it, and worst of all we are entertained by it.

The frightening trend of apathy and disillusionment, the sponsor of the hustle mentality, is creeping up the class scale. The media is peppered with narratives of middle-class black men getting caught up in the hustle. The competition to be more and do more places a greater strain on the dream ideal. It is a restless moment for the black male who holds his dream, negotiates his situations, sacrifices himself, and accepts rejection while watching the attrition of his brothers. He finds that in most spaces he is the last man standing. The singular black male expecting to stand on his own, never questioning what purpose he serves for those who have anointed him as the one, is an interpersonal island. His age, appearance, sexuality, behavior and values are content of constant and fluctuating compromise. The institutional systems of work and education see this champion of his race as an example of what all black males are capable of if they would only apply themselves. The mystery of such a statement reaches back to the dream. It makes no real sense but gives great comfort to those who use it as a lesson for black male conformity and progress.

Integration Matters: Navigating Identity, Culture and Resistance not only urges us to deeply understand all of the above, but propels us to engage agency, and to take the lead in reconceptualizing schools and learning spaces. Gause bears witness to these realities and carefully documents the impact of consciousness, awareness, and responsibility. If the reader can dismiss the weight black men carry or intends to essentialize blackness or maleness, he/she has missed the point of the book, the complexity and intersectionality of identity and its significance in learning. The book chronicles the path set and the paths to be paved for young people in today's society, particularly those marked by any degree of marginalization. Although Gause spotlights black identity, what we learn from his work reaches far beyond one social category, rather it calls for a more comprehensive recognition of race, gender, class, sexual orientation, beliefs, and knowledge production, thus integration of ideology, intention, and individuals matter.

Roymieco A. Carter
Wake Forest University

REFERENCES

Akbar, N. (1992). *The community of self.* Tallahassee: Mind Productions & Associates.
American Council on Education. (July, 2004). *Reflections on 20 years of Minorities in Higher Education and the ACE Annual Status Report.* Washington, DC: Author. http://www.acenet.edu/bookstore Accessed: November 17, 2004.
Anderson, Mark E. (May 1988). *Hiring capable principals: How school districts recruit, groom and select the best candidates.* Eugene, OR: Oregon School Study Council.
———. (1991). *Principals: how to train, recruit, select, induct, and evaluate leaders for America's schools.* University of Oregon: ERIC Clearinghouse on Educational Management.
Antonio, A. L. (2003). Diverse student bodies, diverse faculties. *Academe.* American Association of University Professors. http://www.aaup.org/publications/Academe/2003/03nd/03ndanto.htm Accessed: November 16, 2005.
Asante, Molefi Kete. (1988). *Afrocentricity and knowledge.* Trenton, NJ: Africa World Press.
———. (1990). Kemet, *Afrocentricity and knowledge.* Trenton, NJ: African World Press.
Asante, Molefi Kete, & Abdulai S. Vandi (Eds). (1980). *Contemporary Black thought: Alternative analyses in social and behavioral science.* Beverly Hills, CA: Sage.
Baez, B. (2003). Outsiders Within? *Academe.* American Association of University Professors. http://www.aaup.org/publications/Academe/2003/03ja/03jadbaez.htm Accessed: November 16, 2005.
Banks, J. A., & McGee, C. A. (1989). *Multicultural education.* Needham Heights, MA: Allynn & Bacon.
Barbarin, O. A. (1993). Coping and resilience: Exploring the inner lives of African American children. *Journal of Black Psychology,* 19(4), 478–492.
Benjamin, W. (1969). *Illuminations.* New York: Schocken Books.
Bennett, M. H. (1993). Reforming American mental health. *Psych Discourse,* 24(6), 4–7.
Best, S., & Kellner, D. (1991). *Postmodern theory: Critical interrogations.* London and New York: MacMillan and Guilford Press.

Best, S., & Kellner, D. (1997). *The Postmodern turn.* London and New York: Routledge and Guilford Press.

Biggs, S. A. (1992). The plight of Black males in American schools: separation may not be the answer. *Negro Educational Review*, 43(1–2).

Bohman, J. (1997). Deliberative democracy and effective social freedom. In J. Bohman & W. Rehg (Eds), *Deliberative democracy: Essays on reason and politics.* Cambridge, MA: MIT Press. 321–348.

Bohman, J., & Rehg, W. (1997). Introduction. In J. Bohman & W. Rehg (Eds), *Deliberative democracy: Essays on reason and politics.* Cambridge, MA: MIT Press.

Bonner II, Fred A. (2004). "Black Professors: On the Track but Out of the Loop." *The Chronicle of Higher Education* 50(40). http://chronicle.com/temp/email.php?id=dql1or2m38lt8ei5v0dat c57vkd6ej4l Accessed: June 24, 2004.

Books, S. (2007). Devastation and disregard: Reflections on Katrina, child poverty and educational opportunity. In Sue Books (Eds), *Invisible children in the society and its schools.* New Jersey: Lawrence Erlbaum Associates.

Bourdieu, P. & Passeron, J. (1977). *Reproduction in education, society, and culture.* Trans. Richard Nice. Beverly Hills, CA: Sage.

Bowles, S., & Gintis, H. (1976). *Schooling in capitalist America: Educational reform and the contradictions of economic life.* New York: Basic Books.

Brookins, C. C. (1996). Promoting ethnic identity development in African American youth: The role of rites of passage. *Journal of Black Psychology*, 22(3), 388–417.

Brown, K. (2004). Leadership for social justice and equity. Weaving a transformative framework and pedagogy. *Educational Administration Quarterly*, 40(1), 79–110.

Brown, K. M. (2006). The Educational benefits of diversity: The unfinished journey from "Mandate" in *Brown* to "Choice" in *Grutter* and *Comfort*. *Leadership and Policy in Schools*, 5(4), 325–354.

Burnette, E. (1995). Black males retrieve a noble heritage. *The APA Monitor*, 26(6), 1, 32.

Butler, J. (1990). *Gender trouble: Feminism and the subversion of identity.* New York: Routledge.

——. (1993). *Bodies that matter: On the discursive limits of "sex."* New York: Routledge.

Carbado, D. (1999). *Black men on race, gender, and sexuality.* New York: NYU Press.

Carby, H. (1998). *Race men.* Cambridge: Harvard University Press.

Carlson, D. (1998). Finding a voice, and losing your way! *Educational Theory*, 48(4), 541–554.

——. (2007). Are we making progress? The discursive construction of progress in the age of "No Child Left Behind." In D. Carlson & C. P. Gause (Eds), *Keeping the promise: Essays on leadership, democracy, and education.* New York: Peter Lang.

Carlson, D., & Apple, M. W. (Eds). (1998). *Power, knowledge, pedagogy: The meaning of democratic education in unsettling times.* Boulder, CO: Westview Press.

Carlson, D., & Gause, C. P. (2007). *Keeping the promise: Essays on leadership, democracy, and education.* New York: Peter Lang.

Case, M. A. C. (1995). Disaggregating gender from sex and sexual orientation: The effeminate man in the law and feminist jurisprudence. *Yale Law Journal*, 105, 1–105.

Chafetz, J. S. (1974). *Masculine/feminine or human?: An overview of the sociology of sex roles.* Itasca, IL: FE Peacock Publishers.

Chesley, J. (2007). "Student Engagement and Academic Achievement: A promising connection." In D. Carlson & Gause, C. P. (Eds), *Keeping the promise: Essays on leadership, democracy, and education.* New York: Peter Lang.

Chesley, J. & Lyons, J. E. (2004). Fifty years after *Brown*: The benefits and tradeoffs for African American educators and students. *The Journal of Negro Education*, 73, 298–313.

Clifford, M. (1992). Consulting editor. *The harmony illustrated history encyclopedia of rock.* New York: Harmony Books.
Coleman, L. M., Jussin, L., & Kelley, S. H. (1995). A study of stereotyping: Testing three models with a sample of Blacks. *Journal of Black Psychology,* 21(4), 332–356.
Collins, P. (1990). *Black feminist thought: Knowledge, consciousness, and the politics of empowerment.* Boston, MA: Unwin Hyman.
Connell, R. W. (1992). A very straight gay: Masculinity, homosexual experience, and the dynamics of gender. *American Sociological Review,* 57 (December).
Cooper, C., & Gause, C. P. (2007). "Who's afraid of the big bad wolf?" Facing identity politics and resistance when teaching for social justice. In D. Carlson & Gause, C.P. (Eds), *Keeping the promise: Essays on leadership, democracy, and education.* New York: Peter Lang.
Cooper, C. W., & Allen, R. A. (2006). "Fostering parent engagement in multicultural school communities: Race, reform and the 'Politics of Difference'." Paper presented at the Annual Meeting of the American Educational Research Association. San Francisco, CA.
Coupe, S., & Baker, G. (1983). *The new rock 'n' roll: The A-Z of rock in the 80's.* New York: St. Martin's Press.
Crenshaw, K., Gotanda, N., Pellar, G., & Thomas, K. (1995). *Critical race theory.* New York: The New Press.
Crow, G. M., B. Mecklowitz, & Y. N. Weekes. (1992). *From teaching to administration: A preparation institute.* Lancaster, PA: Technomic.
Cummins, J. (1989). *Empowering minority students.* Sacramento, CA: California Association of Bilingual Education.
——. (1994). The socio-academic achievement model in the context of coercive and collaborative relations of power. In R. DeVillar, C. Faltis, & J. Cummins (Eds), *Cultural diversity in schools: From rhetoric to practice* (pp. 363–390). Albany, NY: SUNY Press.
Cunningham, R. T., & Mizelle, R. (1993). The effects of African-American manhood training. A rites of passage model on the self concept of African American adolescent males. *Psych Discourse,* 24(6), 16–17.
Curry, G. D., & Spergel, I. A. (1992). Gang involvement and delinquency among hispanic and African American adolescent males. *Journal of Research in Crime and Delinquency,* 29(3), 273–291.
Damen, L. (1987). *Culture learning: The fifth dimension on the language classroom.* Reading, MA: Addison-Wesley.
D'Andrea, M. (1995). Addressing the developmental needs of urban, African American youth: A preventive intervention. *Journal of Multicultural Counseling and Development,* 23(1), 57–64.
Dantley, M. (2000). *Including a spiritual voice in the educational leadership and school reform discourse.* Paper presented at the International Leadership Association, November, 2000.
——. (2005). A Christian view of spirituality and educational leadership. In C. M. Shields, M. M., Edwards, & A. Sayani (Eds), *Inspiring practice: Spirituality and educational leadership.* Lancaster, PA: Proactive Publications, 129–144.
——. (2007). Re-radicalizing the consciousness in educational leadership: The critically spiritual imperative toward keeping the promise. In D. Carlson & C. P. Gause (Eds), *Keeping the promise: Essays on leadership, democracy, and education.* New York: Peter Lang.
De La Cancela, V. (1993). Coolin—psychosocial communication of African and Latino men. *The Urban League Review,* 16(2), 33–44.
Delpit, L. (1995). *Other people's children: Cultural conflict in the classroom.* New York: The New Press.

Denzin, N. (1997). Performance texts. In W. Tierney, & Y. Lincoln (Eds), *Representation and the text: Re-naming the narrative voice* (pp. 179–218). Albany, NY: SUNY Press.

Detroits' African-centered academies disarm skeptics, empowers boys. *Black Issues in Higher Education*, Feburary, 1994, 10(26), 18–21.

The Digest of Education Statistics, 1996, U.S. Department of Education, National Center for Education Statistics, *Schools and staffing survey*, 1993–94. http://nces.ed.gov/pubs/d96/

Dimitriadis, G. (2001). *Performing identity/performing culture: Hip Hop as text, pedagogy, and lived practice*. Albany, NY: SUNY Press.

Douglas, B. C. (1993). *Psychotherapy with troubled African American adolescent males: Stereotypes, treatment amenability, and clinical issues*. (Report No. CG025778). ERIC Document Reproduction Service No. ED375360.

Du Bois, W. E. B. (1903). *Souls of black folk*. Reprint (1989). New York: Bantam.

Dyson, M. E. (1997). *Race rules: Navigating the color line*. New York: Vintage Press.

Educational Research Service; National Association of Elementary School Principals; and National Association of Secondary School Principals (1998). *Is there a shortage of qualified candidates for openings in the principalship? An exploratory study*. Arlington, VA: Educational Research Service.

Elam, R. (1995, March 3). Voices of reason and compassion. *The Modesto Bee*, p. A11.

Eskridge, Jr. W. N. (2000). No Promo Homo: The sedimentation of antigay discourse and the channeling effect of judicial review. *New York University Law Review*, 75, 1327–1411.

Fanon, F. (1986). *Black skin, white masks*. London, UK: Pluto Press.

Fine, M. (1997). *Off white: Readings on race, power, and society*. New York: Routledge.

———. (1991). *Framing dropouts: Notes on the politics of an urban high school*. Albany, NY: State University of New York Press.

Ferguson, A. A. (2000). *Bad boys: Public schools in the making of black masculinity*. Ann Arbor, MI: The University of Michigan Press.

Fordham, S. and Ogbu. J. (1986). Black student's school success: Coping with the "Burden of Acting White." *Urban Review* 18(3), 176–206.

Foster, M. (1997). *Black teachers on teaching*. New York: The New Press.

———. (1993). Educating for competence in community and culture. *Urban Education*, 27(4), 370–394.

———. (1992). Sociolingustics and the African American community: Implications for Literacy. *Theory into Practice*, 31(4), 304–311.

———. (1990). The Politics of race: Through the eyes of African American teachers. *Journal of Education*, 172(3), 123–141.

Foucault, M. (1979). *Discipline and punish: The birth of the prison*. Trans. Alan Sheridan. New York: Vintage.

———. (1980). *Power/Knowledge: Selected interviews and other writings, 1972–1977*. Ed. and trans. Colin Gordon. New York: Pantheon.

Fowler, F. C. (2000). *Policy studies for educational leaders: An introduction*. Prentice-Hall: New Jersey.

Franke, K. M. (1995). The central mistake of sex discrimination law: The disaggregation of sex from gender. *University of Pennsylvania Law Review*, 144, 1–99.

Frankenberg, R. (1993). *The social construction of whiteness: White women, race matters*. Minneapolis, MN: University of Minnesota Press.

Freire, P. (1970). *The pedagogy of the oppressed*. New York: Continuum.

———. (1994). *The pedagogy of hope: Reliving pedagogy of the oppressed*. New York: Continuum Publishing Group.

Freire, P., & Macedo, D. (1987). *Literacy: Reading the word and the world*. South Hadley, MA: Bergin & Garvey.
Fulmore, C., Talor, T. Hom, D., & Lyles, B. (1994). Psychological consequences of internalized racism. *Psych Discourse*, 25(10), 12–15.
Gant, L. M., Hwalek, M., & Dix, C. (1994). Increasing responsible sexual behavior among high risk African American adolescent males: results of a brief, intensive intervention. *Journal of Multicultural Social Work*, 3(3), 49–58.
Garfinkel, E. (1988). *Ways men and women in school administration conceptualize the administrative team*. Unpublished doctoral dissertation, Hofstra University, Hempstead, NY.
Gariabaldi, Antoine M. (1988). *Educating Black male youth: A moral and civic imperative: An introspective look at Black male students in the New Orleans public schools*. New Orleans: Orleans Board, 1988. ERIC ED 303 546.
Gause, C. P. (2001). *How African American educators "make sense" of hip hop culture and its influence on public schools: A case study*. Unpublished doctoral dissertation, Miami University, Ohio.
———. (2005a). The ghetto sophisticates: Performing black masculinity, saving lost souls and serving as leaders of the New School. *Taboo: The Journal of Culture and Education*, 9(1), 17–31.
———. (2005b). Navigating the stormy seas: Critical perspectives on the intersection of popular culture and educational leader-"ship." *Journal of School Leadership*, 15(3), 333–342.
———. (2005c). Guest editor's introduction: Edu-tainment: Popular Culture in the making of schools for the 21st century. *Journal of School Leadership*, 15(3), 240–242.
Gause, C. P., Reitzug, U. C., & Villaverde, L. E. (2007). Beyond generic democracy: Holding our students accountable for democratic leadership and practice. In D. Carlson, & C. P. Gause (Eds), *Keeping the promise: essays on leadership, democracy and education*. New York: Peter Lang.
Gilchrist, R. (1992). Holistic counseling. *American Counselor*, 1, 10–13.
Gill, W. (1992). Helping African American males: The cure. *Negro Educational Review*, 43(1–2), 31–36.
Gilroy, P. (1993). *Small acts: Thoughts on the politics of black culture*. New York: Serpent's Tail.
Giroux, H. A. (1981). Hegemony, resistance and the paradox of educational reform. In H. A. Giroux, A. Penna, & W. Pinar (Eds), *Curriculum & instruction: Alternatives in education*. Berkely, CA: McCutchan Publishing Corporation.
———. (1988). *Schooling and the struggle for public life. Critical pedagogy in the modern age*. Minneapolis, MN: University of Minnesota Press.
———. (1995). Is there a place for cultural studies in colleges of education? In H. A. Giroux, C. Lankshear, P. McLaren, & M. Peters (Eds), *Counternarratives: Cultural studies and critical pedagogies in postmodern spaces* (pp. 41–58). New York: Routledge.
———. (1996). *Fugitive cultures: Race, violence, and youth*. New York: Routledge.
Giroux, H. A., & Giroux, S. S. (2004). *Take back higher education: Race, youth and the crisis of democracy in the Post-Civil Rights era*. New York: Palgrave MacMillan.
Givens, M. (2007). Constructions of blackness: A White woman's study of whiteness and schooling. In Carlson, D., & Gause, C. P. (Eds), *Keeping the promise: Essays on leadership, democracy, and education*. New York: Peter Lang.
Gordon, E. W. (2006). Establishing a system of public education in which all children achieve at high levels and reach their full potential. In T. Smiley (Ed.), *The Covenant with Black America*. Chicago, IL: Third World Press.
Gordon, K. A. (1995). Self-concept and motivational patterns of resilient African American high school students. *Journal of Black Psychology*, 21(3), 239–255.

Gordon, R., Piana, L. D., & Keleher, T. (2000). *Facing the consequences: An examination of racial discrimination in U.S. public schools*. ERASE Initiative (Expose Racism & Advance School Excellence). Oakland, CA: Applied Research Center. http://www.arc.org Accessed: October 17, 2001.

Gordon, R. A., & Snowden, P. E. (1993). *School leadership and administration: Important concepts, case studies, and simulations* (4th ed). Indianapolis, IN: WCB Brown & Benchmark.

Gourdine, Angeletta, & Smitherman, G. (1992). "By any means necessary": An interview with Dr. Clifford Watson, ON the Malcolm X Academy and the Black all-male school movement. *Toward the curriculum of struggle*. Trenton, NJ: African World Press.

Gray-Ray, P., & Ray, M. C. (1990). Juvenile delinquency in the Black community. *Youth and Society, 22*(1), 67–84.

Grills, C., & Longshore, D. (1996). Africentrism. *Journal of Black Psychology, 22*(1), 86–106.

Grossberg, L. (1993). Cultural studies and/in new worlds. In C. McCarthy & W. Crichlow (Eds), *Race, identity, and representation in education*. New York: Routledge.

Guthrie-Jordan, M. (1990). *A descriptive study of black public school administrators in Ohio who hold the positions of superintendent, assistant superintendent, or high school principal*. Ph.D. dissertation, Miami University.

Gutmann, A. (1987). *Democratic Education*. Princeton. NJ: Princeton University Press.

Gutmann, A., & Thompson, D. (1996). *Democracy and disagreement*. Cambridge, MA: Harvard University Press.

Hale-Benson, J. (1982). *Black children: Their roots, culture, and learning styles*. Baltimore, MD: John Hopkins Press.

Hamilton, K. (2002). Race in the college classroom. *Black Issues in Higher Education, 19*(2), 32–36.

Hardy, P. & Laing, D. (1988). *Encyclopedia of Rock*. New York: Schirmer Books.

Harper, S. (2006). *Black male students at public flagship universities in the U.S. status, trends and implications for policy and practice*. Joint Center for Political and Economic Studies: Washington, DC: Author.

Harris, S. M. (1995). Psychosocial development and Black male masculinity: Implications for counseling economically disadvantaged African American male adolescents. *Journal of Counseling and Development, 73*(3), 279–287.

Harris, M. (2006). Fostering accountable community-centered policing. In T. Smiley (Ed.), *The Covenant with Black America*. Chicago, IL: Third World Press.

Havinghurst, R. J. (1976). The relative importance of social class and ethnicity in human development. *Human Development, 19*, 56–64.

Heasley, R. (2005). Queer masculinities of straight men: A topology. *Men and Masculinities, 7*(3), 310–320.

Heatley, M. (1993). *The ultimate encyclopedia of rock: The world's most comprehensive illustrated rock reference*. New York: Harper Collins.

Helms, J. E. (1989). Considering some methodological issues in racial identity counseling research. *The Counseling Psychologist, 17*(2), 227–252.

Henke, S. (2000). *Representations of secondary urban education: Infusing cultural studies into teacher education*. Ph.D. dissertation, Miami University, Ohio.

Hernandez, A. (1997). *Pedagogy, democracy and feminism: Rethinking the public sphere*. New York: SUNY Press.

Hill, P. (1992). *Coming of age*. Chicago, IL: African American Images.

———. (1995). Back to the future. *Journal of African American Men, 1*(1), 41–62.

Hofmann, R. (1995). *Using thinking units to initiate the analysis and interpretation of textual data*. Paper presented at the annual meeting of the Qualitative Research in Education Conference, Athens, Georgia.

Hollins, E., King, J., & Hayman, W. (1994). *Teaching diverse populations: Formulating a knowledge base*. Albany, NY: SUNY Press.
Holt, T. (1995). Afterword: Mapping the black public sphere. *The Black Public Sphere: A Public Culture Book*. (Eds), The Black Public Sphere Collective. Chicago, IL: The University of Chicago Press.
hooks, bell. (1989). *Talking back: Thinking feminist, thinking black*. Boston, MA: South End Press.
——. (1990). *Yearning: Race, gender, and cultural politics*. Boston, MA: South End Press.
——. (1994). *Teaching to transgress: Education as the practice of freedom*. New York: Routledge.
——. (2003). *Teaching community. A Pedagogy of hope*. New York: Routledge.
——. (2004). *We real cool. Black men and masculinity*. New York: Routledge.
Hopkins, R. (1997). *Educating black males: Critical lessons in schooling, community, and power*. Albany, NY: State University of New York Press.
Horkheimer, M., & Adorno, T. (1972). *Dialectic of enlightment*. New York: Seabury.
Howard, G. R. (1999). *We can't teach what we don't know: White teachers, multiracial schools*. New York: Teachers College Press.
Hudak, G. M. (2007). Leadership-With: A spiritual perspective on professional & revolutionary leadership in a digital culture. In D. Carlson & C. P. Gause (Eds), *Keeping the promise: Essays on leadership, democracy, and education*. New York: Peter Lang.
Huebner, D. (1998). Education and spirituality. In S. Shapiro & D. Purpel (Eds), *Critical issues in American Education* (2nd ed). Mahwah, NJ: Lawrence Erlbaum Associates, 321–336.
Hunter, M. (1984). Knowing, teaching, and supervising. In P. L. Hosford (Ed.), *Using what we know about teaching* (pp. 169–192). Alexandria, VA: Association for Supervision and Curriculum Development.
Hutchinson, E. (1996). *The assassination of the black male image*. New York: Touchstone Press.
Jackson, M. L. (1992). Drug use patterns among Black male juvenile delinquents. *Journal of Alcohol and Drug Education*, 37(2), 64–70.
Jackson, R. L. (2006). *Scripting the black masculine body: Identity, discourse, and racial politics in popular media*. New York: State University of New York Press-Albany.
Jagers, R. J., & Mock, L. O. (1993). Culture and social outcomes among inner city African American children: An Afrographic exploration. *Journal of Black Psychology*, 19(4), 391–405.
Jagers, R. J., Smith, P., & Mock, L. O. (1997). An Afrocultural social ethos: Component orientations and some social implications. *Journal of Black Psychology*, 23(4), 328–343.
Jeffries, R. B. (1997). *Performance traditions among African-American teachers*. Bethesda: Austin & Winfield.
Johnson, M. C., & Douglas, J. R. (May 1990). Grow-your-own: A model for selecting administrators. *NASSP Bulletin*, 74(526), 34–38.
Johnson, R. (1993). Clinical issues in the use of the DSM-III-R with African American children: A diagnostic paradigm. *Journal of Black Psychology*, 19(4), 447–460.
Jones, C. A. (1993). African-American male adolescent problems: A two way comparison. *Psych Discourse*, 24(6), 16–17.
Jones, R. (2002). Defining diversity. *American School Board Journal*, October, 18–23.
Jones, R. L. (1989). *Black adolescents*. Berkely: Cobb & Henry.
Jones, E. H., & Montenegro, X. P. (1985). *Women and minorities in school administration*. Arlington, VA: American Association of School Administrators, Office of Minority Affairs.
Joseph, J. (1996). School factors and delinquency—a study of African American youth. *Journal of Black Studies*, 26(3), 340–355.

Kellner, D. (1995). *Media culture: Cultural studies, identity and politics between the modern and the postmodern*. London: Routledge.

Kincheloe, J. L. (1999). The struggle to define and reinvent whiteness. *College Literature*, 26, 162–184.

King, A. E. O. (1994). An Afrocentric cultural awareness program for incarcerated African American males. *Journal of Multicultural Social Work*, 3(4), 17–28.

Knight, T., & Pearl, A. (2000). Democratic education and critical pedagogy. *The Urban Review*, 32(3), 197–226.

Kohn, L. P., & Wilson, M. N. (1995). Social support networks in the African American family: Utility for culturally compatible interventions. *New Directions for Child Development*, 68(summer, 95), 35–58.

Kozol, J. (1991). *Savage inequalities*. New York: Crown.

Kreisberg, S. (1992). *Transforming power: Domination, empowerment, and education*. Albany, NY: State University of New York Press.

Kroeber, A. L., & Kluckhohn, C. (1952). *Culture: A critical review of concepts and definitions*. Harvard University Peabody Museum of American Archeology and Ethnology Papers 47.

Kunjufu, J. (1989). *Children are the reward of life*. Chicago, IL: African American Images.

———. (1990). *Countering the conspiracy to destroy Black boys*, vol. III. Chicago, IL: African American Images.

Ladson-Billings, G. (2004). Landing on the wrong note: The price we paid for *Brown*. *Educational Researcher*, 33(7), 3–13.

———. (1994). *The dreamkeepers: Successful teacher of African American children*. San Francisco: Jossey-Bass Publishers.

La Point, V. (1992). Accepting community responsibility for African American youth education and socialization. *Journal of Negro Education*, 61(4), 451–454.

Lather, P. (1992). Critical frames in educational research: Feminist and post-structural perspectives. *Theory into Practice*, 31(2), 87–99.

———. (1997). Creating a multi-layered texts: Women, AIDS, and angels. In W. Tierney & Y. Lincoln (Eds), *Representation and the text: Re-naming the narrative voice* (pp. 233–258). Albany, NY: SUNY Press.

Lawrence, C. R. III (1995). The word and the river: Pedagogy as scholarship and struggle. In Crenshaw, K. et al. (Eds), *Critical race theory: The key writings that formed the movement*. (pp. 336–351). New York. New World Press.

LeCompte, M. D., & Preissle, J. (1993). *Ethnography and qualitative design in education research*. New York: Academic Press.

Lee, C. C. (1982). The school counselors and the Black child: critical roles and functions. *Journal of Non white concerns*, 11(3), 94–101.

———. (1992). *Empowering young Black males*. Ann Arbor, MI: ERIC Counseling and Personnel Services Clearinghouse.

———. (1996). *Saving the native son: Empowerment strategies for young Black males*. Greensboro, NC: ERIC Counseling and Student Services Clearinghouse.

Leistyna, P., Woodrum, A., & Sherblom, S. (1996). *Breaking free: The transformative power of critical pedagogy*. Cambridge, MA: Harvard Educational Review.

Lemelle, A. & Battle, J. (2004). Black masculinity matters in attitudes towards gay males. *Journal of Homosexuality,* 47(1), 39–51.

Lindsey, R., Robins, K. N., & Terrell, R. (1999). *Cultural proficiency: A manual for school leaders*. Thousand Oaks, CA: Corwin Press.

Lomotey, K. (1992). Independent Black institutions—African-centered education models. *Journal of Negro Education*, 61(4), 455–462.

Lovett-Tisdale, M., & Purnell, B. A. (1996). It takes an entire village. *The Journal of Black Psychology*, 22(2), 266–269.

Lugg, C. A. (2007). Sissies, faggots, lezzies, and dykes: Gender, sexual orientation, and a new politics of education? In Carlson, D. & Gause, C. P. (Eds), *Keeping the promise: Essays on leadership, democracy, and education*. New York: Peter Lang.

MacCaskill, Y. (1997). *Kuumba Academy*. Available ftp: Milwaukee Public Schools: ftp.milwaukee.k12.wi.us/schools/kuumba/

Madhubuti, H. R. (1990). *Black men: Obsolete, single, dangerous? In The Afrikan American family in transition: Essays in discovery, solution, and hope*. Chicago, IL: Third World Press.

Magubane, Z. (2002). Black skins, black masks or "The return of the white negro": Race, masculinity, and the public personas of Dennis Rodman and RuPaul. *Men and Masculinities*, 4(3), 233–257.

Majors, R., & Nikelly, A. (1983). Serving the Black minority: A new direction for psychotherapy. *Journal of Non White Concerns*, 11(4), 142–151.

Majors, R., & Billson, J. (1992). *Cool pose. The dilemmas of black manhood in America*. New York: Simon and Schuster.

Maxwell, B. (January 4, 2004). On Campus, grim statistics for African-American men. *St. Petersburg Times*. http://www.sptimes.com/2004/01/04/news_pf/Columns/On_campus_grim_stati.shtml Accessed: April 8, 2008.

McBride, D. A. (1998). "Can the Queen speak?: Race essentialism, sexuality and the problem of authority." *Callaloo* 21, 363–379.

McCarthy, C., & Crichlow, W. (1993). *Race, identity, and representation in education*. New York: Routledge.

McCollum, V. J. M. (1997). Evolution of the African American family personality: Considerations for family therapy. *Journal of Multicultural Counseling and Development*, 25(3), 219–229.

McDougald, E. J. (1923). The Negro woman teacher and the Negro student. *The Messenger*, 7, 769–770.

McLaren, P. (1997). The ethnographer as postmodern Flaneur: Critical reflexivity and posthybridity. In W. Tierney, & Y. Lincoln (Eds), *Representation and the text: Re-naming the narrative voice* (pp. 143–178). Albany, NY: SUNY Press.

McWhorter, J. (2000). *Losing the race*. New York: The Free Press.

Messerschmidt, J. (2000). *Nine lives: Adolescent masculinities, the body, and violence*. Boulder, CO: Westview Press.

Midgette, T. E., & Glenn, E. (1993). African American male academies: A positive view. *Journal of Multicultural Counseling and Development*, 21(2), 69–78.

Miller, N. (1995). *Out of the past: Gay and lesbian history from 1869 to the present*. New York: Vintage Press.

Mincy, R. B. (1994). *Nurturing young Black males . . . challenges to agencies, programs and social policy*. Washington, DC: The Urban Institute Press.

Moore, C. D. (1994). Religiosity and mental health: An Africentric perspective. *Psych Discourse*, 25(4), 10–11.

Morris, L. C. (1997). Spirituality and psychosocial competence among African American college students. *Psych Discourse*, 28(12), 15–21.

Murray, B. (1995). Black psychology relies on traditional ideology. *The APA Monitor*, 26(6), 33–34.

Muse, I., & Thomas, G. J. (Winter 1991). The rural principal: Select the best. *Journal of Rural and Small Schools*, 4(3) pp. 32–37.

Muskopf, B. (1998). *Women, education, and leadership: A narrative of four women.* Ph.D. Unpublished dissertation, Miami University.
Mutisya, P. M. (1996). Demythologization and demystification of African initiation rites: A positive and meaningful education aspect heading for extinction. *Journal of Black Studies,* 27(1), 94–103.
Nagda, B. A., Gurin, P., & Lopze, G. E. (2003). Transformative pedagogy for democracy and social justice. *Race, Ethnicity and Education,* 6(2), 165–191.
National Assessment of Educational Progress (1996). *Reading report card for the nation and states.* Office of Educational Research and Improvement, Washington, DC: U.S. Department of Education.
———. (1998). *Reading report card for the nation and states.* Office of Educational Research and Improvement, Washington, DC: U.S. Department of Education.
———.(2000). *Reading report card for the nation and states.* Office of Educational Research and Improvement, Washington, DC: U.S. Department of Education.
National Center for Education Statistics. (June 1993). Teaching, administrative and other work experience of public school principals. *Issue Brief IB-2-93.*
———. (January 1994). Public and private schools principals: Are there too few women? *Issue Brief IB-1-94.*
———. (April 1996). Where do minority principals work? *Issue Brief IB-2-96.*
Nelson, J. (1985). Fear of Tomorrow. *The Crisis,* 92(4), 29–30.
Nichols, J. (2006). "The realist Nigga: Constructions of Black masculinity within rap music". Master of Arts Unpublished Thesis. University of Maryland-College Park.
Ogbu, J. U., & Wilson, J. (1990). *Mentoring minority youth: A framework.* East Lansing, MI, National Center for Research on Teacher Learning. (Premises ERIC Document Reproduction Service No. 354 293).
Orfield, G., & Lee, C. (2007). *Historic reversals, accelerating resegregation, and the need for new integration strategies.* Cambridge, MA: The Civil Rights Project, Harvard University.
Orfield, G., & Yun, J. (1999). *Resegregation in American schools.* Cambridge, MA: The Civil Rights Project, Harvard University.
Palmer, P. (1998). *The courage to teach: Exploring the inner landscape of a teacher's life.* San Francisco, CA: Jossey-Bass.
Parker, W. M., & McDavis, R. J. (1983). Attitudes of Blacks toward mental health agencies and counselors. *Journal of Non White Concerns,* 11(4), 89–98.
Parker, W. M., & Lord, S. L. (1993). Characteristics of role models for young African American men: An exploratory survey. *Journal of Multicultural Counseling and Development,* 21(2), 97–105.
Peters, M., & Lankshear, C. (1996). Postmodern counternarratives. In H. A. Giroux (Ed.), *Counternarratives: Cultural studies and critical pedagogies in postmodern spaces* (pp. 1–41). New York: Routledge.
Plummer, D. L. (1996). Patterns of coping in racially stressful situations. *Journal of Black Psychology,* 22(3), 302–315.
Pratt, M. A. E. (1993). Racial bias in the juvenile justice system in the United States. *Journal of Intergroup Relations,* 20(3), 46–71.
Prince, K. J. (1997). Black family and Black liberation. *Psych Discourse,* 28(1), 4–7.
Polkinghorne, D. E. (1997). Reporting qualitative research as practice. In W. Tierney, & Y. Lincoln (Eds), *Representation and the text: Re-naming the narrative voice* (pp. 3–22). Albany, NY: SUNY Press.

Powell, J. (2005). A new theory of integrated education: True integration. In J. Boger & G. Orfield (Eds), *School resegregation: Must the south turn back?* (pp. 281–304). Chapel Hill, NC: University of North Carolina Press.

Putnam, H. (1991). A reconsideration of Deweyan democracy. In M. Brint, & W. Weaver (Eds), *Pragmatism in Law and society*. Boulder, CO: Westview Press.

Quantz, R., & O'Connor, T. (1988). Writing critical ethnography: Dialogue, multivoicedness, and carnival in cultural texts. *Educational Theory*, 38(1), 95–109.

Richardson, F. C. (1992). The plight of Black males in America: The agony and the ecstasy. *Negro Educational Review*, 43(1–2), 3–10.

Ridenhour, C. & Jah, Y. (1997). *Fight the power: Rap, race, and reality-chuck d with yusef jah*. New York: Delacorte Press.

Robbins, B. (1993). *The phantom public sphere*. Minneapolis, MN: university of Minnesota Press.

Robbins-Brinson, L. M. (1997). Racism, ethics and cultural competence in psychology. *Psych Discourse*, 28(9), 8–11.

Romanowsky, P., & George-Warren, H. (Eds). (1995). *The New Rolling Stone encyclopedia of rock & roll*. New York: Fireside.

Rose, T. (1991). Fear of a black planet: Rap music and black cultural politics in the 1990s. *Journal of Negro Education*, 60, 32–77.

Rosenwald, G. C., & Ochberg, R. L. (1992). Introduction: Life stories, cultural politics, and self-understanding. In G. C. Rosenwald & R. L. Ochberg (Eds), *Storied lives: The cultural politics of self-understanding* (pp. 1–18). New Haven, CT: Yale University Press.

Rusch, E. (2004). Gender and race in leadership preparation: A constrained discourse. *Educational Administration Quarterly*, 40(1), 16–48.

Russell, K., Wilson, M., & Hall, R. (1992). *Color complex: The politics of skin color among African-Americans*. New York: Doubleday.

Rux, Carl Hancock. (2003). Eminem—The New White Negro. In Greg Tate (Ed.), *Everything but the burden—what white people are taking from black culture* (pp. 15–37). New York: Harlem Moon Broadway Books.

Sadker, M. & Sadker, D. (1986). Sexism in the classroom: From grade school to graduate school. *Phi Delta Kappan*, 67, 512–515.

Sarles, H. (1993). *Teaching as dialogue: A teacher's study*. Lanham, MD: University Press of America.

Shakeshaft, C. (1989). The gender gap in research in educational administration. *Educational Administration Quarterly*, 25, 324–337.

Shakeshaft C., Nowell, I., & Perry, A. (1991). Gender and supervision. *Theory into Practice*, 30(2) 134–139.

Shields, C. M. (2004). Dialogic leadership for social justice: Overcoming pathologies of silence. *Educational Administration Quarterly*, 40(1), 109–132.

Shujaa, M. (1993). Education and Schooling: You can have one without the other. *Urban Education*. 27(4) 328–351.

———. (1996). *Beyond desegregation: The politics of quality in African American schooling*. Nashville, TN: Corwin Press.

Sleeter, C. E., & Grant, C. A. (1999). *Making choices for multicultural education: Five approaches to race, class, and gender* (3rd ed). Columbus, OH: Merrill.

Small, M. (1992). *Break it down: The Inside story from the new leaders of rap*. New York: Carol Publishing Group.

Smiley, T. (2006). *The covenant with Black America*. Chicago, IL: Third World Press.

Smith, E. P., & Brookins, C. C. (1997). Toward the development of an ethnic identity measure for African American youth. *Journal of Black Psychology*, 23(4), 358–377.

——. (2002). Queer fiction of race: Introduction. *MFS Modern Fiction Studies*, 48(4), 787–794.

Somverville, S. B. (2000). *Queering the color line: Race the invention of homosexuality in American culture*. Durham, NC: Duke University Press.

Spencer, M. B. (1991). *Adolescent African American male self esteem: Suggestions for mentoring program content-mentoring program structures for young minority males*. East Lansing, MI, National Center for Research on Teacher Learning. (Premises ERIC Document Reproduction Service No. 359 313).

St. Lawrence, J. S., Brasfield, T. L., Jefferson, K.W., Allyene, E., & Shirley, A. (1994). Social support as a factor in African American adolescents' sexual risk behavior. *Journal of Adolescent Research*, 9(3), 292–310.

Stancell, S. (1996). *Rap whoz who: The world of rap music*. New York: Schirmer Music.

Stanley, C. A. (2007). When counter narratives meet master narratives in the journal editorial-review process. *Educational Researcher*, 36(1), 14–24.

Staples, R. (1983). *Black masculinity, the Black male's role in American society*. San Francisco, CA: The Black Scholar Press.

Stevenson, H. C. (1993). Validation of the scale of racial socialization for African American adolescents: A preliminary analysis. *Psych Discourse*, 24(12), 6–10.

Tate, W. F. (1994). From inner city to ivory tower: Does my voice matter in the academy? *Urban Education*, 29(3), 245–269.

Tatum, B. L. (1996). An analysis of factors contributing to the delinquency of Black youth. *Journal of Black Studies*, 26(3), 356–368.

Taylor, L. C., Henson, I. D., & Wilson, M. N. (1993). Parental influences on academic performance in African American students. *Psych Discourse*, 24(11), 6–10.

Taylor, R. D., Casten, R., Flukinger, S. M. and Roberts, D., & Fulmore, C. D. (1994). Explaining the school performance of African American adolescents. *Journal of Research on Adolescence*, 4(1), 21–44.

Taylor, R. L. (1990). Black youth the endangered generation. *Youth and Society*, 22(1), 4–11.

Terry, J. (1999). *An American obsession: Science, medicine, and homosexuality in modern society*. Chicago, IL: University of Chicago Press.

Thomas, G. (2001). The dual role of scholar and social change agent: Reflections from tenured African American and Latina faculty. In R. O. Maboleka, & A. L. Green (Eds), *Sisters of the academy: Emergent Black women scholars in higher education*. Sterling, VA: Stylus.

Thompson, V. L. S. (1994). A preliminary outline of treatment strategies with African Americans coping with racism. *Psych Discourse*, 25(6), 6–9.

——. (1996). An Africentric, intervention program for African American youth. *Psych Discourse*, 27(4), 7–9.

Tierney, W. (1993). Self and identity in a postmodern world: A life story. In D. McLaughlin & W. Tierney (Eds), *Naming silenced lives* (pp. 119–134). London: Routledge.

Trier, J. (2007). "Critically examining popular culture representations of educators." In D. Carlson & C. P. Gause (Eds), *Keeping the promise: Essays on leadership, democracy, and education*. New York: Peter Lang.

Tutwiler, S. W. (2007). How schools fail African American boys. In Sue Books (Ed.), *Invisible children in the society and its schools*. Mahwah, NJ: Lawrence Erlbaum Associates.

Valdes, F. (1995). Queers, sissies, dykes, and tomboys: Deconstructing the conflation of "sex," "gender," and "sexual orientation" in Euro-American law and society. *California Law Review*, 3–377.

Vontress, C. E., & Epp, L. R. (1997). Historical hostility in the African American client: Implications for counseling. *Journal of Multicultural Counseling and Development*, 25(3), 170–184.

Walker, E. M., & Sutherland, M. E. (1993). Urban Black youths' educational and occupational goals—the impact of Americas' opportunity structure. *Urban Education*, 28(12), 200–220.

Warfield-Coppock, N. (1992). "The rites of passage movement: A resurgence of African-centered practices of socializing African American youth." *Journal of Negro Education*, 61(4), 471–482.

Watts, J. G. (1994). *Heroism and the black intellectual: Ralph Ellison, politics and Afro-American intellectual life*. Chapel Hill, NC: University of North Carolina Press.

Weatherspoon, F. D. (1998). *African-American males and the law: Cases and materials*. New York: University Press of America.

Weis, L. (1988). *Class, race, and gender in American education*. Albany, NY: State University Press.

Weis, L. & Fine, M. (1993). *Beyond silenced voices: Class, race, and gender in United States schools*. Albany, NY: SUNY Press.

West, C. (1993). *Race matters*. New York: Vintage Press.

——. (2004). *Democracy matters. Winning the fight against imperialism*. New York: Penguin Press.

White, J. L., & Parham, T. A. (1990). *The psychology of Blacks: An African-American perspective*. Englewood Cliffs, NJ: Prentice Hall.

Williams, J. (2006). *Enough: The phony leaders, dead-end movements, and culture of failure that are undermining Black America—and what we can do about it*. New York: Three Rivers Press.

Williams, R. L., & Johnson, R. C. (1981). Progress in developing Afrocentric measuring instruments. *Journal of Non White Concerns*, 11(2), 3–18.

Willis, J. T. (1990). *Implications for effective psychotherapy with African-American families and individuals*. Matteson, IL: Genesis Publications.

Willis, P. (1990). *Common culture*. Buckingham: Open University.

Wilson, A. (1991). *Understanding Black adolescent male violence*. New York: Afrikan World InfoSystems.

Wilson, M. N., Kohn, L. P., Curry-el, J., & Hinton, I. D. (1995). The influence of family structure characteristics on the child rearing behavior of African American mothers. *Journal of Black Psychology*, 21(4), 450–462.

Wink, J. (1997). *Critical pedagogy: Notes from the real world*. New York: A. B. Longman.

Woodson, C. G. (1933). *The mis-education of the negro*. Washington, DC: Associated Press.

Yoshino, K. (2002). Covering. *Yale Law Journal*, 111, 769–939.

Zelditch, M. (1962). Some methodological problems of field studies. *American Journal of Sociology*, 67, 566–576.

INDEX

academic achievement. *see also* education
   African Americans' continued lag in, 5, 8, 18–19, 24
   and Afrocentric curriculum, 57
   gap in, 35, 119
   lack of attributable to boredom, 56–57
   Latinos' continued lag in, 18–19
   and segregation, 19, 21, 22, 24
accountability, calls for, 139
achievement
   of African Americans, disregarded in curriculum, 55, 56
   failure to encourage young African American males in, 165
activism, 138–139
activism, collaborative
   keys for administrators, 148–149
   keys for parents, 152–154
   keys for students, 154–156
   keys for teachers, 150–152
   need for educators to engage in, 141, 147
   and transformative leadership, 147
administrators. *see* leaders, educational
administrators, African American. *see* educators, African American
African American community
   competitiveness in, 72
   diversity of, 64
   sexism in, 171
African-American Males and the Law (Weatherspoon), 51
African Americans. *see also* males, African American
   belief of selves as powerless to reify domination, 29
   female. *see* females, African American
   male. *see* males, African American
agents of change, educational leaders as, 147
Akbar, Naim, 52
alcohol, 139
alternative gendered identity, living, 166
anger, of African American males, perceived, 39–40
Apple, M. W., 20
Applied Research Center, 125
Asante, Molefi Kete, 55
assimilation, African American, 4
athletes
   and African American masculinity, 10, 55
   fame and fortune as center of lives of, 70
   as slaves, 69–70
"at-risk" students, 115, 116
attraction and spiritual connections, 166
Ayer, Gertrude, 121

Baldwin, James, 45
Bambaataa, Afrika, 89
banking metaphor, 28
Battle, J., 171
behavior. *see also* expressiveness young African American males; resistance
  interpretation of, 134
Billson, Janet, 52, 132
"Bitter" (Gause), 123–124
bitterness, 124
Black, 77–78, 79–81
Black Enterprise Board of Economists, 57–58
Black Male Educational Academies, 57
Black Male Students at Public Flagship Universities (Harper), 8
body, African American
  commodification of, 107. *see also* entertainment
  stylizing of and acquisition of power, 125
  as tool for labor and procreation, 108
Books, Sue, 35
boredom, 56–57
break dancing, 90, 94
breaks, 94
Brookins, C. C., 56
"Brother Denied" (Gause), 61–62
Brown, Kathleen, 9, 21, 34–35
Brown II, 22
Brown vs. Board of Education, 21, 22
Bruner, J., 167–168
Busta Rhymes, 77

cafeteria, 130
canon, marginalization of those without power by, 98
"Can Young Black Men Be Saved?" (Scott), 44
capitalism
  of African American leadership, 63–64
  hip-hop as tool of, 69
careers, 104–105
Carlson, D., 16, 20, 140, 165
Case Junior-Senior High School
  administrative team, 126–127. *see also* Kirkpatrick, William; Victoria
  African American educators at. *see* Christina; Crystal; Doug; Victoria
  cafeteria, 130
  discipline at, 124, 125, 128–129, 131
  reasons for studying, 7
Casten, R., 56
censorship of gangster rap, 32
Chafetz, J. S., 47–48

Chesley, Joanne, 109–110, 167
Christina
  on "disadvantaged" classification, 112–113
  on mediated images of African Americans, 133
  on parents' questioning of authority, 114
  on policing of students, 129
  on rap, 100, 102–103
  on rap videos, 135
  on students' desire to be rappers, 104
  on teachers shouting at African American students, 118–119
Chuck D, 98. *see also* Public Enemy
church. *see also* faith; religion
  hypocrisy of leaders in, 62
  lack of youth involvement in, 62
church, African American
  corruption in, 84–85
  homophobic values of, 73, 170–171
  importance of to African American leadership, 62
  role in African American community, 84
Cincinnati, Ohio, 70–71
civil rights movement
  impact on African American America, 63
  students' ignorance of, 117
classroom, democratic, 146
class struggles, divisiveness of, 72
clothes, 131
college enrollment, gender gap among African Americans, 8
color, skin
  effects on identity, 111
  importance of acknowledging, 110
community, African American. *see* African American community
competition
  within African American community, 72
  in rap, 94, 95
  self-worship as form of, 17
Cones, J., 54
connectivity, loss of, 16
consensus building, 141
consumerism, rap as vehicle for, 95
control. *see also* discipline; police; policing of African American males; punishment
  emphasis on, 115
coolness. *see also* behavior; disposition, African American male
  and African American masculinity, 49–50
  as end in itself, 49
  perceived as threatening, 132
"Cool Pose," 132. *see also* coolness

courage, required for teaching, 167
The Courage to Teach (Parker), 166, 167
critical consciousness, need for, 121
Critical Legal Theory, 53
critical literacy, 31
critical pedagogy
   and creation of new knowledge and language, 29–30
   and desire to transform, 29
   Freire, 28, 29
   hooks on, 27
   reading of world and word, 30, 31
   and transformation of positions of power, 30
Critical Race Theory, 53
critical reflection, administrators' need for, 9–10
critical self-reflection, 53
critical spirituality, 53
critical theory, 28–29
critique, 27. *see also* critical pedagogy
Crystal
   on dress code and discipline, 131
   on lack of parental involvement, 118
   on lunch, 130
   on paycheck teachers, 112
   on racial differences in discipline, 129
   on rap, 99, 102
   on rap videos, 135
   on students' desire to be rappers, 104–105
   on teachers' expectations of African American students, 111
   on white teachers' lack of respect for African American students, 115
cultural capital, 30
Cultural Proficiency Model, 144
cultural studies, 33
culture
   African Americans' view of, 49
   definition of, 32
culture, African American. *see also* popular culture, African American
   popular concept of, 33
   viewed as limited, 49
culture, dominant. *see* dominant culture
culture, politics of, 143
culture, popular. *see* popular culture
curriculum
   lack of inclusion of African American achievement and experience, 55
   need to integrate popular culture into, 26
   perpetuation of dominant culture, 31
   and power, 19

curriculum, Afrocentric, 57
curriculum, hidden, 31

Dantley, M., 11, 46, 62–63
deconstructive interpretation, 53
Delpit, L., 71
democracy
   benefits of diversity to, 35
   dependence upon habits of democratic public life, 16
   education considered vehicle for developing, 138
   flawed implementation of, 120
   instituted through hierarchical system of denial and oppression, 20
   lack of and segregation, 22
   and necessity of public schools, 160
   teaching as soul of, 111
desegregation. *see also* integration; segregation
   effects of on African American schools and educators, 167
   unpreparedness of white teachers for, 108
despair, 51, 64. *see also* nihilism
"Devastation and Disregard" (Books), 35
Dewey, John, 16
dialogue, 30
differences
   need to recognize, 113–114
   need to seek opportunities to bridge, 16
digital cameras, 17
Dimitriadis, G., 93
"disadvantaged" classification, 112–113
disasters, natural, 110, 118
discipline
   administrative detentions, 128
   and African American males in special education, 127
   at Case Junior-Senior High School, 124, 128–129, 131
   and dress code, 131
   focus on, 115
   influence of image of African American male on, 125
   police interaction with students, 128–129
   problems attributable to boredom, 56–57
   racial differences in, 129
   students as bodies to be controlled, 125
   suspension of African American students, 125
   teachers' use of code of conduct, 129
   treatment of students as outlaws, 128
   zero-tolerance, 127

Discipline and Punish (Foucault), 125
discourse, silences in, 3030
disposition, African American male, 52. *see also* coolness; "Cool Pose"
diversity
　of African American community, 64
　benefits of, 34–35
　importance of in education, 21
　in North Carolina, 23
DJ Grandmaster Flash, 89, 94
DJ Hollywood, 89
DJs, 89
dominant culture
　perpetuation of through curriculum, 31
　silencing of anything outside of, 170
　in teacher education, 27–28
double consciousness, 92–93, 132
Doug
　on accomplishments since desegregation, 117
　on assumptions about rap, 135–136
　on double consciousness, 132
　on gangster rap, 103–104
　on lunch, 130
　on need to recognize cultural differences, 113–114
　on policing of students, 128–129
　on rap, 99–100, 102
　on students' desire to be rappers, 105
　on white teachers, 112, 116–117
downtowns, revitalization of, 3
dream reality/dream identity, 42
dress code and discipline, 131
drinking, 139
drug use, 18, 139
Du Bois, W. E. B., 69, 71–72, 92–93
duffle bag boy, respect for, 65
Dyson, M. E., 105

economic expansion, 3
education. *see also* academic achievement; school; schools
　African American males' continued lag in, 4–5. *see also* academic achievement
　African American males' disengagement from, 70
　cause of, 145
　considered vehicle for developing democracy, 138
　considered vehicle for mobility, 138
　de-emphasis of, 69
　future vision of, 20–21
　gender gaps among African Americans, 8
　importance attached to by African Americans, 116, 118
　increasing difficulty in receiving, 160
　inferiority of for African Americans and poor, 5
　interventions in resistance to, 119–120
　Latinos' continued lag in, 4–5
　marginalization of African American males in, 79
　need to recognize multiple identities, 20
　perceived as irrelevant, 56–57
　as praxis of freedom, 109
　purpose of, 142
　questioning and critique in, 27
　and relations of power, 34
　relative importance of to entertainment, 139
　resistance to, 10, 50
　as responsible for teaching youth to transform culture, 101
education, liberatory, 27
education, online, 16
education, public. *see also* schools, public
　promise of, 140
　promise of as curse, 121
"The Educational Benefits of Diversity" (Brown), 21
"Education and Spirituality" (Huebner), 46
educators. *see also* teachers
　collaborative activism for. *see* activism, collaborative
　current challenges for, 137
　need to be culturally proficient, 144
　need to engage in collaborative activism, 141, 147
educators, African American. *see also* Christina; Crystal; Doug; teachers, African American; Victoria
　Ayer on duty of, 121
　broad conception of role, 116
　on desegregation, 109
　limited study of, 6, 36, 167
　reasons for studying, 7
　views on rap, 99–101, 102–105
educators, social justice, 36
Elementary and Secondary Education Act of 1965, 5
Enough (Williams), 25, 42
entertainment. *see also* music, popular; rap; rappers
　commodification of African American body, 107
　commodification of hip-hop culture, 69

nihilistic construction of African American masculinity, 44
    relative importance of to education, 139
entitlement, sense of, 65
era of idols, 17, 68, 89
European Americans. *see also* parents, white; teachers, white
    as potential enemy, 132
    view of inner city African American males, 10
expressiveness young African American males. *see also* behavior
    hip-hop culture as specific to, 105–106

failure
    culture of, 25
    experience of, 108
faith. *see also* church; pleading the blood; spirituality
    centrality of in African American life, 46
    emphasis on docility and acquiesence, 63
fame
    African American male's desire for, 69
    as center of athletes' lives, 70
family, African American, 102
Fanon, F., 42
fear
    and assault on crime, 125–126
    opposition to rap grounded in, 96–97
    Parker on, 166
    white teachers' of African American students, 125, 132
females, African American
    college enrollment of, 8
    encouraged to be teachers, 116
    objectification of, 69
Feminist Legal Theory, 53
Ferguson, A. A., 92, 110
film industry, 107
Flukinger, S. M., 56
Foster, M., 134
Foucault, M., 125
Frankfurt School, 28–29
Freire, P., 28, 29
"From Humble Beginnings Comes Great Achievement" (Melendez), 18
Fulmore, C., 56

gangs
    Leaders of the New School, 76–77, 85
    in Southeast, 71
gangster rap, 32, 103, 135
Gary, 88

Gause, C. P.
    on democracy, 16, 141
    on educational leadership preparation programs, 146
    family, 159
    mother of, 161–162
    poetry. *see* poetry
    on promise of public education, 140
    reflection on world's view of, 166–167
Gause, Walter T. Sr., 159
Gay and Lesbian Legal Theory, 53
gay culture, commodification of, 172
GED, 80, 82
gender. *see also* masculinity; masculinity, African American
    and challenging of teachers, 133–134
    concept of, 42
    explanation of, 47
    social construction of, 42
gender role, 96
gender role, male, 47–48, 95–96
gender roles, African American, 43–44, 48
generation X. *see* youth
Genovese, E., 50
Gill, W., 56
Giroux, H. A., 20, 33
globalization, impact of on rural farming communities, 3
Gordon, E. W., 58, 119–120
Gore, Tipper, 32
graduate students, 142
graffiti writing, 90–91
Grandmaster Flash, 89, 94
Grandmaster Flash and the Furious Five, 94
Grand Wizard Theodore, 89
green jobs, 3
Greensboro, North Carolina, 160–161
griot, 94, 98
Grossberg, Lawrence, 33
group think, 63
Gutmann, A., 138

habits of democratic public life, 16–17
Hall, R., 111
Harper, Shaun, 8
Harris, M., 125–126
Harris, S. M., 56
Heasley, R., 170, 171
Heifetz, R., 114
hero worship, 10, 55
heteronormativity in constructions of masculinity, 55
hidden curriculum, 31

INDEX

higher education
  African American enrollment in, 8
  and development of democratic classroom, 146
  minority faculty in, 171
  teaching for social justice in, 163
hip-hop. *see also* rap
  adults' views of, 90
  current state of, 93
  explanation of, 90–91
  and formation of multiple identities, 94
  founded on signification, 95
  marginalization of in purest form, 98
  opposition to grounded in fear, 96–97
  popularity among white youth, 169
  as postmodern, 92
  and production of LPs, 93
  prominence in culture, 91
  as situated cultural practice, 93
  as subculture, 90–91
  as tool of capitalism, 69
  view of by dominant culture, 98
  as way of life, 90
  youths' views of, 90
hip-hop culture
  commodification of, 97
  and policing of African American males, 133
  as specific to expressiveness of young African American males, 105–106
Hispanics. *see* Latinos
Historic Reversals (Orfield and Lee), 22, 24
Hollywood, 89
homophobia in African American community, 73, 170–171
homosexuality
  commodification of, 172
  viewed as sign of weakness, 170
hooks, bell
  on African American gender roles, 43–44
  on African American male leaders, 164
  on African American males' need for critical consciousness, 24
  on classroom, 146
  on condition of African American male in America, 25–26
  on critical pedagogy, 27
  on sexist thinking, 171
  on teaching, 109
Hopkins, R., 138
"How Schools Fail African American Boys" (Tutwiler), 26
Hudak, G., 46, 161
Huebner, D., 46

Hurricane Katrina, 118. *see also* disasters, natural
hustler, respect for, 65
hustling as manifestation of resistance, 65

Ice Cube, 101, 102
identities, African American
  need to stop accepting, 43
  performance of, 42–43
identity
  construction of, 94, 135, 167–168
  effects of skin color on, 111
  and marginalization of popular culture, 32
  young people's desire to define, 32
identity, school, 144
identity, sexual, 166
identity, student, 20–21
identity formation
  and need for educational leaders to promote social justice, 56
  postmodern conceptions of, 20–21
images of African American males
  as almost completely negative, 25–26
  consumption of by African American males, 70
  cultural effects of, 44
  dominance of in popular culture, 41
  projected by media, 54, 55
  reinforcement of stereotypes, 133
  and selling of products, 2
  use of for political power, 70–71, 134
  use of to sell rap, 135, 136
images of African Americans
  perpetuated and consumed by African American community, 65
  student leaders on, 66–68
  young people's enactment of, 68–69
immigrants, 2, 3
immigration, slavery as form of, 3
individualism, dangers of focusing on, 160
industry, 4
information as power, 64
integration
  gains of, 119
  losses of, 109–110, 119
  necessity of struggles for, 118
  need to recognize importance of, 35
  negative impact on African American students, 109–110
  of North Carolina, 23–24
  struggle for, 160
  and young people's squandering of opportunities, 159

integration, technological, 16
intelligence, perception of African
    Americans', 26, 108
Internet and activism, 138
interventions in resistance to educational
    experience, 119–120
Iraq, 139

Jackson, Jesse, 63
Jackson, Randall, 108
Jackson, Ronald L. II, 41–42
jails
    African American population of, 51
    schools as feeders to, 79
Jeffries, R. B., 108
Jesus Christ
    as controversial, 63
    words during crucifixion, 45
jobs, 3–4, 69, 103–104. *see also* careers
Joseph, J., 55, 56
justice system, African American males and, 51

Kansas, lawsuits in, 21, 22
Keeping the Promise (Carlson), 165
Kellner, Douglas, 41
King, Martin Luther, 159
Kirkpatrick, William, 126–127, 129
Kitwana, B., 17
knowledge
    creation of, 29–30
    defined by those in power, 19
Kool Herc, 89, 90, 94
Kunjufu, J., 56

Ladson-Billings, G., 22, 28
language of critique, 30
language of possibility, 30
Latinos
    continued lag in education, 4, 18–19
    segregation of, 21, 22
law, African American males and, 51. *see also* jails; police
leaders, African American male. *see also* leadership, African American
    co-optation of, 164–165
leaders, educational
    as agents of change, 147
    belief in need for technical model, 143
    keys for collaborative activism, 148–149
    maintenance of status quo, 9
    need to ask questions, 27
    need to be culturally proficient, 144
    need to develop critical reflexivity, 9–10

leadership, African American
    capitalism of, 63–64
    continued victimization of African
        American community, 64
    and group think, 63
    as heads of corporations, 65
    hypocrisy of, 62
    importance of churches to, 62
    integration into mainstream
        society, 64–65
    neglect of constituency, 72
    slowing of emergence of new
        leadership, 63
leadership, courageous, 165
leadership, revolutionary, 161
leadership, transformative, 141
"Leadership for Social Justice and Equity"
    (Brown), 9
"Leaders of the New School" (gang), 76–77,
    85. *see also* Black; Raheem; RJ; Tiger
"Leaders of the New School" (rap group), 77
learning, sharing of, 31
learning communities. *see also* education;
    schools
    focus on perceptions of dominant
        culture, 27–28
learning environment, coconstructing of, 143
Lee, Chungmei, 22, 24
Lemelle, A., 171
Lester, Julius, 65
lineage
    Gause's, 159
    importance of, 2
Look Out, Whitey (Lester), 65
LP records, 93
Lugg, C. A., 53
lunch, 129–130
Lyons, Henry J., 84, 85
Lyons, J. E., 167

Madhubuti, H.R., 33, 49
Majors, R., 10, 52, 132
male mentality, 52
maleness, heteronormative constructions
    of, 55
males, African American. *see also* Black;
    Raheem; RJ; Tiger
    academic achievement of. *see* academic
        achievement
    achievement gap with African American
        females, 119
    acquisition of power, 125
    condition of, 25–26, 44, 51

disadvantages of, 24–25
distinct characteristics of, 47
and exercise of power, 48, 95–96
feelings of insecurity, 131
and gender role, 43–44, 48, 51, 95–96
images of. see images of African American males
limited opportunities to construct positive self-identities, 134
perceived as angry, 39–40
perception of male role, 47
presence on streets, 74–77
reasons for studying, 7–9
redefinition of manhood, 131–132
resistance of domination, 50
responsibility to transform the world, 102
solutions for transforming condition of, 57–58
stigmatization of, 10–11, 29, 70
strategies for working with, 174–175
transforming lives of, 173–174
view of selves, 54
view of white men as enemy, 132
"Man of Fire-Man of Passion" (Gause), 37–38, 40
marginalization of African American students, 110
Marxists, 29
masculinity
  Chafetz on, 47–48
  heteronormativity in constructions of, 55
  as mentality, 52
  queering of and affirmation of other, 55
  Raheem's concept of, 77, 83
masculinity, African American. see also coolness; "Cool Pose"
  African American males' desire to exhibit, 10
  and athletes, 55
  considered legitimate object of surveillance and policing, 134
  construction of, 42
  contemporary expressions of, 43
  and cultural politics, 96
  and experience with war, 48–49
  hero worship in, 10, 55
  as heteronormative, 49–50
  hip-hop's construction of, 42
  images of used for political power, 70–71
  intersection with queerness and educational leadership, 168
  masking strategies, 52–53
  nihilistic construction of by entertainers, 44
  and proper response to systematic injustice, 96
  and rappers, 55
  reasons for studying, 7–9
  redefinition of, 131–132
  and response to systematic injustice, 48
  and social relations, 96
masculinity, queer, 171
masking strategies, 52–53
Maxwell, Bill, 4–5
media
  and image of African American masculinity. see images of African American males
  youth's connectedness to, 89
media, digital
  African American youth as consumers of, 90
  youth as producers of, 89
Media Culture (Kellner), 41
Melendez, Sara, 18
men. see males, African American
Meredith, James, 159
Midgette, T. E., 57
millennium generation. see youth
Mincy, R. B., 56
minorities. see African Americans; Latinos
money, view of in African American community, 65, 69. see also underground economy
music, popular. see also hip-hop; rap
  attempts to protect young people from, 32
Supermodel, 168–169

narratives
  of African American teachers. see Christina; Crystal; Doug; Victoria
  role of in identity construction, 167–168
  of young African American males. see Black; Raheem; RJ; Tiger
National Assessment of Educational Progress, 5
National Baptist Convention, 84, 85
Nichols, Jason, 97
nihilism, 50, 93. see also despair
No Child Left Behind (NCLB), 5
North Carolina, 4, 23–24, 160–161
North Carolina Greensboro, University of, 8
notoriety, young people's desire for, 17
N. W. A., 101–102, 103

"On Campus, Grim Statistics for African-American Men" (Maxwell), 4–5

opportunities, squandering of, 159
oppression, dichotomies generated by, 40
Orfield, G., 18, 21, 22, 24
other
    image of as tool of production, 2
    rappers as, 98
    tolerance *vs.* affirmation of, 55
outlaws, students treated as, 128
outliers. *see* other
Over-the-Rhine, 70–71

Palmer, Parker, 166, 167
parents, African American, 118
parents, keys to collaborative activism for, 152–154
parents, white
    belief in mediated images of African Americans, 133
    challenging of authority of African American teachers, 114, 133–134
passing, 170
past, resistance of awareness of, 92
paternalism, 72
personal stories. *see* narratives
pleading the blood, 45. *see also* church; faith
poetry
    "Bitter," 123–124
    "Brother Denied," 61–62
    "Man of Fire-Man of Passion," 37–38
    "Today: I Opened My Eyes," 157–159, 165, 166
    "Voiceless Spirit," 87
police
    interaction with Case students, 128–129, 130
    rap's glorification of encounters with, 95
    shooting of Thomas, 71
policies, failed, 120–121
policing of African American males, 133, 134. *see also* police; surveillance
political power
    rap's loss of, 103
    use of image of African American males for, 70–71
    use of immigrants for, 2
political power, African American, 72, 103. *see also* leadership, African American
politics of culture, presence of in schools, 143
poor
    inequity of education for, 5
    overrepresentation in special education, 108

popular culture
    and African American community's perpetuation of and consumption of image, 65
    assault on school and family culture, 9
    dominance of African American males in, 41
    marginalization of, 32
    need to integrate into curriculum, 26
popular culture, African American, 25
poverty, 108. *see also* poor
Powell, J., 19
power
    acquisition of by young African American males, 125
    in cultural studies discourse, 33
    and curriculum, 19
    information as, 64
    opposition to exercise of by African American males, 48, 95–96
power, disciplinary. *see* discipline; policing
power, political. *see* political power
power, relations of, 34
power struggles in educational experience, 119
pragmatism, 63
praxis, definition of, 31
prayer of renewal and faith, 58–59
preachers. *see also* church; leadership, African American
    call to be seen as victims, 62
    Raheem's views of, 78
prison complex economy, 79
professional development, 117
Public Enemy, 101, 102. *see also* Chuck D
punishment. *see also* discipline; special education
    of African American males, 26, 51, 56
    for African American males fulfilling ideal male gender role, 95–96
    and demonization of African Americans, 125
    of resistance, 26

queering, 170
Queer Legal Theory, 53, 54
questioning, 27. *see also* critical pedagogy

race, 47, 105
racism, U.S.'s failure to address, 22
Raheem, 76–77, 78, 83–84
Raising Hell, 94

rap. see also hip-hop
    African American educators' views
        on, 99–101, 102–105, 135
    as anthem of postmodern marginality, 106
    and blackness as symbol of masculinity/
        identity, 96
    Chuck D on, 98
    commodification of, 95, 97, 103. see also
        gangster rap
    as critique of social order, 93
    current state of, 93
    early, 89, 101
    embodiment of postmodern aesthetic, 92
    emergence of gangster rap, 103
    as extension of oral traditions, 94–95,
        102–103
    as form of cultural identity, 92
    Gause's first exposure to, 88
    glorification of encounters with police, 95
    identity constructed on basis of, 135
    as informational medium, 92, 93
    as job, 103–104
    loss of political consciousness, 102, 103
    opposition to grounded in fear, 96–97
    as political machine, 101
    production of counterhegemonic
        discourses, 93
    prominence in culture, 91
    use of African American males' image to
        sell, 135, 136
    as vehicle for consumerism, 95
    as way of life, 99, 100
rappers
    and African American masculinity, 10, 55
    image of, 104
    as other, 98
    as pawns, 104
    students' desire to be, 104–105
"The Realist Nigga" (Nichols), 97
reflection, habit of, 16
reforms, educational, 120
Reitzug, U. C., 141
relations of power, 34
religion. see also church
    importance of in African American politics
        and leadership, 62
    vs. spirituality, 46, 47
remedial courses, overrepresentation of
    African American males in, 56
representation in cultural studies
    discourse, 33
resegregation, 21–22, 23. see also
    desegregation; integration; segregation

resistance
    African American culture of, 50
    of awareness of past oppressions, 92
    to domination, 50
    to education, 10, 50
    in educational experience, 119
    hustling as manifestation of, 65
    interventions for, 119–120
    misinterpretation of, 26
    punishment of, 26
resources, inadequate, 140
respect
    for duffle bag boys and hustlers, 65
    gaining of in rap, 94
rituals, 32–33
RJ, 74–78, 80
Roberts, D., 56
role, male, 47
Rose, T., 90, 96–97
Run-DMC, 94
RuPaul, 168–169
Rusch, E., 142
Russell, K., 111
Rux, Carl, 42

salvation, among peers, 84
same-affection loving, 165–166, 170
Sarles, H., 108
school. see also education
    African American males' reasons for
        avoiding, 75–76
    experiences of Raheem's gang in, 78–79
    Raheem's experience in, 83–84
schooling. see education
schools. see also education
    failure to hire teachers capable of coping
        with reality, 108
    as feeders to prison complex economy, 79
    need to be communities of learners, 114
    need to examine contemporary issues, 11
    need to examine history, 11
    reproduction of racial inequalities, 108
    as reproductions of larger society, 142
    resegregation of. see resegregation
    as social, 31
    and transmission of knowledge defined by
        those in power, 19
    under-resourcing of, 119, 140
schools, public. see also education
    closing of African American, 167
    impact on African American youth, 55
    increasing segregation in, 5. see also
        resegregation

lack of equality in, 24
necessity of in democracy, 160
need to integrate, 20
presence of community values in, 22
reification of perception of African American males, 56
and reproduction of capitalist relations of production, 20
as tailored for white middle class, 55
Scott, Matthew, 44, 57
Scripting the Black Masculine Body (Jackson), 41–42, 108
seamless learning from K-12, 146
segregation. *see also* desegregation; integration; resegregation
   and academic achievement, 19, 21, 24
   increase of in public schools, 5. *see also* resegregation
   and lack of democracy, 22
   of Latinos, 21, 22
   lawsuits challenging, 21, 22
self
   African American experience of as unstable and dualistic, 92
   as relational, 20–21
self-worship as form of competition, 17
Sergiovanni, T., 114
service industry, 4
sexism in African American community, 171
sexual identity, construction of, 166
sexuality, 166
Sharpton, Al, 63, 64
Shields, C. M., 143, 164
shouting at African American students, 116–117, 118–119
signification, hip-hop founded on, 95
silence, of African Americans in education literature, 6, 36, 167
silent, need to listen to voices of, 11
slavery, 3, 69–70
Slavin, R., 115
social justice
   educators for, 36
   need for educational leaders to promote, 56
   teaching for in higher education, 163
social order, rap's critique of, 93
soldiers, African American, 49
The Soul of Black Folk (Du Bois), 69
South/Southeast. *see also* North Carolina
   creation of urban centers in, 3
   increase in gangs in, 71
   relocation of companies to, 4

resegregation of, 21, 71
special education
   and experience of failure, 108
   number of African American males in, 5, 56, 127
   number of minorities in, 19
   number of poor students in, 108
spiritual connections and attraction, 166
spirituality, 46, 47
spirituality, critical, 53
sports industry
   as alternative work arena, 69
   commodification of African American body, 107
   use of African American males in, 69–70
stigmatization of African American males, 10–11, 29, 70. *see also* images of African American males
storytelling
   linked to African American community, 98
   rap's evolution from, 94–95, 102–103
"Student Engagement and Academic Achievement" (Chesley), 109–110
student leaders on images of African Americans, 66–68
students. *see also* youth
   as bodies to be controlled, 125. *see also* discipline; punishment
   engagement with, 26–27
   keys for collaborative activism, 154–156
   moving from language of reformation to transformation, 144
   as teachers in successful classrooms, 26–27
students, African American
   loss of understanding of, 109
   low expectations of, 111–113
   marginalization of, 110
   punishment of (*see* discipline; punishment; special education)
   in special education classes. *see* special education
students, "at-risk," 115, 116
students, graduate, 142
subculture
   hip-hop as, 90–91
   as set in relation to dominant culture, 33
substance abuse, 18, 139
success, African American
   money as marker of, 69
   need for assistance from white majority, 69
Supermodel, 168–169

surveillance
    African American masculinity considered legitimate object of, 134
    environment of, 131. *see also* police; zero-tolerance
suspension. *see also* discipline; punishment
    rate of for African American students, 125
Sutherland, M. E., 56
Sylvester, 169

Taylor, R. D., 56
Taylor, R. L., 56
teacher education
    focus on perceptions of dominant culture, 27–28
    inadequate preparation of teachers, 108
teachers. *see also* educators
    African American women encouraged to be, 116
    desire for students to conform to own images of youth, 125. *see also* discipline; punishment
    keys for collaborative activism, 150–152
    need to be culturally proficient, 144
teachers, African American. *see also* educators, African American
    Ayer on duty of, 121
    challenging of authority of, 114, 133–134, 163
    dismissal of after integration, 167
    narratives of. *see* Christina; Crystal; Doug; Victoria
    perceptions of, 28
teachers, "paycheck," 112
teachers, successful, 26–27
teachers, white
    fear of African American students, 125, 132
    lack of respect for African American students, 115
    low expectations for African American students, 111–113
    perceptions of, 28
    shouting at African American students, 116–117, 118–119
teaching. *see also* critical pedagogy
    courage required for, 167
    as liberatory practice, 109
    need for culturally-relevant styles, 28
    as performative act, 109
    Sarles on, 108
    as soul of democracy, 111
teaching, didactic, 28

technology
    and activism, 138
    African American youth's limited access to, 90
    need for human factor in, 16
    as tool of iniquity, 17
testing
    failure to measure knowledge, 84
    reproduction of class stratification, 79
Thomas, Timothy, 71
Thompson, V.L.S., 138
Three 6 Mafia, 69
Tiger, 77–78, 81–83
"Today: I Opened My Eyes" (Gause), 157–159, 165, 166
transformation
    of lives of African American males, 173–174
    students encouraged in, 144–145
transformative leadership, 147
Tutwiler, Sandra, 26

underground economy
    African American males' engagement in, 70
    amount of money made in, 76
    increase in, 139

Valdes, Francisco, 53, 54
values, 22, 73
values, African American, 68–71
victimhood, price of, 72–73
victims, call to be seen as, 62
Victoria
    on challenging of authority, 133–134
    on coolness, 132
    on discipline matters, 124
    on district's educational mission, 114–115
    on image of African American male, 135
    on lunch problems, 130
    on need to develop teacher leaders, 117
    on need to recognize differences, 113
    on police interaction with students, 130
    on policing of students, 131
    on rap, 100–101, 103, 104
    on student code of conduct, 129
    on teachers shouting at African American students, 119
Villaverde, L. E., 141
"Voiceless Spirit" (Gause), 87
Vygotsky, L., 29

Walker, E. M., 55, 56
war and African American masculinity, 48–49
Warfield-Coppock, N., 55
War on Drugs, 139–140
Washington, Booker T., 71–72
Watts, Jerry, 72
ways of knowing, African, 55
Weatherspoon, F. D., 51
We Real Cool (hooks), 24, 25–26, 43–44
West, C., 50
White, J. L., 54
whiteness, constructed by relationship to blackness, 110
white privilege, 118
whites. *see also* parents, white; teachers, white
  as potential enemy, 132
  view of inner city African American males, 10
Williams, Juan, 25, 42
Willis, J. T., 56
Willis, P., 56
Wilson, M., 111
Wink, J., 30, 31
women. *see* females, African American
word, reading of, 30
work. *see also* careers; jobs
  rap as, 103–104
work ethic, devaluation of, 69
world, reading of, 30, 31

youth
  drug and alcohol use by, 18, 139
  teachers' images of and discipline, 125
  world of, 17
youth, African American
  as consumers of digital media, 90
  and technology, 90
Yun, J., 18, 21

zero-tolerance, 127

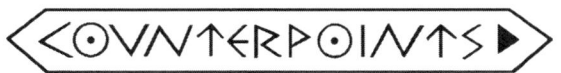

Studies in the Postmodern Theory of Education

General Editors
Joe L. Kincheloe & Shirley R. Steinberg

Counterpoints publishes the most compelling and imaginative books being written in education today. Grounded on the theoretical advances in criticalism, feminism, and postmodernism in the last two decades of the twentieth century, Counterpoints engages the meaning of these innovations in various forms of educational expression. Committed to the proposition that theoretical literature should be accessible to a variety of audiences, the series insists that its authors avoid esoteric and jargonistic languages that transform educational scholarship into an elite discourse for the initiated. Scholarly work matters only to the degree it affects consciousness and practice at multiple sites. Counterpoints' editorial policy is based on these principles and the ability of scholars to break new ground, to open new conversations, to go where educators have never gone before.

For additional information about this series or for the submission of manuscripts, please contact:

        Joe L. Kincheloe & Shirley R. Steinberg
        c/o Peter Lang Publishing, Inc.
        29 Broadway, 18th floor
        New York, New York 10006

To order other books in this series, please contact our Customer Service Department:

        (800) 770-LANG (within the U.S.)
        (212) 647-7706 (outside the U.S.)
        (212) 647-7707 FAX

Or browse online by series:
        www.peterlang.com